Multidimensional Curriculum Enhancing Future Thinking Literacy

Multidimensional Curriculum Enhancing Future Thinking Literacy

Teaching Learners to Take Control of Their Future

By

Hava E. Vidergor

Foreword by David Passig

BRILL SENSE

LEIDEN | BOSTON

All chapters in this book have undergone peer review.

Library of Congress Cataloging-in-Publication Data

Names: Vidergor, Hava E., author.
Title: Multidimensional curriculum enhancing future thinking literacy :
   teaching learners to take control of their future / by Hava E. Vidergor.
Description: Leiden ; Boston : Brill Sense, [2018] | Includes bibliographical
   references and index.
Identifiers: LCCN 2018017326 (print) | LCCN 2018018671 (ebook) | ISBN
   9789004375208 (E-book) | ISBN 9789004375185 (pbk. : alk. paper) | ISBN
   9789004375192 (hardback : alk. paper)
Subjects: LCSH: Curriculum change. | Thought and thinking--Study and
   teaching. | Interdisciplinary approach in education.
Classification: LCC LB1570 (ebook) | LCC LB1570 .V45 2018 (print) | DDC
   375/.006--dc23
LC record available at https://lccn.loc.gov/2018017326

Typeface for the Latin, Greek, and Cyrillic scripts: "Brill". See and download: brill.com/brill-typeface.

ISBN 978-90-04-37518-5 (paperback)
ISBN 978-90-04-37519-2 (hardback)
ISBN 978-90-04-37520-8 (e-book)

Copyright 2018 by Koninklijke Brill NV, Leiden, The Netherlands.
Koninklijke Brill NV incorporates the imprints Brill, Brill Hes & De Graaf, Brill Nijhoff, Brill Rodopi, Brill Sense and Hotei Publishing.
All rights reserved. No part of this publication may be reproduced, translated, stored in a retrieval system, or transmitted in any form or by any means, electronic, mechanical, photocopying, recording or otherwise, without prior written permission from the publisher.
Authorization to photocopy items for internal or personal use is granted by Koninklijke Brill NV provided that the appropriate fees are paid directly to The Copyright Clearance Center, 222 Rosewood Drive, Suite 910, Danvers, MA 01923, USA. Fees are subject to change.

This book is printed on acid-free paper and produced in a sustainable manner.

To my children
Guy, Yohai, Udi and Katia
and grandchildren
Tom, Noa, Adam and Hadas

You have always been a source of pride and joy.
Thank you for your support and encouragement.

Contents

Foreword XI
    David Passig
Preface XIV
Acknowledgements XVII
About the Author XVIII

PART 1
Future Thinking Literacy: The Multidimensional Curriculum Model

1 **Dynamic Curricula Promoting Future Thinking Literacy: The Multidimensional Curriculum Model** 3
   1   Meaningful Learning and Developing 21st Century Skills 3
   2   Conceptual Framework for Curriculum Model Development 5
   3   Developing Thinking Skills 6
   4   The Construction and Components of the Multidimensional Curriculum Model (MdCM) 7
   5   21st Century Thinking Processes Developed by MdCM 10
   6   Effectiveness Data 12
   7   Learning in Future Thinking Societies (LIFTS) Center 13

2 **Teaching Future Thinking Literacy: Curriculum Design and Development** 18
   1   Principles 18
   2   Content and Process 18
   3   Products 19
   4   Designing a Multidimensional Curriculum 19
   5   Additional Key Components 22
   6   Putting It All Together: Developing Future Thinking Literacy 23
   7   Developing a Unit of Study 25

PART 2
Updating the Curriculum in Core Domains

3 **Science and Technology: Genetics** 35
   1   Science and Technology 35
   2   Example Unit and Lessons: Genetics 36

    3 Unit Description 36
    4 Lesson Plans 38
    5 Future Scenario 53

4 **Mathematics: Consumerism and the Percentages** 55
    1 Teaching Math 55
    2 The Percentage 56
    3 Consumerism 56
    4 Example Unit Consumerism and Lessons 57
    5 Unit Description 57
    6 Lesson Plans 58
    7 Future Scenario 67

5 **Language Arts: English as a Foreign Language** 70
    1 Teaching English as a Foreign Language in the Arab Sector in Israel 70
    2 Thinking Maps 71
    3 Guinness World Records 74
    4 Example Unit and Lesson Plans: Extreme Sports 74
    5 Lesson Plans 75
    6 Future Scenario 85
    Appendix: Worksheet (Lessons 4–5) 87

6 **Social Studies: Community Settlements** 89
    1 Social Studies 89
    2 Thinking Hats 90
    3 Three-Stage Application of Six Thinking Hats in MdCM 91
    4 Example Unit and Lesson Plans: My Homeland 91
    5 Lesson Plans 92
    6 Future Scenario 103

PART 3
Multidimensional Curriculum for Non-Core Domains

7 **The Bible: Leaders and Leadership** 107
    1 Leadership, Creative Thinking, and Problem Solving 107
    2 Leadership in the Bible 108
    3 Example Unit and Lesson Plans: Leadership in the Bible 109
    4 Lesson Plans 109
    5 Future Scenario 122

8 Music: The Beatles   125
   1   Music Education   125
   2   Cognitive Contribution   126
   3   Personal and Social Contribution   126
   4   The Beatles   127
   5   Example Unit and Lessons: The Beatles   127
   6   Lesson Plans   128
   7   Future Scenario   140

9 Life Skills: Me Myself and I   142
   1   Life Skills   142
   2   Life Skills in 1st Grade on the Topic of Self   143
   3   Example Unit and Lessons: Me Myself and I   144
   4   Lesson Plans   145
   5   Future Scenario   159
   6   Additional Products and Units   160
   7   Unit on Accepting Others   161
   8   Unit on Violence   162
   9   Future Scenario   163

PART 4
Multidimensional Curriculum Integrating Domains

10 Energy: The Phenomenon-Based Approach   167
    1   Phenomenon-Based Learning   167
    2   Energy   168
    3   Example Unit and Lesson Plans: Energy   169
    4   Lesson Plans   169
    Appendix   179

11 Jerusalem: The Transdisciplinary Perspective   180
    1   Interdisciplinarity and Transdisiplinarity Teaching and Learning   180
    2   Israel's Culture and Heritage and the City of Jerusalem   181
    3   Example Unit and Lessons: Jerusalem   182
    4   Lesson Plans   183
    5   Future Scenario   195

12 Human Rights: Moral Ethical Social Medical and Legal Aspects   198
    1   Blended Learning   198
    2   Designing Blended Learning Environments   199
    3   Flipped Classroom   200

    4   Example Unit and Lessons: Human Rights   201
    5   Lesson Plans   202
    Appendix: Problem Solving Simulation   219

13 Language Arts and Sciences: The Cell Phone   222
    1   Inventive Thinking and Technology: Melioration Creation and Use of 3D Printers   222
    2   Writing in English as a Foreign Language   223
    3   Teaching Physics   224
    4   Example Unit and Lesson Plans: The Cell Phone   225
    5   Lesson Plans   226
    6   Future Scenario   246

14 Women's Status and Rights: Bible and Social Studies   248
    1   Women's Status in the Bible   248
    2   Public Speaking – Debate   249
    3   Example Unit and Lessons: Women's Status and Rights   251
    4   Lesson Plans   252
    5   Invited Guest   268
    6   Example Product   268

PART 5
Multidimensional Curriculum for Special Needs

15 Gifted Learners: Developing Leadership and Global Citizenship   273
    1   Leadership and the Gifted Student   273
    2   Model United Nations   275
    3   Example Unit and Lessons: Developing Leadership and Global Citizenship   276
    4   Lesson Plans   277

16 Learners at Risk: Economics and Globalization   293
    1   Global Economics   293
    2   Students At-Risk in High School   294
    3   Thinking Actively in a Social Context (TASC)   295
    4   Example Unit and Lesson Plans: Economics and Globalization   296
    5   Lesson Plans   297
    6   Future Scenario   308
    Appendix: TASC Wheel   310

Index   313

Foreword

Prospective thinking, or future thinking, as a cognitive ability has been supported by numerous educational and neurophysiological studies. It has now also become apparent that it is not unique to humans and that different animals are also capable of various types of prospective thinking. Studies are supplying us with a clearer picture of how it develops from infancy to become an important survival skill. However, the road to understanding all neurophysiological and psychological processes involved in this human ability is still long. There are numerous issues to be resolved if we are to engage in a meaningful endeavor of teaching it. Nonetheless, what is known to date indicates that it is crucial to introduce it systematically into the curriculum.

In general, brain imaging studies (Atance & Hanson, 2011) indicate that primary prospective thinking, which is simply expectations, begins during early infancy. Only in the first years of elementary school does the ability develop for creating scenarios which serve as the basis for the ability to predict the future. As the child advances in elementary school, the brain is able to take the uncertainty and the innovation which the future holds into account when creating scenarios. Only later does the conceptualization of the future become flexible, useful and adaptive, until it reaches full maturity at the age of twenty-four.

The scientific literature also indicates that there are three landmark points in the semantic and conceptual process undergone by children until full *future orientation* maturation at the age of five to seven:

1 At the first landmark point children understand the past before they understand the future, i.e. they semantically learn the word "yesterday" before they learn the word "tomorrow" (Benson, 1994).
2 At the second point, children understand the future before the past, i.e. they refer spontaneously mainly to the present, then to the present and the future, and only after that to the present, the future and the past.
3 Finally, at the third point, the past and the future are understood simultaneously (Suddendorf, 2003). Children have difficulty understanding history and this is another good reason why history should be taught in schools at a later age.

Empirical evidence collected through advanced brain imaging technologies is beginning to support the assumption that the prediction ability at older ages is carried out by other brain mechanisms, in addition to the basic ones that initiate the process. One of the characteristics of the development of prospective thinking ability is that it takes many years to mature. We still do not have an in-depth understanding as to why this skill is drawn out and delayed for so long time its maturation. It is assumed that prospective thinking ability involves many components of the brain's mechanisms. It is therefore reasonable to assume that it takes time for the brain to entwine the parts together, send longer than usual axons to distant places and work in collaboration and simultaneously with other components in a manner that will ensure the inferences will be sufficiently reliable.

What is clear at this point is that after the child reaches the age of seven his/her ability to assess occurrences in the future and to plan his/her steps accordingly becomes much more complex. After his/her awareness of others matures, the ability to create scenarios of future possibilities does not remain bund merely to the physical world. The scenarios which s/he is able to generate become more hypothetical and sophisticated due to a mechanism that continues to develop (Barsalou, 2008). This requires a *complex and focused computational ability*, which involves a wide variety of cognitive activations in different brain areas, such as the reenactment of motor, perceptual and introspective experiences that are received from the world through the body and the senses.

Introspective experiences are internal experiences in the form of feelings, motivations, intentions, meta-cognition, etc. These experiences are constructed in the neural networks in two stages (Barsalou, 2011):

1. In the first stage, a command is given to store information arriving from different places in the brain in the long-term memory, after it was received by the senses and changed its shape to *introspective* experiences.
2. In the second stage, another command is given in which only a few of these experiences are reenacted in order to generate a simulation of experiences of other and new events that might develop in the future – what is termed a *prediction*.

This book joins the efforts of many in the literature to develop learning processes that can enhance the development of the prospective thinking skill in different stages. The author introduces a pedagogical model with which we can teach this skill with great efficiency during the years of schooling. It is an important goal as it holds the prospects of the next generations to solve future challenges and carry society on to its next stage in evolution.

References

Atance, C. M., & Hanson, K. L. (2011). Making predictions: A developmental perspective. In M. Bar (Ed.), *Predictions in the brain: Using our past to generate a future* (Chapter 23, pp. 311–324). Oxford: Oxford University Press.

Barsalou, L. W. (2008). Grounded cognition. *Annual Review of Psychology, 59*, 617–645.

Barsalou, L. W. (2011). Simulation, situated conceptualization and prediction. In M. Bar (Ed.), *Predictions in the brain: Using our past to generate a future* (Chapter 3, pp. 27–39). Oxford: Oxford University Press.

Benson, J. B. (1994). The origin of future orientation in the everyday lives of 9–36 month-old infants. In M. M. Haith, J. B. Benson, R. J. Roberts, & B. F. Bennington (Eds.), *The development of future oriented processes* (pp. 375–407). Chicago, IL: University of Chicago Press.

Suddendorf, T., & Busby, J. (2003). Mental time travel in animals? *Trends in Cognitive Sciences, 7*, 391–396.

David Passig
(Bar-Ilan University, Ramat Gan, Israel)

Preface

This book is the product of four years of supervising graduate students at a teacher education college in Israel. The students designed and taught units of study based on the Multidimensional Curriculum Model (MdCM), followed by research on its contribution to the development of higher order thinking skills, knowledge, motivation and learning strategies, as well as students' perceptions concerning the contribution of MdCM to their learning. It coins a new term: "future thinking literacy" which brings together all the components of the MdCM and illustrates how they lead to the enhancement of future thinking and develop future thinking literacy, which are necessary skills students need to acquire in order to succeed in adult life.

The book presents the theory of how students of different ages can best be taught, and translates this theory into practice, in the shape of innovative teaching practices and the form they should take in today's schools. The book aims to serve as a resource for teachers in elementary and secondary schools who wish to update and expand their teaching range, by providing them with practical examples and advice on different ways of promoting thinking, and future thinking literacy.

Part 1 introduces future thinking literacy and the Multidimensional Curriculum Model (MdCM). Chapters 1 and 2, provide an introduction to the entire book. *Chapter 1* describes the construction, components, thinking processes and tools of the Multidimensional Curriculum Model, and reviews the results and implications of the most recent quantitative and qualitative studies. Chapter Two focuses on the design of MdCM-based curricula in order to provide a guiding template for the units described in following chapters. It posits that studying at any age, from first to twelfth grade, should be relevant, multi or transdisciplinary, incorporate 21st century skills, use innovative pedagogies, and prepare students to control their future by practicing future thinking and developing future thinking literacy.

The rest of the book is divided into four parts, each one dealing with a different aspect of the curriculum, i.e. core domains, non-core domains, integration of domains, and curriculum for special needs students. Each chapter commences with a short overview of the strategy in focus. It is followed by an example MdCM-based unit illustrating the application of personal, global, and time perspectives, teaching strategies, thinking process, and products. Each chapter ends with a future scenario written by student projecting themselves into the future and imagining life regarding the topic in question.

Part 2 demonstrates the use of the MdCM to update existing themes and units in the core curriculum. It offers various ways of incorporating the personal, global and time perspectives in the basic domains along with special tips for differentiation based on ability and special needs. Within this section, Chapter 3 focuses on science and technology and illustrates the teaching of genetics to secondary school students in novel ways based on the model. Chapter 4 discusses teaching mathematics to elementary school students, focusing on percentages through the relevant topic of consumerism. Chapter 5 provides the theory on thinking maps and demonstrates how English as a foreign language was taught using them. Chapter 6 elaborates on the six thinking hats and suggests a three-step process for teaching social studies to elementary students on the topic of community centers.

Part 3 relates to three non-core domains, leadership, music, and life skills, and demonstrates how the MdCM can be applied to enhance learning and integrate into the core-curriculum as well remain in stand-alone domains. Chapter 7 provides an insight into teaching about leadership and leaders in the Bible, as well as providing the theory and practice of creative problem solving. Chapter 8 uses the model to teach secondary school students music, using the Beatles and their songs. Chapter 9 illustrates teaching first grade elementary students to think about themselves, not only in the past and present, but also in the future, meaning five years ahead.

Part 4 addresses differentiation, designing interdisciplinary units based on the MdCM model, along with suggestions and ideas for incorporating thinking strategies, and enhancing language skills. Chapter 10 examines phenomenon-based learning and illustrates the design of a unit on energy, focusing on the phenomenon and using project- and problem-based learning to address issues related to it, providing students with a wide perspective and understanding of future prospects of development. Chapter 11 takes the topic of Jerusalem and challenges elementary students to solve problems taking into consideration its transdisciplinary nature. Chapter 12 introduces blended learning and more specifically, the flipped classroom technique, providing theoretical, as well as practical aspects. The unit demonstrates the instruction of a unit on human rights in upper secondary school, selecting videos that students are required to watch prior to lessons, as preparation for group work on different topics related to human rights. Among the teaching methods used are decision making, problem solving, debating, and designing a mock trial – all dealing with moral, ethical, social, medical, and legal aspects of human rights. Chapter 13 takes up the relevant topic of the cell phone and explores teaching writing skills in English as a foreign language, as well as applying inventive or entrepreneurial thinking. The unit highlights motivating and challenging ways of teaching writing, as well as designing and 3D printing of a future model of the cell phone. Chapter 14 addresses the topic of women's status and rights from the combined perspectives of the Bible study and social studies. The focus of this unit is debating, inviting students in middle school to present argument for and against granting rights to women, as well as predicting how women's status will change in the near or far future, based on accumulated knowledge from the biblical times to the present day.

Part 5 demonstrates how MdCM could be used to address the special needs of gifted learners with high abilities, and weak learners who need special scaffolding. Chapter 15 deals with enhancing leadership among gifted students and provides the theoretical and practical aspects of using the Model United Nations (MUN), as well as developing future thinking literacy at the highest level. Chapter 16 concludes the book, addressing economics in the topic of globalization, among high school learners at risk. It provides an overview of students at risk and illustrates the use of the TASC tool to develop thinking in a more structured manner.

Acknowledgements

I would like to express my gratitude to my graduate students teaching in Jewish and Arab schools. You have designed inspiring units of study, taught them enthusiastically in your classes, and thoroughly investigated different aspects. I could not have completed this project without your practical input and unlimited belief in the model.

I would like to thank Gordon Academic College of Education, and more specifically the Research Authority, for supporting this project and generously contributing to the funding which made the publication possible.

I would like to thank Brill Sense, and especially Michel Lokhorst and Jolanda Karada. It was a pleasure working with you knowing that the book is in good hands and the final product would be impeccable.

I would also like to thank my editor, Micaela Ziv. You handled the manuscript with great care and professional manner.

Last but not least, I beg forgiveness of all those who have been with me over the course of the years and whose names I have failed to mention.

About the Author

Hava Vidergor

PhD, is a senior lecturer of curriculum and instruction in the Graduate School at Gordon Academic College of Education, and Arab Academic College, Haifa, Israel. She began her career as an English teacher, and taught English as a foreign language for 30 years at all levels. She received an MA in educational leadership with distinction from University of Alabama at Birmingham, and a PhD in Education from Haifa University, Israel. Her research interests center on curriculum planning and design, innovative teaching strategies and gifted education. She has published numerous papers and presented widely in international conferences. She is the editor (with Carole R. Harris) of *Applied Practice for Educators of Gifted and Able Learners*, and of *Innovative Teaching Strategies and Methods Promoting Lifelong Learning in Higher Education: From Theory to Practice* (with Orly Sela), and the author of *Enhancing the Gift of Leadership* (with Dorothy Sisk). She designed a new graduate program called Innovation in Education promoting teacher entrepreneurship in applying new pedagogies and creating and investigating blended learning environments. Her Multidimensional Curriculum Model (MdCM) focusing on developing high order thinking and future thinking literacy in K-12 students is currently applied in Israel and internationally. havavi@gordon.ac.il

PART 1

Future Thinking Literacy: The Multidimensional Curriculum Model

∴

CHAPTER 1

Dynamic Curricula Promoting Future Thinking Literacy: The Multidimensional Curriculum Model

Dynamic curricula for the 21st century should focus on meaningful learning, developing thinking skills and creativity, looking at issues from a broad multidisciplinary or transdisciplinary perspective, incorporating the use of technology. They should also stress the acceptance of others, develop social responsibility and understanding of future developments. *All these components form future thinking literacy.* Learning in future thinking societies requires innovative and dynamic curricula. The dynamic aspect of such curricula may appear in all areas: planning and design, teaching and learning, products and assessment. Designed units should be broad and open enough for students to choose a topic they find relevant and allow them to express their talents and capabilities in presenting the newly acquired knowledge and in designing a project for the benefit and betterment of society.

1 Meaningful Learning and Developing 21st Century Skills

Kauffman (1976) said 40 years ago that schools need to pay careful and explicit attention to the question of the kind of education that would best prepare children and adolescents for the world in which they will actually live as adults. This implies that today's education needs to prepare the individual for tomorrows' demands. Trilling and Fadel (2009) refer to the essential skills students will require in the 21st century as the "7C's", including: (a) critical thinking and problem solving; (b) communication; (c) collaboration; (d) computing and ICT; (e) career; (f) cross-cultural understanding; (g) creativity and innovation. Higgins (2014) argues that education needs to fit local contexts in a global world and meet the specific needs of students in diverse cultures.

In the Israeli context, educational leaders have met the above challenges by acknowledging the "7Cs" model and adding an additional layer to it by introducing the concept of "meaningful learning". Meaningful learning is defined by the Israeli Ministry of Education (2013) as a learning process that results in a significant and lasting change in individuals' behavior and function. For this purpose, learning combines emotional, social and cognitive experiences (involving independent learning in social contexts) based on three components: Value for student and society, student and teacher involvement, and relevance to the student. Meaningful learning can be implemented and facilitated using strategies such as: inquiry and project-based learning; problem-based learning, debate, cohort learning, digital pedagogy, interdisciplinary learning incorporating arts, focus on values and dilemma discussions, and reflection. A recent document by the Israeli Ministry of Education (2016) outlines the policy for research and development for a future pedagogy, addressing trends, challenges, principles and recommendations. At the core of the concept, then, lies the realization that a significant, ongoing change in function and behavior occurs when the learners learn actively and within a context relevant to the application of whatever is being learned. Factors facilitating change include: personalized learning, using technologies in higher-order thinking activities, and collaborative authentic learning, focusing on four clusters: (1) access to information; (2) clear thinking and effective communication; (3) personal skills, and (4) understanding of the environment, society and individual. To support new learning paradigms as suggested by the Ministry new settings are required – ones that will support flexible learning tasks, diverse activities – from outdoors exploration to computer-based virtual reality engines, collaborative learning efforts and activities, and a shift of focus from teaching to learning.

The Multidimensional Curriculum Model (MdCM) (Vidergor, 2010, 2015a, 2017) offers a systematic framework for conceptualizing meaningful learning and designing curricula for all grade levels and school types. The model invites students to explore big multi/transdisciplinary issues from personal, global and time perspectives in blended learning environments that incorporate technology.

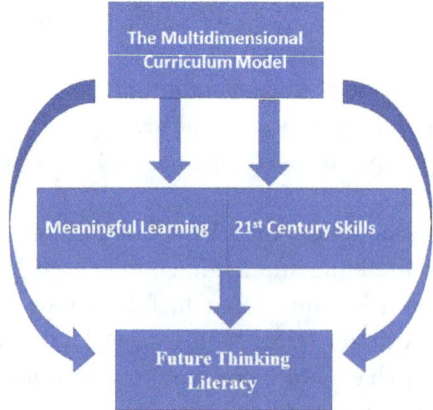

FIGURE 1.1 *Future thinking literacy*

Based on this new model, we present a new paradigm for learning, one that will reshape learning processes at all levels in the education system: from teacher preparation, to teaching, and facilitation practices in schools for groups and individual students – a new and enhanced learning experience that fosters meaningful learning on the one hand, and preparation for the challenges of the future on the other. The model will be constantly developed, updated and applied to practice in "Future Thinking Centers" named LIFTS supporting learning in all grade levels. The LIFTS center is based on the MdCM and offers a world-innovation in the area of pedagogies and planning promoting future thinking literacy. As a multifaceted professional development and teaching-learning center, it will offer ample resources of research, best practices, and tools for constant improvement for learners at all levels. This concept will be explained in detail later on in the chapter.

2   Conceptual Framework for Curriculum Model Development

2.1   *The Constructivist Approach Underlying MdCM*

The theoretical support for the MdCM is derived from several constructivist sources: general learning theory and development, current curriculum models for teaching gifted and able students, and teaching and learning of the future. The latter two will be briefly introduced.

2.2   *Current Curriculum Models*

MdCM draws part of its conceptual framework from curriculum models designed for gifted and talented students, but is intended for students of all levels and grades. (1) The Integrated Curriculum Model (ICM) (Van Tassel-Baska & Stambaugh, 2006; Van Tassel-Baska & Little, 2011) comprises three dimensions: (a) advanced content; (b) issues-themes; and (c) process-product. (2) The Parallel Curriculum Model (PCM) (Tomlinson, Kaplan, Renzulli, Purcell, Leppien, & Burns, 2002; Tomlinson & Jarvis, 2009) offers four parallel ways of thinking about curriculum development: core curriculum, interdisciplinary curriculum, personal involvement, and practice as an expert. (3) Future Problem-Solving Program (FPSP) (2001) focusing on creative problem-solving processes and projection of future development trends, to teach and learn the skills necessary to adapt to a changing world and shape the future.

2.3   *Teaching and Learning the Future Model*

David Passig (2001), an Israeli futurist, suggests that learning about the past is not enough. He goes on to explain that in order to survive in a fast-changing world, people need to make active use of their imagination to create possibilities beyond traditional paradigms in order to discover, explore, invent and investigate new directions in the present. In order to train students to think about the future and include a time perspective dimension in their reasoning and problem-solving processes, students need to practice the historical and current review of issues or topics, leading to designing short-term (5 years) and long-term (20 or 50 years) predictions. Students are invited to investigate three aspects: (a) the development of a product; (b) the development of a concept; and (c) the development of a perception (Passig, 1995).

3   Developing Thinking Skills

Ample suggestions for programs and teaching strategies address the development of thinking skills (Dwyer, Hogan, & Stewart, 2014; Ritchhart & Perkins, 2008; Savery, 2014; Segal, Chipman, & Glaser, 2014). Very few models relate to future thinking, incorporate a personal view on an issue, concept or product, a global understanding of related events, and predict its development over time (Passig, 1995, 2001). This capability or skill turns out to be essential for adults as well as students in our time. Planning ahead, or planning for the future, regarding different time spans (Passig, 2004) depending on student age and level, can and should be taught in schools. Planning for the future involves looking at things from different perspectives, and relies on basic skills of inquiry and problem solving.

All teaching strategies and methods used in this program involve the use of *High Order Thinking Skills* (HOTS). The revised Bloom's Taxonomy (Anderson & Krathwohl, 2001) identified remembering, understanding and applying as low order thinking skills, and analyzing, evaluating and creating as high order thinking skills. They explained that high order thinking skills are involved in the creation of new knowledge, which is created while utilizing problem-solving, critical and creative thinking skills and strategies. Passig (2007) added a higher order skill which is situated between evaluating and creating named melioration. He explained that melioration is the competence to borrow a concept from a field of knowledge supposedly far removed from his or her domain, and adapt it to a pressing challenge in an area of personal knowledge or interest. One stage before actual creation, this competence improves an existing concept or object to solve a need or a problem.

Higgins, Hall, Baumfield, and Moseley (2005) introduce several types of frameworks for thinking dealing with: instructional design (pedagogy), productive thinking (philosophy), cognitive structure and/or development (psychology), and all-embracive frameworks. Vickery (2013) mentions several approaches to the teaching of thinking skills, one of which is the infusion approach. The infusion approach (Leat & Higgins, 2002) employs pedagogy and makes thinking explicit by teaching students to find patterns, consider similarities and differences, conjecture and justify, reason, consider different perspectives, make decisions, solve problems, and evaluate.

Most of the classical scientific inquiry skills, such as asking questions, formulating hypotheses, planning experiments, or drawing conclusions are also classified as high order thinking skills (Zohar & Dori, 2003). Other examples of cognitive activities that could be classified as high order thinking activities are: argumentation, comparison, problem solving, dealing with differences of opinion, decision making, and identification of hidden assumptions (Zohar & Nemet, 2002).

Perkins, Tishman, Ritchhart, Donis, and Andrade (2000) discussed the relationship between content knowledge in a specific subject and thinking. They asserted that control or knowledge of a specific domain develops thinking in that domain. In addition, they concluded that creativity is also domain-dependent. Meta-cognitive thinking happens simultaneously, involving critical and creative skills and procedures (Marzano, Brandt, Hughes, Jones, Presseisen, Rankin, & Suhor, 1988). Ritchhart and Perkins (2008) add that thinking requires teachers to use a different language and model thinking in their teaching, by asking their students key questions such as 'What is going on?' and 'How do we know?' and creating opportunities for students to engage in thinking routines.

4 The Construction and Components of the Multidimensional Curriculum Model (MdCM)

The model created by Vidergor (2010) focuses on inviting students to examine issues and concepts from varying perspectives, utilizing individual and collaborative work models to hone a deep understanding and broad perspective on issues learned, thus leading them toward the level of expert reasoning within selected themes and disciplines. The model is comprised of 6 dimensions as illustrated in Figure 1.1.

4.1 *Content Dimension*
The content dimension is comprised of themes, issues, and concepts addressed, whether restricted to a single subject matter, or more preferably

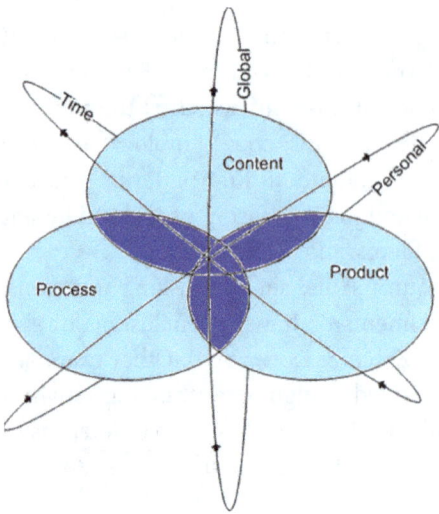

FIGURE 1.2   *The Multidimensional Curriculum Model (MdCM)*
SOURCE: VIDERGOR, 2010

to overarching larger interdisciplinary or multidisciplinary concepts. Selecting broad concepts that are relevant to students' lives is crucial to generating involvement and motivation for both students and teachers. The larger concepts or themes can be broken down to sub-concepts or smaller subjects that students would be challenged to explore, but then put together again to enable a more holistic view of the issue or concept addressed. Taking into consideration the interconnectivity of the dimensions, the concepts/issues/themes or products used need to play a meaningful role in the lives of students and all humans.

4.2   *Process Dimension*

The process dimension pertains to the actual acquisition-adaptation processes taking place within given time and space settings: theme or concept investigated. It incorporates teaching strategies used by the teacher to enhance learning and to develop skills much needed in the 21st century. Among suggested strategies are: enhancing productive thinking skills, problem finding and problem solving, promoting creativity, independent learning and investigative competencies. It incorporates working on more than one perspective or dimension in a blended learning environment incorporating technology.

4.3   *Product Dimension*

The product dimension reflects the new knowledge, skill or know-how gained and accumulated, researching the concept or issue using the various perspectives selected. Products may be varied and based on the interests and strengths of students. They need to be accompanied by pre-designed tools for self, peer and teacher evaluation. Students need to be offered opportunities to undertake individual, pair, or group projects and products. As teachers aim to enhance students' creativity, products suggested by students can take many forms, auch as written action plans, speeches, maps, flow charts, prediction models, role plays, poems, songs, illustrated books, computer games, written scenarios, and so forth.

The MdCM (Vidergor, 2010, 2015a) suggests three additional key dimensions orbiting around, interconnecting and focusing on three different perspectives: personal, global and time. These may guide learning activities around each theme explored.

4.4 Personal Perspective Dimension

This dimension focuses on personal identity. It stresses personal involvement and self-awareness of students and infuses interest and intrinsic motivation. The main questions asked include: How do I feel about the subject/issue? Where am I in the process? How could I make things better for myself and society? The personal perspective is dynamic in the sense of developing the awareness of students on how they are influenced by the processes, and how they can participate or influence such processes in the future for their own benefit, or the benefit of society. Awareness of the personal perspective could be used as an introductory activity or assignment, but would be helpful for applying comparison and contrast procedures after constructing the global and time perspectives. It is essential to use the personal perspective as the basis for the time perspective to enable future thinking.

4.5 Global Perspective Dimension

The world has become one large village and incidents occurring in one country affect all or many others in numerous fields. Students need to be taught to examine issues, not only from the micro to macro, but also to analyze events and concepts by examining similarities and differences, involving cultural, geographical, and other aspects influencing global events and trends. The questions asked in this perspective are: "Where do the leading countries stand on the issue in question?" or "Where does the world stand in the issue in question?". Awareness of the global perspective will be helpful in the design of the time perspective in older children.

4.6 Time Perspective Dimension

This dimension focuses on ongoing and rapid changes experienced in our time. It stresses the fact that students engaged in issues and themes, dealing with advanced contents, focusing on the process and product and need to be aware of the past, present and future aspects. The main questions asked are: Where does it come from? How did it start? What is the situation now? And what is the future direction? This dimension enhances students' awareness and prepares them to better predict and cope with future changes based on past and present knowledge. They are introduced to certain tools which can help them with their analyses and predictions, as well as thinking about possible personal or global consequences (Vidergor, 2010, 2015a).

5 21st Century Thinking Processes Developed by MdCM

Numerous existing definitions of teaching of thinking reflect the wealth and complexity of human thinking (Yoad, 2010). This complexity led researchers to define thinking processes in varied ways such as inquiry, combination and oral discourse, which are included in creative thinking (Perkins et al., 2000). Marzano et al. (1988) gave examples of thinking processes such as: designing a concept, understanding, decision making and problem solving. Vidergor (2010, 2015a) organized the thinking processes into three main dimensions: scientific thinking involving inquiry processes; creative thinking involving problem finding and problem solving; and future thinking, which is characterized as personal view of a subject, incorporating its development over time with consideration of past and present occurrences. The first two match the 21st century skills all students are supposed to develop in order to prepare for life. Future thinking is a new process of thinking, which needs to be addressed for building future orientation and better capabilities of surviving and thriving in this constantly changing world.

5.1 *Scientific Thinking – Inquiry*

There are various definitions regarding the aspects of scientific thinking. Hativa (2003) states the common ground, which is examining questions regarding a certain content by performing scientific experiments. Zohar (1996) adds the disciplinary aspect of scientific thinking involving certain thinking skills: defining a problem, formulating hypotheses, planning an experiment, analysis of experiment results, and drawing conclusions. Halpern (1998, 2014) elaborated on that and explained that critical thinking skills are considered high order thinking skills as they involve judgment, analysis, and synthesis, and are not applied in a mechanical manner. She proposed a taxonomy of skills as a guide for instruction, comprising: (a) Verbal reasoning skills; (b) Argument analysis skills; (c) Hypothesis testing; (d) Likelihood and uncertainty; and

(e) Decision making and problem solving skills applying creative thinking. In addition, Martin and Halpern (2011) found that explicit instruction of critical thinking is more effective compared to embedded instruction.

5.2   Creative Thinking – Problem Identifying and Problem Solving

Definitions of creativity tend to vary (Ferrari & Wyse, 2015). Perkins et al. (2000) relate to creative thinking as a sub-type of critical thinking, the contrast between them lying more in the aims than in the processes. Hativa (2003) states that critical thinking is based on standards of objectivity, strategies and techniques involving problem solving, reflectivity, and practicality which leads to decisions and actions. De Bono (1970, 2006) coined the term 'parallel thinking' or 'lateral thinking', and described the divergent and convergent thinking processes which are the basics of the creative thinking process and problem solving. Problem solving skills as described in the Future Problem Solving Program Coach's Handbook (2001) include: (a) identifying the problem; (b) defining the problem; (c) suggesting varied solutions; (d) suggesting criteria for evaluation of best solution; (e) applying criteria to select the best solution; and (f) designing an action plan.

5.3   Future Thinking Literacy

Passig (2004) refers to Future Time Span (FTS) as a state of mind that characterized thinkers in ancient times. With the help of FTS they succeeded in making future evaluations and in assessing their significance and implications, basing their thinking on the information that was available to them, on their value emphases, and on their personal styles. Passig (2013) suggests that the ability of children to project their personal selves into the future is the most important component on which future-orientation can be developed. He explains that the earlier form of future thinking – creating expectations based on personal experience (or personal perspective) – already exists in very young children, and gradually develops till the age of 24 when one can use the average future time span of three years. He adds that tapping into the collective wisdom (global perspective) with accessible documented past offers endless opportunities to predict the future more accurately than ever. Passig (2004) further determines that awareness of FTS can be developed using a model comprising four strategies, four levels of awareness, and five time-spans. The four strategies of research are: (1) Predictions by building a model of development over time; (2) Scenarios that design several options of occurrence; (3) Future Imagery creating a collectivist view (global perspective); and (4) Wild Cards in which thinking about illogical things that might happen are followed by unconventional solutions. The four levels of awareness are:

1. Continuity between events;
2. Connection between events;
3. Duration of events; and
4. Acceleration/deceleration of activities.

The five ranges of time awareness are:

1. *Immediate range* – up to five years;
2. *Short range* – five to ten years;
3. *Median range* – ten to thirty years;
4. *Long range* – thirty to fifty years; and
5. *Very long range* – fifty to one hundred years.

The MdCM (Vidergor, 2010, 2015a) includes all three types/processes of thinking: Scientific thinking – inquiry; Creative thinking – problem identifying and problem solving; and Future thinking. The combination of all three types of thinking enhances future thinking literacy.

6 Effectiveness Data

A recent study (Vidergor, 2017) aimed to assess the effectiveness of the MdCM in the development of high order thinking skills and future thinking in a sample of 394 elementary and secondary school students in Israel. The study employed a quantitative quasi-experimental pre-post design, using a study module based on MdCM, comparing intervention group to control group. Thinking skills were measured using a thinking questionnaire comprising 3 dimensions: Scientific thinking – focusing on inquiry skills, creative thinking – relating to problem finding and problem solving, and future thinking – concerning personal and time perspectives. Findings indicate improvement in measured thinking skills in the intervention group by 40% compared to 4% in the control group. Most improved skills were future thinking and creative thinking. Differences were detected according to type of school. It is suggested that when used regularly, the MdCM incorporating innovative teaching-learning strategies and embedded thinking tools could improve all thinking skills, mainly scientific and future thinking, among students of different age groups.

A second study (in process) assessed the contribution of MdCM to students' knowledge, motivation and learning strategies. Initial results show that research group has increased knowledge on subject matter by 10% more compared to the control group. Knowledge was assessed pre- and post-intervention and was divided into 3 types: declarative, procedural, and conditional/situational knowledge. All three types of knowledge increased and resulted in covering the material by 80% on average. Motivation was broken down into the dimensions of intrinsic motivation and task value. Learning strategies consisted of critical thinking, individual learning, and team work. Significant differences were detected between research and control group in motivation and learning strategies in general and all their dimensions.

Data from a qualitative study (in process) regarding elementary and secondary students' perceptions of studying based on the MdCM (Jewish N = 108; Arab N = 84) are currently being analyzed. Thirty (30) units of interdisciplinary and multidisciplinary study have been developed in the course of three years, and taught by graduate students in Jewish and Arab elementary and secondary schools focusing on different topics such as genetics, biodiesel, the mobile phone, Jerusalem, me myself and I, the percent, economy, senses, the Druze, my village, and the biometric database. Interviews with teachers experiencing the design process and teaching using the MdCM are conducted to assess the strengths and difficulties they experience in order to better understand how the model and its various components can be adapted to cater to all types and levels of students. Initial findings indicate enhanced students' awareness of thinking tools and thinking processes, preference for teaching-learning strategies used in the MdCM, and the contribution of group work and team work to the students' social skills.

7   Learning in Future Thinking Societies (LIFTS) Center

The proposed LIFTS Center is innovative, as it adopts a different view of the role of a support center for learning communities applying MdCM. The center will support and facilitate the development and implementation of the model at all levels – beginning with research, teacher preparation (colleges), practicing teachers (by collaborating with schools), and most importantly – at the level of the school and the individual pupil (by providing infrastructure to support learning activities in and out of schools). The center will be located in elementary and secondary schools and will be supported by LIFTS Centers in teacher education colleges serving as a research and development center, offering professional development for teachers, teacher trainees, and modelling an enrichment center for students. It will also advise elementary and secondary schools on the implementation of LIFTS Centers based on the MdCM.

LIFTS Centers at school will be designed as open spaces inviting students to investigate large relevant topics applying different perspectives (personal, global and time). It will enable students to work in a blended learning environment offering various models according to student's needs, ability and interest. Students will be able to work individually on a project supervised by an expert teacher, as well as work in small groups to solve a problem and suggest a solution to be presented and applied to an authentic audience out of school. The center will be equipped with the latest technology including video conferencing and 3D printers. It will also have an assessment system showing real-time progress of individual students. Areas will be devoted to one-on-one tutoring, individual learning cubicles creating intimate spaces for contemplation and reflection. Large thinking walls will enable students to jot down ideas and will record creative thinking processes.

Design of the learning environment is crucial, but is not enough. Learning at a LIFTS Center has to be supported by MdCM as the main curriculum design model enabling students to experience Project-Based Learning, Problem-Based Learning and Phenomenon-Based Learning, develop their thinking skills and creativity, and think about the future. Sharing ideas about the near or far future with peers or other audiences will form collaborations and will result in innovative projects for the benefit of the local community, sometimes having national or even international impact. A LIFTS Center at school visited by every student at least once a week for several hours could promote student ability, knowledge, motivation and learning strategies. Systematic thinking about the future in many areas using various tools will prepare students become independent thinkers, confident in their ability, and having a sense of control in life.

References

Anderson, L. W., & Krathwohl, D. R. (Eds.). (2001). *A taxonomy for learning, teaching, and assessing: A revision of Bloom's taxonomy of educational objectives*. New York, NY: Longman.
de Bono, E. (1970). *Lateral thinking: Creativity step by step*. New York, NY: Harper & Row.
de Bono, E. (2006). *Lateral thinking: The power of provocation manual*. Clive: de Bono Thinking Systems.
Dwyer, C. P., Hogan, M. J., & Stewart, I. (2014). An integrated critical thinking framework for the 21st century. *Thinking Skills and Creativity, 12*, 43–52.
Ferrari, A., & Wyse, D. (2015). Creativity in education: An overview of the implications of creativity in curricula. In D. Wyse, L. Hayward, & J. Pandya (Eds.), *The Sage handbook of curriculum, pedagogy and assessment*. London: Sage Publications.

Future Problem Solving Program. (2001). *Future problem solving program coach's handbook.* Lexington, KY: Author.

Halpern, D. F. (1998). Testing critical thinking for transfer across domains. *American Psychologist, 53*, 449–555.

Halpern, D. F. (2014). *Critical thinking across the curriculum: A brief edition of thought & knowledge.* New York, NY: Routledge.

Hativa, N. (2003). *Teaching processes in the classroom.* Tel Aviv: Academic Publishing for Teachers Professional Development. [in Hebrew]

Higgins, S. (2014). Critical thinking for 21st-century education: A cyber-tooth curriculum? *Prospects, 44*(4), 559–574.

Higgins, S., Hall, E., Baumfield, V., & Moseley, D. (2005). *A meta-analysis of the impact of the implementation of thinking skills approaches on pupils* (Project report). London: EPPI-Centre, Social Science Research Unit, Institute of Education, University of London.

Kauffman, D. I. (1976). *Teaching the future.* California, CA: ETC.

Leat, D., & Higgins, S. (2002). The role of powerful pedagogical strategies in curriculum development. *Curriculum Journal, 13*(1), 71–85.

Martin, L. M., & Halpern, D. F. (2011). Pedagogy for developing critical thinking in adolescents: Explicit instruction produces greatest gains. *Thinking Skills and Creativity, 6*, 1–13.

Marzano, R. J., Brandt, R. S., Hughes, C. S., Jones, B. F., Presseisen, B. Z., Rankin, S. C., & Suhor, C. (1988). *Dimensions of thinking: A framework for curriculum and instruction.* Alexandria, VA: ASCD.

Ministry of Education. (2013). *Quality teaching: Learning and development space.* Jerusalem: Ministry of Education. [in Hebrew]

Ministry of Education. (2016). *Research and development of future span pedagogy: Trends, challenges, principles, and recommendations.* Jerusalem: Pedagogical Administration. [in Hebrew]

Passig, D. (1995). *To teach and learn the future: Futuristic educational and training systems.* Tel Aviv: Bar-Ilan University. [in Hebrew]

Passig, D. (2001). To study and to teach the future. *Journal of Jewish Education, 66*(3), 41–50. [in Hebrew]

Passig, D. (2004). Future time span as cognitive skill in future studies. *Futures Research Quarterly, 19*(4), 27–47.

Passig, D. (2007). Melioration as a higher thinking skill to enhance intelligence. *Teachers College Record, 109*(1), 24–50.

Passig, D. (2013). *Forcognito- the future mind.* Tel Aviv: Mishkal-Yediot Ahronot Books and Hemed Books. [in Hebrew]

Perkins, D., Tishman, S., Ritchhart, R., Donis, K., & Andrade, A. (2000). Intelligence in the wild: A dispositional view of intellectual traits. *Educational Psychology Review, 12*(3), 269–293.

Ritchhart, R., & Perkins, D. (2008). Teaching students to think: Making thinking visible. *Educational Leadership, 65*(5), 57–61.

Savery, J. R. (2006). Overview of problem-based learning: Definitions and distinctions. *The Interdisciplinary Journal of Problem-Based Learning, 1*(1), 9–20.

Savery, J. R. (2015). Overview of problem-based learning: Definitions and distinctions. In A. Walker, H. Leary, C. Hmelo-Silver, & P. A. Ertmer (Eds.), *Essential readings in problem-based learning: Exploring and extending the legacy of Howard S. Barrows* (pp. 5–15). Lafayette, IN: Purdue University Press.

Segal, J. W., Chipman, S. F., & Glaser, R. (2014). *Thinking and learning skills: Volume 1: Relating instruction to research.* London: Routledge.

Tomlinson, C., & Jarvis, J. (2009). Differentiation: Making curriculum work for all students through responsive planning and instruction. In J. Renzulli, J. Gubbins, K. McMillan, R. Eckert, & C. Little (Eds.), *Systems and models for developing programs for the gifted and talented* (2nd ed., pp. 599–625). Mansfield Center, CT: Creative Learning Press.

Tomlinson, C. A., Kaplan, S. N., Renzulli, J. S., Purcell, J., Leppien, J., & Burns, D. (2002). *The parallel curriculum: A design to develop high potential and challenge high-ability learners.* Washington, DC: Corwin Press.

Trilling, B., & Fadel, C. (2009). *21st century skills: Learning for life in our times.* San Francisco, CA: Jossey-Bass Publishers.

Van Tassel-Baska, J., & Little, C. A. (Eds.). (2011). *Content based curriculum for high ability learners.* Waco, TX: Prufrock Press.

Van Tassel-Baska, J., & Stambaugh, T. (2006). *Comprehensive curriculum for gifted learners* (3rd ed.). Boston, MA: Allyn & Bacon.

Vickery, A. (2013). *Frameworks for thinking: Developing active learning in the primary classroom.* London: Sage Publications.

Vidergor, H. E. (2010). The multidimensional curriculum model. *Gifted and Talented International, 25*(2), 153–165.

Vidergor, H. E. (2015a). The multidimensional curriculum model. In H. E. Vidergor & C. R. Harris (Eds.), *Applied practice for educators of gifted and able learners* (pp. 199–214). Rotterdam, The Netherlands: Sense Publishers.

Vidergor, H. E. (2015b). The ambassador: Leadership for gifted and able students. In H. E. Vidergor & C. R. Harris (Eds.), *Applied practice for educators of gifted and able learners* (pp. 587–602). Rotterdam, The Netherlands: Sense Publishers.

Vidergor, H. E. (2015c). Relate-create-donate: Promoting social responsibility in second language teaching and learning. In H. E. Vidergor & C. R. Harris (Eds.), *Applied practice for educators of gifted and able learners* (pp. 559–572). Rotterdam, The Netherlands: Sense Publishers.

Vidergor, H. E. (2017). Effectiveness of the multidimensional curriculum model in developing high order thinking skills in elementary and secondary students. *Curriculum Journal, 29*(1), 95–115. doi:10.1080/09585176.2017.1318771

Vidergor, H. E., & Sisk, D. A. (2013). *Enhancing the gift of leadership: Innovative programs for all grade levels*. Ulm: International Center for Innovation in Education Press.

Yoad, Z. (2010). *Thinking in the learning process during the knowledge era*. Tel Aviv: Maalot Publishing. [in Hebrew]

Zohar, A. (1996). *To learn, think, and learn to think*. Jerusalem: Branco Weiss Publishing, Ministry of Education, Pedagogical Management, Curriculum Division. [in Hebrew]

Zohar, A., & Dori, Y. (2003). Higher order thinking skills and low-achieving students: Are they mutually exclusive? *The Journal of the Learning Sciences, 12*(2), 145–181.

Zohar, A., & Nemet, F. (2002). Fostering students' knowledge and argumentation skills through dilemmas in human genetics. *Journal of Research in Science Teaching, 39*, 35–62.

CHAPTER 2

Teaching Future Thinking Literacy: Curriculum Design and Development

The Multidimensional Curriculum Model (MdCM) develops future thinking literacy in general and does so by combining several perspectives and tools, as illustrated in chapter one of this book. It also follows and innovates curriculum design for the 21st century. This chapter focuses on curriculum design and development based on MdCM. It reviews principles of development and design of units of study; defines the different components and additional key components; and illustrates how applying principles and components together results in forming future thinking literacy.

1   Principles

Curriculum design and development in the 21st century needs to follow certain principles, processes and products to create meaningful learning.

The following seven principles comprise up-to-date curriculum design:

1 Constructivism
2 Transdisciplinarity
3 21st century skills
4 Blended learning incorporating technology
5 Teaching-learning strategies
6 Social responsibility/service learning
7 Putting it all together: Future thinking literacy

Designing using MdCM follows these principles and incorporates them into the teaching-learning content, process and products.

2   Content and Process

The processes of teaching and learning should focus on students' construction of new knowledge in blended learning environments using technology. During the learning process, students should investigate an issue, concept or product of their choice, from different aspects or perspectives, working in small groups on a project and trying to solve authentic problems. While working on the project, students also need to investigate the past and present in order to be able to prepare for the future. Another major concern in the process of learning and thinking about possible products should be suggesting how a proposed project can be of help to authentic or relevant audiences. Learning in this way will develop their 21st century skills and will result in meaningful and multi-category products.

3   Products

Products should vary from project to project, not only illustrating the accumulated knowledge, but also realizing the talents and strengths of the members of the group. Almost every lesson should have a mini-product. The final product of a project should be multicategorical, meaning it should, for example, present a model, a drawing, or an exhibition with some written explanation of why it was chosen, what each part represents etc. Types of products need to be suggested by the teacher and students prior to working on the project. Criteria for the assessment of mini- and final products need to be mutually agreed upon by teacher and students and displayed throughout the project, for students to be able to follow them and assess their work while creating it and use it as a final self-evaluation tool before presenting it. Peer evaluation of the product could also be used with cautioun, and with clear directions in order to avoid misunderstandings and offending of students.

4   Designing a Multidimensional Curriculum

Designing a multidimensional curriculum needs to take into consideration many components such as: content, thinking processes, thinking strategies, thinking tools, assessment tools, products, and evaluation/reflection (Vidergor, 2015a). Figure 2.1 illustrates the different components focusing on the three types of thinking – scientific, creative, and future thinking broken down to thinking strategies, thinking tools, assessment, product and reflection on learning.

4.1   *Interdisciplinary/Multidisciplinary/Transdisciplinary Content*
Content should be interdisciplinary, multidisciplinary, or transdisciplinary, employing comprehensive concepts, issues, theories, phenomena, or commonly

Content	Relevant multi/transdisciplinary content (concept, issue, phenomenon, product, object etc.)		
Thinking Process	Scientific Thinking Inquiry	Creative Thinking Problem Finding and Problem Solving	Future Thinking Construction and Analysis of Concept
Thinking Strategies	• Forming a research question • Proposing hypotheses • Collecting information • Organizing information • Using graphic presentation • Inferring/drawing conclusions	• Defining problem • Suggesting solutions • Finding criteria • Identifying perspectives • Selecting best solution • Encountering different angles • Empathizing (Being in someone's shoes)	• Defining & identifying components • Classifying & analyzing • Comparing • Identifying connections • Identifying processes • Organizing in sequence • Evaluating • Meliorating • Creating • Predicting development
Tools	• TASC thinking wheel • Inquiry stages	• Six thinking hats • Types of problems • Problem-solving stages • S.C.A.M.P.E.R.	• Thinking maps • Future scenarios
Assessment Tools	• Building criteria for product evaluation with students • Using formative and summative assessment • Incorporating self, peer and teacher evaluation		
Products	• Mini Research	• Problem solution • Action plan • Improved model	• Concept maps • Development model • Time line • Future model • Future scenario
	Multi categorical (combined) written, oral, creative, or other		
Reflection	Meta cognition/personal reflection on thinking process • General questions on learning process • Questions regarding thinking strategies		

FIGURE 2.1 *Components of the Multidomensional Curriculum Model (MdCM) (revised according to Vidergor, 2015a)*

known products, such as the topic of biodiesel, which involves biology, chemistry, technology, economics, agriculture, and environmental studies (recycling, alternative energy).

4.2 *Thinking Processes*
The thinking process is divided into three types of thinking: scientific thinking using inquiry, creative thinking involving problem finding and problem solving, and future thinking focusing on construction and analysis of concepts or phenomena.

4.3 Thinking Strategies

Thinking strategies are derived from three main thinking processes. Thinking strategies developed under scientific thinking are: formulating a research question and hypothesis, collecting and organizing information, representing it graphically and inferring from it; Creative thinking involves the stages of problem solving: defining the problem, suggesting solutions, defining criteria for selecting the best solution, designing an action plan using various perspectives and angles. It also includes encountering different angles and empathizing when making decisions. Future thinking incorporates: defining & identifying components, classification & analysis, comparison, identifying connections and processes, organizing in sequence, evaluating, creating, and predicting development.

4.4 Tools for Developing Thinking Skills

Tools for developing scientific thinking would be the TASC Thinking Wheel (Wallace, 2001, 2015), which means putting thinking in order and around a wheel, as well as using inquiry stages for researching a topic. Developing creative thinking requires use of complex problems characterized as Type IV, V, or VI problems (Maker, Zimmerman, Paz Gomez-Arizaga, Pease, & Burke, 2015), employing the problem-solving stages (FPSP, 2001), and examining perspectives using six thinking hats (De Bono, 2006) in order to discuss different authentic dilemmas. Developing future thinking involves illustrating issues using thinking maps (Hyrele, 2011), and writing future scenarios. S.C.A.M.P.E.R (Eberle, 1996) which stands for Substitute, Combine, Adjust, Modify, Put to other uses, Eliminate, and Reverse can be used for melioration and creation of new/future products combining creative thinking and future thinking.

4.5 Assessment Tools

Assessment tools for product evaluation need to be designed and mutually agreed upon with students. They should include both formative and summative assessment, and incorporate self, peer and teacher evaluation, readily available to students online in real time.

4.6 Products

The final product for the process of scientific thinking is the mini-research project, which could be individual or collaborative in part. Problem, solution and action plan will be considered as final products of the creative thinking development. As for the development of future thinking, suitable products could be: concept maps, a development model timeline, innovative entrepreneurship designing a new model, and a future scenario. Products need to be multicategorical (written, oral, creative) in order to best represent the acquisition of new knowledge and various perspectives by individual students, for example giving a TEDEx short talk on the topic studied followed by a model and short description of a new invention.

4.7   Reflection and Evaluation

Students need to be taught how to reflect on the process of learning using meta-cognition/personal reflection on the thinking processes, asking general questions, and questions regarding the use of different thinking strategies. Students need to learn how to use both self and peer evaluations in order to evaluate the process and products.

5   Additional Key Components

Four additional key factors necessary to achieve meaningful learning using the MdCM are teaching strategies, personalization of learning, developing social responsibility, and understanding the new teacher's role.

5.1   *Teaching-Learning Strategies Incorporating Technology*

Teaching strategies utilized in the MdCM to prepare students for adult life include project-based learning (Bell, 2010; Grant, 2002; Gultekin, 2005; Partnership for 21st Century Skills, 2008) and problem-based learning (Isaksen & Treffinger, 2004; OECD, 2015; Savery, 2006, 2015), which both create flexible blended learning environments, enhancing the use of technology and authentic use of language, and dealing with relevant issues (Christensen, Horn, & Staker, 2013). They explain that school, as we know it today, has to change its physical and organizational structure (schedule/timetable) to fit the learning needs of the students and comply with the latest strategies. Within blended learning environments students will use mobile phones as part of Bring Your Own Device, using game-like apps, tablets, learning apps (An, 2014), and MOOCs (Brahimi & Sarirete, 2015), rotating between the classroom and computer room, flipping learning and working on selected personal projects with mentor teachers in specific time slots and designed spaces. Two other powerful tools which will aid learning are collaborative game-based leaning (Sung & Hwang, 2013), and the use of 3D printers (Schelly, Anzalone, Wijnen, & Pearce, 2015) for the development of creative thinking and entrepreneurship. Communicating with guest scholars and debating current and future issues will enable students to obtain a deeper and broader perspective of the topic, issue or concept in question.

The teaching aspect and teacher preparation must take into account Pedagogical Content Knowledge (PCK) and Technological Pedagogical Content Knowledge (TPACK) (Koehler & Mishra, 2009), while exposing the teachers to the innovative MdCM teaching strategies and tools, focusing on the incorporation of technological devices and tools mentioned above, which could enhance learning.

5.2   *Personalization/Individualization of Learning*
Using the above mentioned strategies will allow for personalized or individualized learning (Houchens et al., 2014), including self-regulated (Zimmerman, 2000), multi-age grouping (Cornish, 2006; Nishida, 2009) based on students' talents, curiosity and areas of interest (Mitra & Rana, 2001), creating engagement and flow of creativity (Shernoff, Csikszentmihalyi, Schneider, & Shernoff, 2003), developing multiple intelligences (Gardner, 2003), catering to different learning styles (Schmeck, 2013), and addressing personal and cultural diversity (Banks, 2015).

5.3   *Developing Social Responsibility and Leadership Skills*
In their book *Enhancing the Gift of Leadership*, Vidergor and Sisk (2013) stress the need to teach leadership and enhance students' characteristics for their own benefit and for the benefit of society. Teaching leadership to our students aims at developing and enhancing their skills so that they become thinking, responsible, creative and proactive leaders who are aware of other people's needs (Vidergor, 2015b). Incorporating social responsibility in second language learning, for example, enabled the creation of a more meaningful teaching-learning environment, inspiring students to take responsibility for their own and their peers' learning (Vidergor, 2015c).

6   Putting It All Together: Developing Future Thinking Literacy

Using all six principles or components of a curriculum in one model adding the perspective of time promotes future thinking literacy. According to Vidergor (2010) the MdCM: (a) demonstrates effective use of several perspectives (*personal, global and time*) developing students' lifelong and life-wide learning skills; (b) offers opportunities to develop awareness of relevant and authentic multidisciplinary/transdisciplinary issues; (c) encourages the creation of a holistic view which prepares students for the future; (d) focuses on how experts think while taking into consideration developments and connections over time; (e) engages students in problem finding; (f) develops

TABLE 2.1 Compatibility of the multidimensional curriculum model and future span pedagogy

Content and curriculum	Learning practices	Evaluation	Teaching practices	Products	Organization learning environment	Leadership and values	Connectivity
Future thinking literacy	Learning and evaluation of micro-skills	Personal/individual evaluation	Teacher as pedagogical consultant	Multicategorical	Flexible timetable	Application of social and multicultural responsibility	Synchronized collaborative learning
Systems thinking literacy	Flipped classroom	Peer evaluation	Teacher as expert in instruction for understanding	Collaborative	Flexible combination of subject areas		Participation in global communities of learning
Digital/technological literacy	Creative-productive learning	Evaluation of meaningful learning (inquiry, project, problem solution)	Teacher as learner in communities of learning	Incorporating technology	Blended learning environments		Collaborative online peer learning
Global citizenship and multiculturalism	Project and problem-based learning		Teacher as part of an integrative team supporting learning	Mini research			
				Thinking map/s			
				Project			
Personal learning plan/curriculum	Online learning		Teacher as mentor	Model			
	Interest-based curriculum and self-regulation			Development timeline			
				Action plan			
	Multi-age learning			Future scenario			

creativity and innovation while solving problems (*creative thinking*) based on inquiry (*scientific thinking*); (g) demonstrates systematic ways of investigating development through time and looking for connections between events (*future thinking*); (h) develops the ability to write, present information orally and use foreign languages; (i) develops social interaction and team work while respecting cultural and personal differences; (j) develops self-regulation, motivation and personal as well as social responsibility; and (k) promotes constant growth while using different assessment tools.

The model is suitable for all grade levels and ranges of student abilities, encouraging students to develop according to their capabilities. Products, although varied in level, reflect student progress addressing complexity and future thinking literacy in the personal, global, and time perspectives. Breaking the traditional structure of classroom and schedule, teachers and students can communicate on an individual and group basis using face to face or e-learning platforms. The MdCM is compatible with the latest Future Time Span pedagogy published by the Israeli Ministry of Education (2016).

7 Developing a Unit of Study

While planning and designing a unit of study based on the MdCM one should take into consideration the following aspects: Student level, the chosen perspectives, unit and lesson length, content, aims, thinking process and thinking strategies, learning environment, opening/exposure, teaching strategies, learning activities and grouping, learning materials, products, assessment, modification for special needs students, and Enrichment for gifted and able students.

The thread woven across the unit should focus on developing students' future thinking literacy. This is different from traditional unit planning in several aspects lying at the core of MdCM guiding teachers to:

1. Select a multidisciplinary or transdisciplinary topics;
2. State the selected perspectives (personal, global or time);
3. Use all three processes of thinking (scientific, creative, and time) and break them down into thinking strategies;
4. Use several thinking tools suggested by MdCM;
5. Incorporate innovative teaching-learning strategies like problem-based, project-based and phenomenon-based learning; and
6. Plan activities for enriching gifted and able students in the regular classroom, as well as cater for the special needs students.

All these components directed towards the development of future thinking literacy, challenge students to think about the future, and write the future scenario, taking into consideration their newly constructed knowledge on the studied topic or phenomenon.

7.1 Student Level

Student level needs to be considered when planning the unit and lessons. Nowadays, grade level is less important, as students must be treated individually. There is also the option of grouping the students in multi-age or interest groups, where grade levels are less significant.

7.2 The Chosen Perspectives

The unit needs to contain at least two perspectives out of the three i.e. personal, global perspective, and time perspective. Lessons need to planned so that the two perspectives are addressed for 4 to 6 lessons each, in order to enable students to experience learning using the chosen perspective. Teachers could offer the choice of perspective to high school students. It is advised to start with the personal or global perspective and then focus on the time perspective, depending on the topic and student level.

7.3 Unit Length

Unit length is determined by many factors. Based on the experience of planning, designing and supervising the implementation of more than 30 units, the shortest length still covering the material, and working on two perspectives using thinking tools and different teaching strategies, is between 12–15 single lessons of 45 minutes each.

7.4 Lesson Length

Lesson length needs to be flexible, enabling students to work on their projects and products. Sometimes a lesson could be short and last for only 45 minutes, and sometimes a double lesson is needed in order to complete an assignment and not disrupt the process of thinking, planning and designing projects.

7.5 Content

The topic and subtopics of the lesson indicate what material is covered. The topic of the lesson should derive from the more general topic which needs to broad enough to let students choose their subtopics according to their interest. Content needs to evolve around big multidisciplinary and transdisciplinary issues such as migration, energy, family, capital city, etc. which could be investigated from many different angles.

7.6 *Aims*

Aims for the unit in general and for each lesson or group of lessons should be specified very clearly and should be very operative. Aims should start with "students will do/learn/be exposed to/acquire/perform/present etc.

7.7 *Thinking Processes Developed*

The three processes developed in MdCM are scientific thinking, creative thinking, and future thinking. The designed unit should include all three. Each lesson, or group of lessons should specify exactly which thinking process will be developed by students.

7.8 *Thinking Strategies Developed*

Thinking strategies are derived from the thinking process. If, for example we would like to develop students' scientific thinking using inquiry, we will choose from the following strategies: forming a research question and hypotheses, gathering information, organizing information, creating a graphic representation of information or results, inferring and drawing conclusions. Students must also be exposed to certain tools that will help them learn and develop these thinking strategies. Suggested tools for scientific thinking-inquiry would be the inquiry stages and the TASC thinking wheel.

7.9 *Learning Environment*

The learning environment consists of the physical environment, meaning the organization of the class, having one or more teachers present, learning in or out of class, using the computer room, using labs etc. The second aspect relates to the learning climate which enables students to investigate freely, ask questions, enjoy learning, challenge themselves, choose according to their interests, work at the right pace etc. Nowadays it is of the outmost importance to incorporate technology into the learning environment, open the physical environment and stretch it beyond the four walls of the classroom, and create a flow and variety of spaces students can work in at school. It is also advised to incorporate some distance learning, enabling students to work from home on their individual or group projects.

7.10 *Opening/Exposure*

The first lesson or double lesson should serve as an introduction to the general subject or issue addressed by the unit. It should invite and motivate students to learn about this new issue/concept/product/phenomenon from different aspects or angles. Activities need to be challenging, interesting and fun. Among suggested activities are: watching video clips, experimenting, listening to a guest speaker and asking questions, a field trip, putting together pieces of information to create a collage or sequence of events, looking for as many facts as possible on the internet and presenting them creatively, etc.

Each single or double lesson should also have a short ten-minute exposure to the subtopic addressed in that session. Activities should vary from one lesson to another. If a new tool is introduced i.e. the TASC thinking wheel, exposure might take longer and use a topic other than the one in question, just as an example of using the tool. Then a double lesson should be planned to enable students practice the tool after exposure, applying it to their chosen topics relating to the unit.

7.11 *Teaching Strategies*
The teaching strategy selected should fit the aims, thinking processes and strategies to be developed. Thinking strategies recommended by MdCM are inquiry-based learning, project-based learning, problem-based learning, and blended learning. All teaching strategies can be incorporated i.e. using blended learning environments with different types of lab and station rotation for developing projects. While working on the projects students will use inquiry stages to learn about an issue or phenomenon and will define and solve authentic problems suggesting solutions that will contribute to society.

7.12 *Learning Activities and Grouping*
Learning activities are the actual activities students perform during lessons. They are directly derived from and are in accordance with the teaching strategies. Learning activities are presented using verbs explaining what student will do i.e. Students will work in small groups and define the problem. Learning activities need to be listed according to sequence indicating whether the activity is to be performed individually, in pairs, in small groups, or a plenary.

7.13 *Learning Materials*
Learning materials are the sources available to students from which they will be able to extract the information students need to know or practice i.e. books, websites, encyclopedias, newspapers, textbooks, videos, workbooks, worksheets etc. Learning materials need to be varied and multicategorical (printed and electronic). They need to complement learning activities. Not all materials have to be supplied by the teacher, as students need to experience looking for information individually and in groups. In case of very young students, more guidance will be needed.

7.14   *Products*
Products are divided in two: 1. the small products of lessons during the process of learning, and 2. the final product. The small products representing the learning process will be connected to the thinking tools i.e., the TASC wheel, the six thinking hats, stages of problem solving, thinking maps, and timeline. The final product could be the action plan illustrating the application of a selected solution, or a future scenario.

7.15   *Assessment*
All products, whether small or final, must be accompanied by an assessment tool. Assessment tools should vary from checklists to rubrics. Each product needs to have at least five criteria for evaluation. Preferably, the final product should have between five to ten criteria. Criteria for assessment of products should be elicited from students and clearly displayed during the learning process so they will be able to assess their work in real time and work towards delivering the best product reflecting their talents and knowledge. Methods of evaluation can vary from self, to peer to teacher assessment, sometimes combining more than one type. The teacher should pay specific attention to peer evaluation, modeling it and making sure students practice the right way of using it, giving positive feedback for revision during the process without offending their classmates.

7.16   *Modification for Special Needs Students*
Modification of activities is crucial for students with special needs. These students, who are now included in regular heterogeneous classes, must be accommodated so that they can learn the material properly in a manner that acknowledges their strengths and their difficulties. Special attention should be paid to learning styles, dyslexia, dysgraphia, and physical impairments. Modifications need to be carefully thought out and planned, otherwise they will result in less meaningful solutions such pairing or grouping students with special needs with other students who will end up doing the activities and the actual learning.

7.17   *Enrichment for Gifted and Able Students*
Enrichment for gifted and able students is very important. These children tend to finish their assignment earlier than other students, and when they do so, teachers should challenge them to work up to their potential. This means the teacher needs to plan, motivate, and help students choose from a number of extra activities they would be interested in further investigating or addressing. Ability grouping could also work in this case, but teachers need to be careful

not to always resort to the most common solution of asking the more able students to help the weaker ones.

8 Note

Units presented in the coming chapters will follow the template for developing units of study addressed in this chapter. The exemplary units were developed by experienced graduate Jewish and Arab teachers studying in two colleges of teacher education in Israel, supervised by the developer of the model. All units were implemented in classes varying from first grade to eleventh grade, addressing different topics, large concepts and issues. They were planned and designed for heterogeneous classes, as well as for gifted and able students in a special pullout program, and weak high school students preparing for a matriculation exam. Although units follow the template of MdCM, some units will highlight and elaborate on the application of innovative teaching strategies or thinking tools.

References

An, H. (Ed.). (2014). *Tablets in K-12 education: Integrated experiences and implications.* Hershey, PA: IGI Global.

Banks, J. A. (2015). *Cultural diversity and education.* New York, NY: Routledge.

Bell, S. (2010). Project based learning for the 21st century: Skills for the future. *The Clearinghouse, 83,* 39–43.

Brahimi, T., & Sarirete, A. (2015). Learning outside the classroom through MOOCs. *Computers in Human Behavior, 51,* 604–609.

Christensen, C. M., Horn, M. B., & Staker, H. (2013). *Is K-12 blended learning disruptive? An introduction of the theory of hybrids.* San Mateo, CA: Clayton Christensen Institute. Retrieved February 18, 2016, from www.christenseninstitute.org

Cornish, L. (2006). Introduction. In L. Cornish (Ed.), *Reaching EFA through multi-grade teaching: Issues, contexts and practices* (pp. 1–8). Armidale: Kardoorair Press.

de Bono, E. (2006). *Lateral thinking: The power of provocation manual.* Clive: De Bono Thinking Systems.

Eberle, B. (1996). *SCAMPER: Games for imagination development.* Waco, TX: Prufrock Press Inc.

Gardner, H. (2003). *Intelligence reframed: Multiple intelligences for the 21st century.* New York, NY: Basic Books.

Grant, M. M. (2002). Getting a grip on project-based learning: Theory, cases and recommendations. *Meridian: A Middle School Computer Technologies Journal, 5*(1), 1–3. Retrieved February 19, 2017, from http://www.ncsu.edu/meridian/win2002/514/project-based.pdf

Gultekin, M. (2005). The effect of project based learning on learning outcomes in the 5th grade social studies course in primary education. *Educational Sciences: Theory and Practice, 5*(2), 548–556.

Houchens, G. W., Crossbourne, T. A., Zhang, J., Norman, A. D., Chon, K., Fisher, L., & Schraeder, M. (2014). *Personalized learning: A theoretical review and implications for assessing kid-friendly student outcomes.* Bowling Green, KY: Western Kentucky University.

Hyerle, D., & Alper, L. (2011). *Student successes with thinking maps.* Thousand Oaks, CA: Corwin Press.

Isaksen, S. G., & Treffinger, D. J. (2004). Celebrating 50 years of reflective practice: Versions of creative problem solving. *Journal of Creative Behavior, 38,* 75–101.

Koehler, M. J., & Mishra, P. (2009). What is technological pedagogical content knowledge. *Contemporary Issues in Technology and Teacher Education, 9*(1), 60–70.

Maker, C. J., Zimmerman, R., Paz Gomez-Arizaga, M., Pease, R., & Burke, E. M. (2015). Developing real-life problem solving: Integrating the DISCOVER problem matrix, problem based learning, and thinking actively in a social context. In H. E. Vidergor & C. R. Harris (Eds.), *Applied practice for educators of gifted and able learners.* Rotterdam, The Netherlands: Sense Publishers.

Ministry of Education. (2016). *Research and development of future span pedagogy: Trends challenges principles and recommendations.* Jerusalem: Pedagogical Administration. [in Hebrew]

Mitra, S., & Rana, V. (2001). Children and the internet: Experiments with minimally invasive education in India. *British Journal of Educational Technology, 32,* 221–232.

Nishida, Y. (2009). *The challenge of multiage primary education in public education.* Saarbrucken: VDM Verglag, Dr. Mueller.

OECD. (2015). *Draft pisa 2015 collaborative problem solving framework.* Retrieved January 10, 2017, from www.oecd.org/pisa/pisaproducts/pisa2015draftframeworks.htm

Partnership for 21st Century Skills. (2008). *P21 framework definitions.* Retrieved February 1, 2017, from www.21stcenturyskills.org

Savery, J. R. (2006). Overview of problem-based learning: Definitions and distinctions. *The Interdisciplinary Journal of Problem-Based Learning, 1*(1), 9–20.

Savery, J. R. (2015). Overview of problem-based learning: Definitions and distinctions. In A. Walker, H. Leary, C. Hmelo-Silver, & P. A. Ertmer (Eds.), *Essential readings in problem-based learning: Exploring and extending the legacy of Howard S. Barrows* (pp. 5–15). Lafayette, IN: Purdue University Press.

Schelly, C., Anzalone, G., Wijnen, B., & Pearce, J. M. (2015). Open-source 3-D printing technologies for education: Bringing additive manufacturing to the classroom. *Journal of Visual Languages & Computing, 28*, 226–237.

Schmeck, R. R. (Ed.). (2013). *Learning strategies and learning styles.* New York, NY: Springer Science & Business Media.

Shernoff, D. J., Csikszentmihalyi, M., Schneider, B., & Shernoff, E. S. (2003). Student engagement in high school classrooms from the perspective of flow theory. *School Psychology Quarterly, 18*, 158–176.

Sung, H. Y., & Hwang, G. J. (2013). A collaborative game-based learning approach to improving students' learning performance in science courses. *Computers & Education, 63*, 43–51.

Vidergor, H. E. (2010). The multidimensional curriculum model. *Gifted and Talented International, 25*(2), 153–165.

Vidergor, H. E. (2015a). The multidimensional curriculum model. In H. E. Vidergor & C. R. Harris (Eds.), *Applied practice for educators of gifted and able learners* (pp. 199–214). Rotterdam, The Netherlands: Sense Publishers.

Vidergor, H. E. (2015b). The ambassador: Leadership for gifted and able students. In H. E. Vidergor & C. R. Harris (Eds.), *Applied practice for educators of gifted and able learners* (pp. 587–602). Rotterdam, The Netherlands: Sense Publishers.

Vidergor, H. E. (2015c). Relate-create-donate: Promoting social responsibility in second language teaching and learning. In H. E. Vidergor & C. R. Harris (Eds.), *Applied practice for educators of gifted and able learners* (pp. 559–572). Rotterdam, The Netherlands: Sense Publishers.

Vidergor, H. E., & Sisk, D. A. (2013). *Enhancing the gift of leadership: Innovative programs for all grade levels.* Ulm: International Center for Innovation in Education Press.

Wallace, B. (2001). *Teaching thinking skills across the primary curriculum.* London: David Fulton Publishers (A NACE-Fulton Pub).

Wallace, B. (2015). Using the TASC thinking and problem-solving framework to create a curriculum of opportunity across the full spectrum of human abilities: TASC – thinking actively in a social context. In H. E. Vidergor & C. R. Harris (Eds.), *Applied practice for educators of gifted and able learners* (pp. 113–130). Rotterdam, The Netherlands: Sense Publishers.

Zimmerman, B. J. (2000). Becoming a self-regulated learner: An overview. *Theory Into Practice, 41*(2), 64–70.

PART 2

Updating the Curriculum in Core Domains

CHAPTER 3

Science and Technology: Genetics

This chapter focuses on science and technology and illustrates the application of MdCM to teach a unit on genetics. The application of thinking tools and personal and future perspectives with 9th grade students resulted in the future scenario indicating integration of knowledge and the ability to take genetics into the future, predicting developments based on past and present.

1   Science and Technology

Science and technology constitute a major part of human culture and everyday reality and are important for our development and understanding of modern society. Developing scientific literacy including knowledge about the world, development of thinking skills, values and behavior, are crucial for general education needed today and in the coming future (Ministry of Education, 2015).

The curriculum for science and technology according to the Israeli Ministry of Education (2015) aspires to develop citizens with scientific-technological literacy, curiosity, and the ability to learn independently and use scientific-technological knowledge and thinking skills to understand phenomena in the world surrounding us, solve problems, make decisions, and take a stand on everyday issues relevant to home, school and workplace environments. The curriculum focuses on STS – Science, Technology, and Society combining chemistry, biology, physics, and technology. Its purpose is to develop: (a) thinking skills such as: inquiry, comparing and contrasting, forming hypotheses, constructing new knowledge, drawing conclusions, presenting knowledge and dissemination; (b) communication and collaboration skills including critical discourse, receiving and giving feedback, expressing ideas and thoughts, and use of digital and non-digital media for sharing. All of this aims to equip graduates to cope successfully with future challenges in a dynamic, constantly changing world.

The curriculum in Life Sciences or Biology (Keinan & Associates, 2014) focuses on the understanding of processes and phenomena in ecological systems and includes three major subjects: the cell, systems and processes in living creatures, and ecological systems relying on accepted principles in life sciences. These principles, woven into teaching and learning throughout the program will give students a world-wide perspective of life sciences.

Keinan and associates (2014) explain that the curriculum includes three main topics: The cell, systems and processes in living creatures, and ecological systems relying on accepted principles in life sciences today. These principles are woven through the curriculum in order to create a wide perspective of life sciences among students.

2 Example Unit and Lessons: Genetics

The unit described in this chapter is based on chemistry and life sciences for 9th grade students. The original program includes inquiry and problem solving, scientific literacy, technological literacy, and development of high order thinking skills. The unit focuses on the subject of genetics, which deals with the principles of heredity. Genetics is considered a basic, complicated, vast, and interdisciplinary subject which relates to: science, technology, health, psychology, environmental sciences, law, ethics, and religion. The unit was designed in congruence with the curriculum suggested by the Israeli Ministry, but enriching the learning process by adding the components of the Multidimensional Curriculum Model (MdCM).

3 Unit Description

The unit was designed for 9th grade middle school students studying in a heterogeneous class, of medium socioeconomic status (SES), consisting of 16 girls, and 12 boys, in total 28 students. It comprises 12 lessons dealing with various issues related to genetics such as: principles of heredity, transferring inherited traits from generation to generation, acquired and inherited traits, DNA structure, genetic coding of information in DNA translated into protein and how it affects the hereditary traits of living creatures, as well as how the environment influences them. The unit also deals with genetic mutations and their influences, ways of avoiding damage to the DNA and hereditary diseases. Another issue dealt with in this unit is human intervention in processes related to heredity and innovative technologies developed for the purpose of intentional melioration, genetic engineering, cloning, the human genome; advantages and disadvantages of such intervention, and moral and bio-ethical issues deriving from it. Interdisciplinary subjects were investigated individually when students were requested to look at the personal perspective. In a different section of the unit, students are invited to inquire, solve problems and make decisions, working in small groups, utilizing peer evaluation. The unit strongly emphasizes thinking processes including scientific, creative, and future thinking. It emphasizes two perspectives: personal, and time, combining the thinking processes with independent study and inquiry and problem-based learning. Unit products, which are creative, varied and multicategorical, reflect the process, and follow mutually agreed upon criteria for evaluation.

The first part introduces students to the topic of genetics, by reading an article about a boy who was born with six fingers. Students are asked to discuss the article in relation to genetics and hereditary traits. Using different thinking maps, students write associations, compare and contrast themselves with another family member, classify hereditary and acquired traits. Then, students are introduced to basic concepts in genetics (gene, chromosome, DNA structure and function of hereditary matter, biological rank and location on the organization level). Learning is accompanied by short videos, presentations, and work on the digital portfolio, as well as the chemistry and life sciences textbooks. Using a Flow Map, students investigate the connection between the cells and the hereditary information they possess and the representation of hereditary traits. They also develop scientific literacy relating to health issues in a social context dealing with Down syndrome, combining scientific knowledge and inference of data from a graph.

The second part examines the subject from the personal perspective. Students learn about the concept of mutation and the contribution of mutations and genetic diversity to the biological variety through videos. Students work in groups and investigate the influences of harmful factors on DNA and the proper function of the body. Students present the collaborative product via a poster containing a written explanation of the immediate, indirect, and long term health damage caused by the harmful factor. They use a flow chart to describe the connection between exposure to the harmful factor and its influence on the DNA and the type of damage in human beings, and draw personal conclusions regarding protection of their DNA. These conclusions should include suggestions for means of protection and rules of behavior that will prevent or reduce the damage. Additional activities dealing with the personal perspective are genetic engineering, in which small groups of students need to gather and organize information about genetic engineering and its application using videos and the textbook. Each group submits one application of genetic engineering (plants, drugs, environment) stating their opinion on the effect of transgenic food on human beings, or on questions such as: Why am I worried that transgenic plants and animal are dangerous for my health? What fears do I have relating to nurturing plants and animals using genetic engineering? In the second part students address cloning, and cloning in humans by watching a film showing the cloning of Dolly. Then students use the six thinking hats in groups of six, reading an excerpt from Huxley's *Brave New World* which in 1932 predicted the possibility of cloning human beings with desirable traits. Students then relate to the bio-ethical issue using the six thinking hats, and need to reach a consensus regarding the decision whether to allow or ban cloning. The group decision will be presented to class creatively following the pre-determined criteria.

The third part explores the time perspective. Students individually seek and collect information on famous genetic scientists. Then students place their scientist on a timeline in chronological sequence. Students become acquainted with scientists and their discoveries, identify connections between processes and design an identity card for their selected scientist, presented via PPT. The final activity combines all scientists to present one sequence of events from the past to the present. This strengthens student awareness of discoveries, preparing them to predict and better cope with future changes based on knowledge from the past and present. In the final product – the future scenario, students project themselves into the future, in this case 2032 or 2068, and write a story incorporating the past and current present to illustrate how the world of genetics will influence human beings.

4 Lesson Plans

Student Level
9th grade heterogeneous class, medium SES

Chosen Perspectives
Personal and time perspectives. Suggestions for the global perspective will follow.

Unit and Lesson Length
12 lessons of 45 minutes each

Lesson 1–2: Introduction to Genetics from a Personal Perspective

Content
- Introduction to genetics
- What does genetics deal with?
- Hereditary and acquired traits

SCIENCE AND TECHNOLOGY: GENETICS

Aims
- Student will define genetics and its branches.
- Student will use thinking maps to define and summarize hereditary and acquired traits.
- Student will compare his/her own traits with those of a family member.

Thinking Processes Developed
Construction and analysis of concept

Thinking Strategies Developed
Defining and identifying components; comparison; classification and analysis

Learning Environment
Science lab equipped with computer and projector

Opening/Exposure
- Students read the article "Born with six fingers".
- Class discussion: What could hint that this is connected to hereditary traits? What is heredity?
- Students use the Bubble Map to write associations about heredity.

Teaching Strategies
Inquiry-based learning

Learning Activities and Grouping
Students will:

1. Ask questions about their own traits.
2. Look for answers in textbook and on websites.
3. Use the Double Bubble Map to compare their traits with those of a family member.
4. Look for information regarding hereditary and acquired traits.
5. Work in pairs to analyze and classify hereditary and acquired traits using the Tree Map.
6. Watch the video on BrainPOP about genetics.
7. Answer the quiz on genetics on BrainPOP.

Learning Materials
- Textbook

- Thinking maps
- Video from BrainPOP about genetics
- Test yourself about genetics on BrainPOP

Product/s
- Bubble Map
- Double Bubble Map
- Tree Map

Assessment
Criteria for evaluating thinking maps: Relevant representation, number of components, correct use of concepts

Modification for Special Needs Students
1. Teacher will help special needs students with activities
2. Teacher will pair a weak student with a stronger one

Enrichment for Gifted and Able Students
Read the chapter in the book and look for additional information online to answer the following question: Can human behavior affect the representation of diabetes?

Lesson 3: Introduction Continued

Content
- Hereditary matter – organization and function, what do parents transfer to their children?
- What is a gene?
- Chromosomes and homological chromosomes.
- Level of organization in nature – biological ranking, the place of DNA and the gene in the organization hierarchy.
- The nucleotide, the amino acid and the genetic code.
- Down Syndrome.

Aims
- Student will recognize the structure, organization, and function of DNA.
- Student will define a gene.
- Student will recognize homological chromosomes.
- Student will recognize levels of organization and places of DNA and genes in these levels (cell, nucleus, chromosome, DNA, gene).

SCIENCE AND TECHNOLOGY: GENETICS

Thinking Processes Developed
1 Scientific thinking – inquiry
2 Construction and analysis of concept

Thinking Strategies Developed
– Defining and identifying components
– Organizing in sequence
– Forming hypotheses
– Collecting information from graphs and drawing conclusions

Learning Environment
1 Science lab
2 Computer lab/BYOD classroom

Opening/Exposure
Presentation on chromosomes
DNA structure – 2 videos
https://www.youtube.com/watch?v=vyeYEiWGtQ8
https://www.youtube.com/watch?v=2BwEqpsDrCU

Teaching Strategies
Scientific thinking – inquiry

Learning Activities and Grouping
Students will:

1 Work in pairs to organize chromosomes in DNA.
2 Work individually in a computer room on the voyage of DNA (Listen to TED talk and write main point) https://www.youtube.com/watch?v=E5X6Qy772YU
3 Work in pairs to design a Flow Map of connection between body cells and hereditary information and representation of hereditary traits.
4 Work in pairs to raise hypotheses from a graph on mothers' age and the odds of delivering a baby with Down Syndrome (Textbook + Worksheet).

Learning Materials
– YouTube videos on DNA
– Definitions of chromosome, gene, homological chromosome
– Connection between body cells and hereditary information and representation of hereditary traits – textbook
– Textbook – graph about Down Syndrome + worksheet

- TED Talk – https://www.youtube.com/watch?v=E5X6Qy772YU

Product/s
- Flow Map of connection between body cells and hereditary information and representation of hereditary traits.
- Completed worksheet about Down Syndrome.

Assessment
- Flow Map: at least four components, proper language, correct representation of information, correct sequence
- Worksheet: raising at least two hypotheses, drawing at least 2 conclusions, relevant use of accurate terms, correct use of language

Modification for Special Needs Students
- Designing flow chart on computer
- Answering the questions on worksheet orally

Enrichment for Gifted and Able Students
Choose one and study the process:

- From DNA to traits
- From DNA to protein

Lesson 4–5: Personal Perspective

Content
From gene to trait – mutation changes in DNA and their implications

Aims
- Student will understand what a mutation is and its contribution to human diversity.
- Student will recognize the effects of harmful factors on the DNA to control proper function of the body.
- Student will understand the importance of personal avoidance or reduction of direct exposure to the sun and mutagens.

Thinking Processes Developed
Scientific thinking – inquiry

SCIENCE AND TECHNOLOGY: GENETICS

Thinking Strategies Developed
– Collecting and organizing information
– Analysis – identifying components and connections

Learning Environment
– Science lab
– Computer lab

Opening/Exposure
What is a mutation? Video by Davidson Institute of Science Education:
http://davidson.weizmann.ac.il/online/maagarmada/life_sci/%D7%9E%D7%94%D7%99-%D7%9E%D7%95%D7%98%D7%A6%D7%99%D7%94-%D7%92%D7%A0%D7%98%D7%99%D7%AA
Video – Sickle cell anemia
https://www.youtube.com/watch?v=VkhYL-BxJhQ

Teaching Strategies
Inquiry-based learning

Learning Activities and Grouping
Students will:

1. Work individually using the textbook to understand that skin complexion is transferred from gene to trait.
2. Work in small groups and choose one of the following materials causing mutations: nickel and cadmium in batteries, beryllium in metal industries, asbestos, radon gas, cigarette smoke, UV rays, sun rays.
3. Gather information online and from textbooks, draw a flow chart describing the connection between the hazardous material and its effect on DNA and on the human body, relating to the most affected age group in society.
4. Draw personal conclusions regarding ways of protecting themselves and rules of behavior.
5. Prepare a poster containing the health hazard, the flow chart, most affected group, and personal conclusions and behavior rules.

Learning Materials
– Textbook
– Digital portfolio for high school – sciences www.ebaghigh.cet.ac.il

Product/s
Collaborative poster containing the health hazard, the flow chart, most affected group, and personal conclusions and behavior rules.

Assessment
Criteria for evaluation of poster: Presenting the changes in DNA and their implications, explanation of the health hazard, flow chart, relating to the most affected age group/s in society, personal conclusions and suggestion for prevention, team work, creative presentation, overall poster appearance.

Modification for Special Needs Students
Dysgraphic students could do the poster on the computer, or record themselves instead of writing the answers to the questions. Dyslectic students could have a partner/group member record from the textbook, or use text-to-speech software when accessing online information. Weak students could be paired with stronger ones.

Enrichment for Gifted and Able Students
- Enrichment activity from textbook – From DNA to protein
- Learning more about sickle cell anemia

Lesson 6: Personal Perspective

Content
- Genetic engineering
- Applications of genetic engineering (medicine, environment)

Aims
- Student will define genetic engineering.
- Student will recognize applications of genetic engineering.
- Student will investigate one application of genetic engineering.
- Student will understand the relationship between scientific research and technology in medicine and the improvement of personal quality of life.

Thinking Processes Developed
Scientific thinking – inquiry

Thinking Strategies Developed
- Collecting and organizing information
- Inferring

Learning Environment
Science lab

Opening/Exposure
What is genetic engineering?
https://www.youtube.com/watch?v=j1rLh5oTA9o
https://www.youtube.com/watch?v=QT8dAYQpoUY

Teaching Strategies
- Inquiry-based learning
- Blended learning – lab rotation

Learning Activities and Grouping
Students will alternate between science lab and computer lab to investigate genetic engineering.
　Computer lab: In pairs, students will investigate genetic engineering and will summarize what they have learnt in one paragraph. (20 min.).
　Science lab: In pairs, students will read relevant pages in the textbook referring to genetic engineering and its applications and answer some questions. (20 min.).
　In science lab: Students will choose one area (medicine – genetically engineered medication, or environment – genetically engineered plants) and will list possible implications or health hazards to their own lives.
　Students will present in groups the selected application orally and in writing and express their opinions and reservations about the effects on their own lives.

Learning Materials
- Videos relating to genetic engineering
- Textbook

Product/s
Written and oral presentation of application and personal effects

Assessment
Written and oral presentation: Accuracy of definition, accuracy of facts, selection of one application, presentation of a personal opinion, written and presented in first person, presenting at least three relevant reservations on the effect of genetic engineering in that area. In addition, delivery should also take into account clarity of speech, and fluency.

Modification for Special Needs Students
Dysgraphic students could use the computer for work and presentation, or could present orally with no writing. Students could watch the videos on genetic engineering and write 3–4 sentences on what they have learnt.

Enrichment for Gifted and Able Students
Conduct a WebQuest on genetic engineering individually or in pairs.

Lesson 7: Personal Perspective

Content
- Cloning
- For and against cloning
- The six thinking hats

Aims
- Student will define cloning.
- Student will engage in ethical dilemma regarding cloning in human beings.
- Student will make a decision on cloning in human beings using the six thinking hats.

Thinking Processes Developed
Creative thinking – decision making

Thinking Strategies Developed
- Identifying perspectives
- Encountering different angles

Learning Environment
Science lab

Opening/Exposure
Cloning
http://www.brainpop.co.il/category_12/subcategory_130/subjects_2688/
Cloning Dolly the sheep
http://www.brainpop.co.il/category_12/subcategory_130/subjects_2689/
The Six Thinking Hats
http://www.debonogroup.com/six_thinking_hats.php

Teaching Strategies
- Problem-based learning – decision making
- Blended learning – lab rotation

Learning Activities and Grouping
1. Students will read an excerpt from *Brave New World* by Huxley.
2. Students will alternate between science lab and computer lab: (20 min.).
3. In the computer lab, students will explore the bio-ethical issue of cloning in human beings
4. In the science lab, in groups of 6, students will use the six thinking hats to make a decision for or against cloning in human beings.
5. Students will present their decisions to the class.

Learning Materials
- Textbook
- Excerpt from *Brave New World* by Huxley
- Digital portfolio – Bio-ethical issue of cloning in human beings http://mybag.ebaghigh.cet.ac.il/content/player.aspx?manifest=%2fapi%2fmanifests%2fitem%2fhe%2f6579fdec-d22d-4b7c-a3fa-8a9553ad0a41#?page=content-1
- PDF explaining the process of the six thinking hats

Product/s
Presentation of a decision for or against cloning in human beings

Assessment
- Process: team work, collection of information, completion of computer assignment.
- Presentation: clear decision, presenting different angles (according to hats), all group members participated, interesting, creative, within three minute time limit.

Modification for Special Needs Students
- Teacher mediation
- Mixed ability grouping

Enrichment for Gifted and Able Students
Conduct a WebQuest on human cloning

Lesson 8–9: Time Perspective

Content
The history of genetics – development of genetics over time

Aims
- Student will recognize the general history of genetics (famous scientists contributing to the field).
- Student will put discoveries in sequence.
- Student will identify connections between events and processes.
- Student will understand how these discoveries led to changes in the area of genetics.

Thinking Processes Developed
- Scientific thinking – inquiry
- Future thinking – construction and analysis of concept

Thinking Strategies Developed
- Collecting and organizing information
- Organizing in sequence
- Graphic representation in timeline
- Defining and identifying components
- Identifying connections
- Identifying processes

Learning Environment
- Science lab
- Computer lab
- Library

Opening/Exposure
PPT presentation showing different genetic scientists

Teaching Strategies
Future-based learning

Learning Activities and Grouping
Individual student will:

1 Choose one scientist from the presentation and explore his/her life.

2 Design an identity card for the selected scientist (photo, first and family name, year of birth, place of birth, childhood, family, education, discovery and year, effect of discovery on the field, and awards/prizes.

In groups students will:

3 Design a timeline for the development of genetics, placing the individually selected scientists according to chronological sequence. Students will add scientists who do not have identity cards. Students will explore the discoveries in genetics in terms of: (a) connections between events; (b) continuity between events; and (c) acceleration of events.
4 Look at connections with other discoveries, developments in technology, major historical events, etc.
5 Prepare a PPT presentation or a poster of the timeline depicting at least 10 scientists and their discoveries.

Learning Materials
Genetics towards the third millennium – video
http://www.amalnet.k12.il/meida/biolog/bi000430.htm

– Textbook
– Worksheet – Identity card
– Worksheet – Instructions for preparing a timeline

Product/s
– Individual: Identity card
– Group: Timeline

Assessment
– Identity card: Includes all sections, accurate information, aesthetically presented, clear explanation of discovery.
– Timeline: Presents ten scientists, correct sequence, shows year and main discovery for each scientist, accompanied by written text: Explaining (1) (a) connections between events; (b) continuity between events; and (c) acceleration of events; and (2) connections with other discoveries, developments in technology, major historical events, etc.

Modification for Special Needs Students
– Individual: Identity card – less writing and more photos to describe the scientist
– Group: Mixed ability grouping

Enrichment for Gifted and Able Students
Genetics towards the third millennium – video
http://www.amalnet.k12.il/meida/biolog/bioo0430.htm

Lesson 10–11: Time Perspective

Content
DNA fingerprint – Genetics helping to solve crimes

Aims
Student will solve a real-life problem related to a criminal act involving a genetic fingerprint

Thinking Processes Developed
Creative thinking – problem finding and problem solving

Thinking Strategies Developed
– Defining problem
– Suggesting solutions
– Identifying criteria
– Selecting the best solution

Learning Environment
– Science lab
– Computer lab
– Library

Opening/Exposure
Scenario presentation: A true story about an Israeli lawyer murdered in 2006 which remained a mystery for two years. In 2008 a young man was arrested on the suspicion of a motorcycle theft, and was identified as the murderer who had committed the crime two years earlier, when he was only 15 years old.

Teaching Strategies
Future-based learning – creative problem solving

Learning Activities and Grouping
Students will look for more information on the presented scenario

SCIENCE AND TECHNOLOGY: GENETICS

In groups: You are assigned to investigate the case of the murder of Lawyer Anat Fliner. You have to suggest a possible solution that will be accepted by the court for the conviction of the murderer.
Note: Any scenario of a criminal act can be used.
Pay attention to the following instructions:

1. Draw a table listing what you know about the case, and what is unknown
2. Define the problem. Start with "How can we...?"
3. Suggest at least five solutions.
4. Identify at least four criteria for selecting the best solution.
5. Select the best solution based on the criteria.
6. Suggest an action plan.
7. Support your decision with at least two sources from the internet.
8. Present the process and action plan to the class.

Learning Materials
- Worksheet presenting the case scenario
- News website
  http://www.ynet.co.il/articles/0,7340,L-4367340,00.html
- DNA fingerprint on Digital Portfolio
  http://mybag.ebaghigh.cet.ac.il/content/player.aspx?manifest=%2fapi%2fmanifests%2fitem%2fhe%2f0a97d8d8-3074-491e-b734-295fbc23641d#?page=content-1
- Identification and forensic science
  http://www.ynet.co.il/articles/0,7340,L-3999256,00.html
  http://www.ifsi.org.il/
  http://www.ynet.co.il/yaan/0,7340,L-13533-PreYaan,00.html
- Textbook

Product/s
Written and oral presentation of the problem solving process

Assessment
Students presented the following (orally and in writing):

1. A table listing what they know about the case, and what is unknown.
2. A definition of the problem starting with: How can we...?
3. At least five solutions.
4. At least four criteria for selecting the best solution.

5　The best solution according to the criteria.
6　An action plan.
7　Support for their decision from at least two internet sources.

Modification for Special Needs Students
– Dyslectic students could help the group orally.
– Weak students will summarize the process in short sentences.

Enrichment for Gifted and Able Students
Look up a similar case and describe how the suspect was convicted using DNA fingerprinting.

Lesson 12: Time Perspective- Future Scenario

Content
Genetics in the future

Aims
– Student will think about life in the future relating to genetics.
– Student will predict life in the (near or far) future relating to genetics.

Thinking Processes Developed
Future thinking – construction and analysis of concept

Thinking Strategies Developed
Predicting development

Learning environment
Science lab

Teaching Strategies
Future-based learning

Learning Activities and Grouping
In groups of five, students write a scenario illustrating how genetics will influence human beings, guided by the following instructions:

1　Project yourself into the selected future time-span (medium – 12 years from now, or far – 50 years from now).

2   Write at least one page.
3   Write in first person.
4   Add two characters.
5   Relate to all three periods of time (past, present and future).
6   Try to be creative.
7   The plot has to show changes or development.
8   Mention processes.
9   Mention connection between processes.
10 Use appropriate register.

Present to the class.

Learning Materials
– Worksheet
– All information learnt in this unit

Product/s
Future scenario

Assessment
Ten criteria based on the instructions

Modification for Special Needs Students
Mixed ability grouping. Telling the story, without writing.

Enrichment for Gifted and Able Students
Think about a "wild card" scenario which is unlikely to happen and write a scenario.

5   Future Scenario

Today is May 28th 2087. My name is Paul Wein and I live in L.A., California. I work in a human cloning institute and manage the baby department. I will tell you a little bit about my work. I started working in this institute 15 years ago, after reading an article I had found in the attic. The article was from 2003 about a scientist named Ian Wilmut who had cloned a sheep called Dolly. The article told his story and the story of Dolly the sheep who died that year. It explained how Dolly was cloned from a cell taken from its mammary gland, using the technique called somatic cell nuclear transfer. The experiment succeeded and Dolly carryied the same genetic data as one of the sheep. At this moment, I knew what I wanted to do when I grew up. Twenty years later, in 2023 human cloning was approved by the government and they started teaching it at universities.

I studied cloning at UCLA and finished 7 years later with honors. I founded the institute with my partner, George Grinwald, later to become a professor in the future. Our beginning was very difficult. I will not lie. I, myself, was inexperienced, and the clients who were interested in cloning fr various reasons, were concerned with the moral issues. A few months later they opened up to the idea and dared to come and meet us at the institute. As the process of cloning takes a long time, we became close friends, actually like family. Over time, the genetic cloning business developed, and has become very popular and profitable. Today, I can proudly say that I chose the right profession. In short, I enjoyed sharing my experience with you, the readers, and hope next time we meet at the Nobel Prize ceremony on December 10th.

Note

The unit was developed by Riva Almog under the supervision of Hava Vidergor.

References

Keinan, N., Ben-Horin, D., Minis, S., Atidia, R., & Mintz, R. (2014). *Chemistry and life sciences for 9th grade teacher's guide*. Tel Aviv: Educational Technology Center Publishing. [in Hebrew]

Ministry of Education. (2015). *The updated curriculum of science and technology*. Jerusalem: Department of Planning and Curriculum Development. Retrieved August 1, 2017, from http://cms.education.gov.il/EducationCMS/Units/Tochniyot_Limudim/science_tech/TochnitMeodkenet [in Hebrew]

CHAPTER 4

Mathematics: Consumerism and the Percentages

This chapter presents teaching math in elementary school using MdCM. Teaching math is a challenge as it needs to be relevant. It illustrates teaching the topic of percentage using consumerism to make math more interesting and authentic, as well as incorporate high order thinking and expose students to thinking tools which could be transferred to other subjects and areas in daily life.

1   Teaching Math

According to Hecht, Torgesen, Wagner, and Rashotte (2001) teaching and learning math is performed in two channels, conceptual and procedural representing respectively understanding and skills. When teaching math, the question of balance between the two arises. This also connected to the learning process and the development of meta-cognitive skills as part of that process.

Hiebert and Carpenter (1992) explain that the declared aims of teaching math include constructing expertise in the taught material. Initially, students are required to present visual and concrete understanding. Later, as expertise increases, they are able to rely on more abstract representations, where basic knowledge becomes recall of facts. Teaching math by focusing on understanding of mathematical concepts alongside required procedures will develop students' thinking flexibility and enable the transfer of existing knowledge constructs to newer ones. They further state that in order for understanding to occur, connections must be created between students' systems of inner representations and their knowledge schemes, and the outer representations of the learned material. As they become more complex, and form a more densely woven net, containing more knowledge networks, the students' understanding will increase. Difficulties in understanding may occur when there are 'holes' in the 'nets' of knowledge, or connections between representations are not sufficiently established. The process of understanding is dynamic, and each time knowledge connections are organized in a different way, where the new or re-organized knowledge is better that before and is dependent on existing networks (Hiebert & Carpenter, 1992).

Conceptual knowledge is not easy to define, but very easy to recognize. A student with conceptual knowledge can develop thinking flexibility and control the transition from quantities to numbers, understand the essence of math, its typical seriality, and the mathematical validity it entails. This is the ability to think about math and about the world, and draw comparisons between math and the outside world, which indicates actually understanding the essence of this discipline (Gersten & Chard, 1999).

Math is a powerful tool for solving actual problems in science and in daily life. One of the aims of teaching math is to promote students' ability to decide on their own how to use the available toolbox, which includes a collection of the concepts, activities, and tools acquired. The creation of this decision-making ability is expressed in the organization of a situation or problem, choice and adaptation of tools and mathematical models for its solution, presentation of real-life situations or students' imagination, analysis of situation from a mathematical perspective, and presentation of possible solutions while using interdisciplinary considerations (Pilo & Peled, 2013).

2 The Percentage

Problem with percentages appear in many areas in everyday life, in business transactions, calculating concentration of mixtures, sales announcing discounts, public opinion polls report viewing percentage, labels on food products report fat percentage, and so forth. According to Shmuely (1993) although percentage is widely used, it seems to be hard to learn and use it properly, as the concept is more complicated than it appears. Teaching percentage should consider the fact that students encounter it in everyday life and develop preconceptions. It is advised to address this and assess students' pre-acquired knowledge and design the instruction accordingly. The aim is to develop content knowledge and understanding of content knowledge while teaching.

3 Consumerism

The connection between consumerism and mathematics is inseparable from reality and everyday life, as consumers very often need to apply thinking manipulations based on calculations, estimates, and recognition of numbers, in order to examine profitability and protect their rights. The new math curriculum for elementary school stresses the need for knowledge of algorithms along with oral calculation abilities combining estimates, control, and calculation understanding. One of the topics presented in the new curriculum is data inquiry and it recommends engaging students in performance tasks such as: phrasing questions, making assumptions, collecting, organizing and analyzing data, presenting them, and drawing pertinent conclusions. All this along should use a variety of calculating skills such as estimates, control based on calculating ability, and arithmetic comprehension (Israeli Consumerism Council, 2010).

4 Example Unit Consumerism and Lessons

The unit was developed for 6th grade students in elementary school. It was taught for two months and dealt with the topic of consumerism developing mathematical thinking and understanding of the concept of percentage and its everyday life applications. The unit is designed according the MdCM using the personal and time perspectives in 10 lessons.

The unit emphasized scientific, creative and future thinking processes. It incorporated concept construction, inquiry, decision making, problem solving and more. Thinking products reflected content, process, and concepts learned creatively in various way, using alternative assessment based on pre-determined criteria.

5 Unit Description

The first part began by eliciting students' existing knowledge of the topic of percentage. Each group of students received a set of advertisements relating to consumerism. Students classified the ads according to selected criteria, and organized the information in a table summarizing data from all groups.

The second part engaged students in examining the subject of consumerism from a personal point of view presenting a dilemma: to buy a school uniform from an elite designer brand or an unknown label. Each student responded. All responses were collected and analyzed and collective findings were presented in a graph. Conclusions were drawn relating to the consumerism of the class. In groups, the students used the six thinking hats to make a decision for or against buying brand outfits. Data was collected and presented in a diagram converted to percentages. Finally, students had to write instructions on how to become a smart consumer.

The third part examined consumerism from the time perspective. Students investigated how consumerism developed over time, from the time when there were no computers or internet, to the present, when a large portion of consumer purchase is conducted online. The aim was to create a timeline and calculate the percentage of development. While investigating, students identified processes, arranged in sequence, tried to find connections between processes, and designed the time line. In addition, students raised and defined problems concerning consumerism in the future, found multiple solutions, and selected the best solution, suggesting an action plan for its application. Finally, student wrote future scenarios based on acquired knowledge on consumerism. They projected theselves to the near or far future and wrote a scenario in groups based on criteria. This final product summarized their knowledge and also enabled them to experience future thinking and predicting what the world might be like in the future regarding consumerism.

6   Lesson Plans

Student Level
6th grade students in a heterogeneous class, medium SES

The Chosen Perspectives
Personal and time perspectives
   Unit and Lesson length: 10 lessons of 45 minutes each

Lesson 1: Introduction to Consumerism from a Personal Perspective

Content
– Introduction to consumerism through percentage

Aims
– Student will be introduced to the topic of percentage.
– Student will understand the meaning of percent.
– Student will recognize the concept of percent.
– Student will identify types of ads.
– Student will classify ads according to criteria.
– Student will explain the meaning and relevance of chosen criteria.

Thinking Processes Developed
Scientific thinking – inquiry

Thinking Strategies Developed
– Organization of knowledge
– Classification

- Knowledge representation
- Drawing conclusions

Learning Environment
Classroom

Opening/Exposure
Students get into groups and receive different ads connected to consumerism

Teaching Strategies
Inquiry-based learning

Learning Activities and Grouping
Student will:

- Suggest at least 4 criteria for organizing the ads.
- Classify ads based on suggested criteria.
- Draw a table summarizing the classification process.

Learning Materials
Ads from newspapers and the internet

Product/s
A table classifying the ads

Assessment
- Each table has at least 4 different criteria for classification
- All ads were classified

Modification for Special Needs Students
Students will receive a table with criteria and will have to match the ads

Enrichment for Gifted and Able Students
Students will rank the ads from the lowest to the highest discount

Lessons 2–3: Personal Perspective

Content
Awareness of consumerism

Aims
- Student will recognize basic concepts of smart consumerism.
- Student will develop the ability to estimate using simple percent 10% of quantity 20%, 25%, 50%, 100%, and 200%.
- Student will learn how to use percentage in static conditions (partial quantity out of integral quantity).
- Student will calculate the partial quantity when the whole quantity is given.
- Student will investigate everyday life situations requiring the use of percent.

Thinking Processes Developed
Scientific thinking

Thinking Strategies Developed
- Construction of concept
- Analysis
- Classification
- Comparison

Learning Environment
Classroom computers with calculating app (percent and fractions)

Opening/Exposure
- Watching a video named: Before you buy you think and review http://www.consumers.org.il/item/think_and_review
- Personal writing: I have always dreamt to buy/own a _____ because _____.
- Introduction to thinking maps: https://vimeo.com/100521066

Teaching Strategies
Inquiry-based learning

Learning Activities and Grouping
Students will work in groups to design a diagram on how numbers are transformed into percentages.

Each student will create a thinking map representing his/her idea of percentages in everyday life (Bubble Map, Circle Map, or Tree Map).

Learning Materials
- Thinking maps video
- Smart consumer video
- Calculating app

Product/s
- Diagram (group)
- Thinking map (individual)

Assessment
- Diagram: has at least 5 calculations transferring a number part of a whole to a percentage, all calculations are correct, 3 calculations are correct.
- Thinking map: shows at least 3 areas of everyday life, followed by and explanation and an example.

Modification for Special Needs Students
- Diagram: weaker students will be paired with stronger ones. Dyslectic students will be able to reply orally, or use the computer.
- Thinking map: weak students will be presented with only one type of map (circle map) and will be asked to write associations of using percentages in real life.

Enrichment for Gifted and Able Students
Using the Divergent Thinking Map to describe different areas of life in which we need to use percentages

Lessons 4–5: Personal Perspective

Content
What do I need to do to become a smart consumer?

Aims
- Student will learn how to use percentage in dynamic situations (discount or price increase)
- Student will develop critical thinking regarding advertising and sales
- Student will increase awareness of deception in advertising

Thinking Processes Developed
Scientific thinking

Thinking Strategies Developed
- Organizing information
- Drawing conclusions

Learning Environment
Classroom + computers

Opening/Exposure
Video "The power to change" http://www.consumers.org.il/item/power_to_change

Teaching Strategies
Inquiry-based learning

Learning Activities and Grouping
The teacher tells a story about sales in different shops.
    Students work in groups to fill in the worksheet relating to sales, calculating percentage of discounts and comparing prices of different products.
    In groups, students:

1. Discuss how the ads work on people's perceptions and try to deceive them into thinking that the discount is much higher than it is in reality.
2. Suggest some ideas on being smart consumers.
3. Design an ad explaining to people how to be smart consumers and present them to class.

In plenary, students will formulate a set of rules on how to be a smart consumer.

Learning Materials
– Video
– Worksheet
– Story

Product/s
– Worksheet (in pairs)
– Advertisement: Suggestions for being a smart consumer (in groups)

Assessment
– The worksheet is filled and at least 6 out of 10 calculations are correct
– Each group has at least 3 suggestions for being a smart consumer
– Criteria: Clear, gives examples in percentage, colorful, interesting, relevant

Modification for Special Needs Students
Using calculators or apps to calculate the discount in percentages

Enrichment for Gifted and Able Students
Examining rules related to display of prices and discounts in other countries

Lessons 6–7: Time Perspective

Content
The development of consumerism from the past to the present

Aims
Student will recognize the development of consumerism

Thinking Process Developed
Future thinking

Thinking Strategies Developed
– Constructing a concept
– Classification and analysis
– Identifying connections
– Identifying processes
– Organizing in sequence

Learning Environment
– Classroom
– Computer room/using mobile phones

Opening/Exposure
Students will read an article about consumerism in Israel:
http://lib.cet.ac.il/pages/item.asp?item=2310

Teaching Strategies
Project-based learning

Learning Activities and Grouping
Working in groups of 5, students will:

1 Look for facts and dates relevant to the development of consumerism.
2 Interview family members (grandparents, parents) about consumerism.
3 Arrange the facts in chronological sequence.
4 Analyze facts to find connections between events/facts to look for processes.

5 Analyze facts in connection to other developments and look for connections between processes.
6 Calculate the time between major events/development and will present it as a percentage (part of the total number of years investigated).

Learning Materials
– Articles
– Interviews
– Websites

Product/s
Timeline

Assessment
– The timeline has at least 10 major events/dates
– Dates are explained briefly in 1–2 sentences
– Dates are accurate
– Dates are organized in chronological sequence
– The timeline presents at least 3 calculations of time duration between events in percentages

Modification for Special Needs Students
– Weak students will receive a ready-made time line with marked events. Students will have to find the dates and add a short explanation.
– Students will have to calculate 2–3 time spans between events in percentages.

Enrichment for Gifted and Able Students
Comparison of Israeli and American timelines

Lessons 8–9: Time Perspective – Problem Solving

Content
Finding solutions for consumerism

Aims
– Student will be aware of different problems concerning consumerism.
– Student practice problem solving.
– Student will learn how to work in a team to solve a problem.
– Student will understand how to select the best solution.

Thinking Processes Developed
Creative thinking – problem solving

Thinking Strategies Developed
- Defining problem
- Suggesting solutions
- Finding criteria
- Selecting the best solution

Learning Environment
- Classroom
- Computer room/BYOD classroom

Opening/Exposure
Video- current consumerism model:
http://www.mako.co.il/news-money/consumer-q1_2017/Article-caa4e0324ae2a51004.htm

Teaching Strategies
Problem-based learning within project-based learning

Learning Activities and Grouping
In groups of 5, students will:

1. Brainstorm problems related to consumerism.
2. Select one problem and define it.
3. Suggest at least 5 different solutions.
4. Think of criteria for selecting the best solution.
5. Select the best solution based on criteria, filling in a table (see appendix).
6. Calculate the percentage of results for each solution out of a total of 100%.
7. Write a short action plan for implementation of the solution.
8. Present the process, the best solution and the action plan in plenary.

Learning Materials
- Article
- Internet

Product/s
- Problem solving process

– Action plan

Assessment
– Problem solving process: follows all stages of problem solving, clear presentation, relevant problem, relevant criteria for best solution selection
– Action plan: has at least 3 different stages or suggestions, clear, relevant to solution

Modification for Special Needs Students
– Weak students will work in mixed ability groups
– Dyslectic students can record the process instead of writing. They can also prepare a PPT presentation of the process and/or action plan

Enrichment for Able and Gifted Students
Try to find a combination of 2 best solutions and write an extended action plan

Lesson 10: Time Perspective – Future Scenario Writing

Content
Incorporating percentage in a future scenario of consumerism

Aims
– Student will experience thinking about the future.
– Student will learn how to predict future events based on past development and the current state of an issue.
– Student will use percentage as an integral part of the scenario.

Thinking Processes Developed
Future thinking

Thinking Strategies Developed
Predicting development

Learning Environment
Classroom

Opening/Exposure
– What is a future scenario?

– Instructions and criteria for writing a future scenario incorporating percentage.

Teaching Strategies
Project-based learning

Learning Activities and Grouping
In groups of 5, students will:

1. Recall what they have learnt about percentage.
2. Recall what they have learnt about consumerism.
3. Write a future scenario following the pre-determined criteria.
4. Present the future scenario to the class.

Learning Materials
Template of a future scenario

Product/s
Future scenario

Assessment
Criteria: located in the future (near or far), at least one page long, mentions past, present and future, has at least 2 characters, there is a plot, uses percentages, is relevant and mentions accurate facts, is creative, mentions processes, mentions connections between processes.

Modification for Special Needs Students
Recording or filming the scenario

Enrichment for Able and Gifted Students
Writing a longer, more elaborate scenario

7   **Future Scenario**

It is now 2057. Pablo woke up this morning when his brain phone rang. It was his boss Ian. It was a recorded message asking him to come immediately, in person, to the conference room in the company building. It was urgent! Pablo walked out of his room and a face woke up on the wall. It was 'Molly' the program he had bought yesterday. "Good morning, Pablo. Ian has sent a message and I sent it to you on the brain phone. Have you listened to it? Or do I need to run it again?" "No thank you, Molly." Pablo replied. He dressed quickly and left the house. The air-car was already waiting for him. He remembered that in a museum he had once seen an old car that couldn't fly. It was called a Ferrari. "It must have been much more difficult to get from place to place back then", he thought. While the automatic driver drove the car to its destination, Pablo was reading the digital newspaper. One article caught his eye. It was about a credit company named 'Segev'. This international company had lost a very large sum of digital money on a product that could be bought everywhere online. Wherever the product was not purchased, the company lost money. It seemed that the public still liked to buy physically – to see the product and hold it in their hands. This is something that was very common many years ago, and was still very difficult to change. Now Although online buying much better, still in many places in the world people prefer the old way.

When Pablo reached the office, he saw and heard Ian on the brain phone: 'This is Ian speaking. Our new product is a failure. I don't know what's wrong, but people don't like the product. Also, this week there have been a few problems with the genetic identification system and people have been charged without buying anything. Do you have any idea why this is happening?' All international department managers were there in room in hologram form, discussing the problem. They hadn't yet found any solutions. When Pablo left the building later that evening, he saw an announcement in the digital newspaper saying that next year there would be worldwide celebrations to mark the centennial of the first credit card issued by the Bank of America.

Note

The unit was developed by Galit Atias and Hava Zachrov under the supervision of Hava Vidergor.

References

Gersten, R., & Chard, D. (1999). Number sense: Rethinking arithmetic instruction for students with mathematical disabilities. *The Journal of Special Education, 33*(1), 18–28.
Hecht, S. A., Torgesen, J. K., Wagner, R. K., & Rashotte, C. A. (2001). The relations between phonological processing abilities and emerging individual differences in

mathematical computation skills: A longitudinal study from second to fifth grades. *Journal of Experimental Child Psychology, 79*(2), 192–227.

Hiebert, J., & Carpenter, T. P. (1992). Learning and teaching with understanding. In D. A. Grouws (Ed.), *Handbook of research on mathematics teaching and learning* (pp. 65–97). New York, NY: Macmillan.

Israeli Consumer Council. (2010). *Education and information: Fairness in consumerism*. Retrieved on August 10, 2017, from http://www.consumers.org.il/category/information-and-education [in Hebrew]

Pilo, R., & Peled, A. (2013). Development of modeling skills among elementary school students. *Strong Number, 24*, 51–68. [in Hebrew]

Shmueli, N. (1993). *The perception of percentage* (MA thesis). Tel Aviv University, Tel Aviv. [in Hebrew]

CHAPTER 5

Language Arts: English as a Foreign Language

Teaching English as a foreign language to elementary school students is challenging, especially when it is not their second, but third language. This chapter illustrates the design of a unit of study based on MdCM teaching English to Arab elementary school students in Israel. The subject selected was extreme sports and the language structure focused on was adjectives and their superlatives. This chapter specifically addresses thinking maps as a thinking tool, showing how students are introduced to and taught how to use the different maps to represent acquired knowledge graphically.

1   Teaching English as a Foreign Language in the Arab Sector in Israel

According to the Israeli Ministry of Education (2015), teaching English as a foreign language (EFL) should be strengthened in all schools and grade levels. Application of the Meaningful Learning reform emphasizes enriching language skills, focusing on vocabulary, thinking skills including text analysis, drawing conclusions, and comparison of data.

For the Arab minority in Israel, English is a third language. Their first language is Arabic. However, Arabic speakers in Israel also need to acquire Hebrew as a second language since it is the language of the dominant group in the country. In addition, they have to learn English because it is a global language. In a study on how to ensure that Arabic-speaking students indeed acquire an adequate command of English, Abu Rabia (2003) found that the Arab minority students in Israel possessed instrumental and positive attitudes toward learning English. In addition, he proposed that, for Arab students, familiar content facilitated reading comprehension. He suggested that "the cultural familiarity of the text, and individual interest in the text, are powerful predictors of reading comprehension in L3 in the case of Arabs learning English as a third language" (p. 353).

Nevertheless, Shin (2006) documented that the majority of EFL teacher education programs have placed more emphasis on developing students' oral and reading skills than on their writing skills. Namely, writing has often been the last skill to be taught after listening, speaking, and reading. Moreover, he added that the writing of EFL learners often presents difficulties that differ from those found in the writing of native English-speaking students. "These include culturally conditioned rhetorical patterns that are familiar to a native speaker as well as unfamiliar grammatical errors that are simply not found in native speaker writing" (p. 326). Thus, teachers often find it difficult to provide feedback on foreign language writing. They are confused whether to start correcting all errors or to leave the errors untouched because there are simply too many of them.

Consequently, teachers should use various strategies to promote their students' writing skills. Zenkov and Harmon (2009) argued that the act of writing is itself a multimodal practice that draws on visual and actional modes. Thus, students are more ready to engage with writing tasks about different topics if teachers use images as a starting point and as an ongoing focus.

2   Thinking Maps

In their book, *Student Successes with Thinking Maps* (2011), Hyerle and Alper perceived thinking maps as a way for learners to become aware of and translate their cognitive processes into any learning atmosphere, from early childhood to adult workplaces. In addition, they argued that thinking maps could be defined as a mixture of three types of visual tools that educators and business people commonly use: mind mapping, brainstorming webs, graphic organizers and thinking process tools such as concept mapping.

Similarly, Gallagher's theoretical review (2011) suggested that thinking maps are similar to concept maps. Nevertheless, he suggested that while concept maps center themselves on specific details of a concept, thinking maps organize or display a larger picture. Moreover, Long and Carlson (2011) argued that thinking maps differ from graphic organizers because they are used to promote "more strategic thinking" and encourage students to focus on the processes used to produce the "correct" answer. That is, unlike graphic organizers that generally involve only surface level details, thinking maps invite students to make meaning of an abstract idea by reducing it on paper.

According to Hyerle and Alper (2011) thinking maps are consistent, which means that "each map has a unique and consistent form that visually reflects the cognitive skill being defined" (p. 10). In addition, "the thinking skill and the graphic primitive for each map provide flexibility in form and numerous ways the map can be configured" (p. 10). Thus, thinking maps are developmental so that learners of all ages can begin with a blank sheet of paper and expand the map to show their thinking (Hyerle & Alper, 2011). Moreover, all the maps may be used and integrated together "for solving multistep problems comprehending overlapping reading text structure and during phases of the writing process" (ibid., p. 11). Therefore, students may employ thinking maps for multistep problem solving, decision making, and organizing, extending, and developing ideas in any context (Hyerle & Alper, 2011). In this manner, the learner "sees and reflects upon the pattern of content" (ibid., p. 11).

Hylere and Alper (2011) explained that thinking maps are grounded in "eight cognitive universals processes that our brains use every day such as sequencing, hierarchical classification, part to whole, causation, comparing and contrasting, describing, analogies and defining in context" (p. 14). Likewise, Long and Carlson (2011) stated that each thinking map serves a different purpose and therefore students must be aware of the appropriate use of each. For example, a *Bubble Map* requires the use of only single adjectives to describe the topic, while a *Circle Map* allows for more complex thoughts and descriptions by allowing nouns, adjectives and even complete sentences to describe the given topic. Additionally, Holzman (2004) suggested that learners could use thinking maps to facilitate learning in different subjects. For example, *Flow Maps* can be used for describing the life of a virus, or problem solving in math.

Hyerle and Alper (2011) described four additional types of thinking maps: dialogic, metaphorical, systems, and evaluative. Gallagher (2011) argued that dialogic maps help define ideas or things in context and are helpful when presenting a point of view. Metaphorical maps help to explain analogies, whereas systems or Flow Maps show steps and patterns within complex processes or show causes and effects of events and predict outcomes. However, evaluative or bubble maps are used to describe qualities or compare and contrast qualities.

Furthermore, Hyerle and Alper (2011) claimed that thinking maps promote independent work among learners. They argued that students can successfully use maps as independent learners and thinkers. They added that teachers should assist students to develop strategies that enable them to become independent learners and this is exactly what thinking maps do. They foster learner independence since they allow students to work by their own (Long & Carlson, 2011).

However, in order to ensure that students are using thinking maps correctly, teachers should teach the use of the different maps. "Because a thinking map is designed for a specific purpose, it is imperative that students understand the correct manner in which to use them" (Long & Carlson, 2011, p. 3). For example, a *Bubble Map* requires students to use only single adjectives to describe the topic, while a *Circle Map* allows for complex descriptions. Then, "once a thinking map has been demonstrated to the class, students work cooperatively with the teacher to develop a new thinking map" (ibid., p. 3). Long and Carlson

(2011) felt sure that this method allowed students to see the creation of the thinking maps step by step, thereby promoting an understanding of the use of thinking maps. Thus, for example, if a student was asked to define in context, she or he would choose to use the *Circle Map*. After completing this step, the teacher could let the students owork independently and create their own maps (Long & Carlson, 2011).

Through using visual maps students can develop the administrative functions necessary to develop language and support social participation in a learning community (Hyerle & Alper, 2011). As Hyerle and Alper (2011) put it, the maps keep words and ideas until students decide what to do with them. That is, the maps are devices that allow students to p;ut abstract thinking into a form that will convey knowledge to their teachers and each other clearly and systematically. Hence, thinking maps serve as "a device for mediating thinking, listening, talking, reading, writing, problem solving, and the acquisition of new knowledge and understanding" (Hyerle & Alper, 2011, p. 41).

2.1   *Studies on Thinking Maps*

In a study that investigated the use of thinking maps regarding the increase of student achievement, Long and Carlson (2011) found that thinking maps make an excellent addition to any classroom because "they teach students to think critically about subjects and form connections between subject disciplines" (p. 5). In addition, they proposed that thinking maps provide a method that can help students organize their thoughts and ideas when it comes to preparing for exams.

Hyerle and Alper (2014) argue that thinking maps enable learners to communicate what and how they are thinking. They add, "Through this language, learners convey, negotiate, and evolve meanings with others and within themselves, through visual patterns of thinking" (p. 9). Therefore, the use of thinking maps promotes collaborative leadership in-group work and encourages the use of the group members' cognitive strengths to solve problems and engage in planning. Moreover, Hyerle and Alper (2014) confirm the benefits of using Thinking Maps in collaborative work. They state, "Leaders using Thinking Maps say that their work with groups is more effective and efficient and their level of thinking is enhanced" (p. 74).

Additionally, Hyerle and Alper (2014) noted that the thinking maps modality appears to have roots that are innate to the brain. Therefore, this modality helps create and shape new memories. Thinking maps can create new memories by identifying the thinking needed and then creating the maps accordingly to help shape the memory. In other words, thinking maps can help store ideas into the memory as one creates them. Moreover, thinking maps are helpful because "the brain remembers patterns, especially when linked to images" (p. 75).

Long and Carlson (2011) found that thinking maps can broaden students' critical thinking skills and enhance their understanding of the content being presented. They note that Hyerle's thinking maps allow students "to express their thoughts and ideas non-linguistically" (p. 1) since they allow students to construct their thoughts in different ways (kinesthetically, verbally, etc.). Moreover, Long and Carlson (2011) concluded that the eight Thinking Maps are unique in the sense that they allow students to feel more connected to the material, as they give them the opportunity "to map out their thought process on paper, which leads to an increase in connections between content and experience" (p. 5). Furthermore, they declared that thinking maps encourage students to construct new knowledge about a topic based on prior knowledge. Therefore, Long and Carlson (2011) infer that "students who utilize thinking maps will see improvements in their academic progress with regards to higher order thinking and content connection" (p. 5).

3   Guinness World Records

The Guinness World Book of Records is published every year and contains updated records documented in different areas of human ability and man-made products. The book is very prestigious and many people would like to set records and be included and mentioned in it. Over the years it has become an expression of extreme measures. It was first published by Arthur Guinness in 1955. It is translated to many languages, and in each version the local records are added. Several world records were removed and some were blocked for ethical reasons, as publishing them could cause harm to people's health and safety (Glenday, 2016).

4   Example Unit and Lesson Plans: Extreme Sports

4.1   *Unit Description*

The unit was aimed to develop thinking skills in foreign language learning in elementary school using Guinness World Records to teach adjectives, comparatives and superlatives in an authentic whole language approach. The unit consisted of 13 lessons, where the first was an introductory lesson and other lessons were taught in double lesson periods of 90 minutes. The unit dealt with different aspects of Guinness World Records focusing on the acquisition of tools and views from different perspectives. The first five lessons were devoted to scientific thinking, mainly focusing on thinking maps from a personal perspective. Students were introduced to and learned to use five out of the eight maps suggested by Hyerle. Lessons 6–7 were devoted to creative thinking, exposing students to thinking hats. Lessons 8–11 focused on developing future thinking, designing a timeline and writing a future scenario related to world records. Foreign language learning was incorporated as an authentic subject which invites students to use language structures necessary for expressing themselves orally and in writing when discussing the subject from different perspectives.

5 Lesson Plans

Student Level
Sixth grade students from the Arabic-speaking sector studying in a private Christian school. English is their third language

The Chosen Perspectives
Personal perspective and time perspective

Unit Length and Lesson Length
11 lessons of 45 minutes each
   Note: Students already know how to form comparative and superlative forms of short and long adjectives.

Lesson 1: Introduction to Guinness World Records

Content
Guinness World Records

Aims
– Student will recognize the concept of "record".
– Student will be exposed to records in different categories.
– Student will learn to form sentences using adjectives.

Thinking Processes Developed
Scientific thinking – construction and analysis of concept

Thinking Strategies Developed
Classification and analysis

Learning Environment
Classroom

Opening/Exposure
– What do you think of when you hear the word 'record'?
– Drawing a Circle map with all associations.
– What do you expect to see?
– Presenting photos of athletes and records in different fields of sports.

Teaching Strategies
Inquiry-based learning

Learning Activities and Grouping
In pairs students:

– Look for the names of different fields of sports.
– Look for the names of athletes.
– Match the sentences with the pictures.
– Fill in the worksheet.
– Instructions: Form sentences that describe each of the following pictures. All the pictures are latest world records.

Learning Materials
– Pictures
– Textbook: Essential Links
– Worksheet

Product/s
– Matching pictures and sentences
– Worksheet

Assessment
Matching Picture: Low – Matching 5 photos out of 10
                    Medium – matching 6–7 photos
                    High – matching 8 or more photos
Worksheet: Low – writing 1–2 sentences using adjectives
                    Medium – Writing 3–4 sentences using adjectives
                    High – Writing 5 or more sentences using adjectives

Modification for Special Needs Students
Select adjectives from a given list

Enrichment for Gifted and Able Students
Select one photo from the ones that you matched and write 3–4 sentences describing it and the difficulties the athlete faced.

Lessons 2–3: Personal Perspective

Content
- World records
- Thinking maps

Aims
- Student will understand the components of extreme sports.
- Students will use different thinking maps to analyze, compare, and contrast extreme sports and regular sports.
- Student will present ideas using thinking maps.
- Student will learn new vocabulary related to extreme sports.

Thinking Processes Developed
Scientific thinking

Thinking Strategies Developed
- Construction of concept
- Analysis
- Classification
- Comparison

Learning Environment
Classroom

Opening/Exposure
Presentation of thinking maps: Circle Map, Tree Map, Bubble Map and Double Bubble Map

Teaching Strategies
Inquiry-based learning

Learning Activities and Grouping
In plenary: students think about associations regarding extreme sports using the *circle map*.

Student can use the textbook, internet and other sources to gather information.

1. In pairs: Students describe one extreme sport using the *Bubble Map*.
2. Students write 3 sentences using adjectives.
3. Students choose a field of sports they practice and compare it to the extreme sport using the *Double Bubble* Map.
4. Students write 3 sentences using comparatives.
5. Using the *Tree Map* students try to identify as many extreme sports as possible and classify them according to groups.
6. Students present one chosen map to the class.

Learning Materials
– PDF template of thinking maps
– Textbook

Product/s
Thinking maps

Assessment
Thinking maps:

a. *Bubble Map* – has at least 4 adjectives, correct spelling, adjectives are used correctly in sentences
b. *Double Bubble Map* – has at least 3 different components and 2 similar ones, spelling is correct, sentences use comparatives correctly
c. *Tree Map* – there are at least 3 classification groups, there are at least 2 fields of extreme sports under each group, correct spelling

Modification for Special Needs Students
The maps will be partially filled in and weak students will have to complete them

Enrichment for Gifted and Able Students
Gifted and able students will use the *Bridge Map* to analyze the components of extreme sports

Note: Student used four thinking maps in these lessons (thinking maps can be found on the official website http://www.thinkingmaps.org/official/index.html)

Lessons 4–5: Personal Perspective

Content
- World records: Advantages and disadvantages
- For and against training for world records
- Thinking maps

Aims
- Student will understand the positive and negative consequences of setting world records.
- Student will present ideas using thinking maps.
- Student will learn new vocabulary related to world records.
- Student will state opinion about world records in English or Arabic.

Thinking Processes Developed
Scientific thinking

Thinking Strategies Developed
- Construction of concept
- Analysis
- Comparison
- Identifying connections (cause and effect)

Learning Environment
Classroom

Opening/Exposure
Watching a video clip about setting a world record of living in the coldest place on earth
https://www.youtube.com/watch?v=pReyPGHw4sQ

Teaching Strategies
Inquiry-based learning

Learning Activities and Grouping
Students will:

- Think individually about the consequences of living in the coldest place in the world.
- Read the passage from the book describing the world record of living in the coldest place in the world.
- Get into groups of 5 and discuss and write down the consequences.
- Use the multi Flow Map for describing causes and effects (see Appendix).
- Discuss being for or against setting world records and present to class.

Learning Materials
- Video clip
- Textbook
- Thinking map

Product/s
- Worksheet: multiflow thinking map
- Presentation of arguments for and against setting world records

Assessment
- Multiflow thinking map – showed at lease two causes and two effects
- Presentation – had a least 2 arguments for and against, was clear, correct use of adjectives and comparatives.

Modification for Special Needs Students
The Multiflow Map will be partially filled in and weak students will have to complete it

Enrichment for Gifted and Able Students
Describe the coldest place in the world and use the new vocabulary and at least two comparatives

Lessons 6–7: Personal Perspective

Content
Using comparative adjectives in decision making about world records

Aims
- Student will be exposed to the six thinking hats
- Student will use the six thinking hats for decision making
- Student will present decision in class

Thinking Processes Developed
Creative thinking

Thinking Strategies Developed
- Identifying perspectives
- Empathy – being in someone's shoes and seeing things from different angles

Learning Environment
Classroom

Opening/Exposure
- Presenting the six thinking hats
- Working on decision making in a school related dilemma

Teaching Strategies
Project-based learning

Learning Activities and Grouping

- Students read the scenario.
- Students get into groups of 6, each selecting a thinking hat.
- Students discuss the scenario using the thinking hats.
- Students reach a unanimous decision.
- Students work on presenting the decision creatively.
- Students present the decision to the class.

Learning Materials
Six Thinking Hats:
Scenario – You are Rami's parents Rami is 12 years old. He came to tell you that he would like to set a new Guinness World Record. He is an excellent athlete and he practices every day. He would like to set a record in wall climbing. Wall climbing is dangerous, even though the climber has to use safety equipment. He would like to climb the highest wall which is 370 meters tall and located in Groningen, Holland.

As his parents, you need to decide using the six thinking hats if you are going to allow him to climb the highest wall and become the first child to do so.

Note: Part of the conversation could be led in native language. The product should be presented in English.

Product/s
- Process of decision making using the six thinking hats
- Creative presentation

Assessment
- Decision making process: All hats are documented, arguments fit the type of hat, decision was unanimous
- Creative presentation: Clear, correct language, use of adjectives and comparatives, creative, interesting, all students participated

Modification for Special Needs Students
- Weak students could use less English in documenting the process.
- Presentation could be shorter and show only one use of adjective or comparative.

Enrichment for Gifted and Able Students
Gifted or able students will work as a separate group. All group members will have to use all hats in the process. For instance, when the red hat dealing with feelings is addressed, all group members will have to wear the red hat and relate to the situation etc.

Lessons 8–9: Time Perspective

Content
- Extreme sports in the past and present.
- Use of comparatives.

Aims
- Student will recognize the history of extreme sports.
- Student will explore and document significant dates in extreme sports.
- Student will understand the process of development of extreme sports.
- Student will look for connections between events relating to extreme sports.

Thinking Processes Developed
Future thinking – construction and analysis of concept

Thinking Strategies Developed
- Defining and identifying components
- Classification and analysis
- Organizing in sequence

- Comparison
- Identifying connections
- Identifying processes

Learning Environment
Computer room

Opening/Exposure
Presenting different photos of extreme sports

Teaching Strategies
Inquiry-based learning

Learning Activities and Grouping
In groups of 3–4 students choose one extreme sport.

1. Look for information on the internet
2. Find at least 10 significant dates related to the selected extreme sport.
3. Prepare a timeline and mark the dates.
4. Write a short description of each event
5. Compare events and look for processes
6. Look for other developments
7. Present the timeline

Learning Materials
- Photos
- Timeline

Product/s
Timeline

Assessment
Timeline: deals with selected extreme sport, presents 10 dates, explanation is short and clear, presentation mentions comparison, connections and processes, at least 3 comparatives and superlatives are used correctly.

Modification for Special Needs Students
Weak student will get a timeline template. The teacher will help with selection of the extreme sport. Work is in mixed ability groups, they will have to contribute at least one date and explanation.

Enrichment for Gifted and Able Students
Students could choose between adding more dates to the outline, or preparing an additional outline for a different extreme sport.

Lessons 10–11: Time Perspective

Content
- The future of extreme sports
- Using comparatives and superlatives in the future tense

Aims
- Student will recognize the difficulties in extreme sports, tools, funding, and keeping healthy.
- Student will practice thinking about the future.
- Student will use comparatives and superlatives in the future tense.

Thinking Processes Developed
Future thinking

Thinking Strategies Developed
Predicting development

Learning Environment
Classroom

Opening/Exposure
Video clip on rappelling
https://www.youtube.com/watch?v=h9E93DOWiws
Future scenario – criteria for writing

Teaching Strategies
Future-based learning

Learning Activities and Grouping
In the same groups of 3–4, students will:

a Read the text from the textbook – Interview with an extreme sports athlete
b Students will write a future scenario on the selected sport.
c Present the scenario to the class.
d Discuss the common and different aspects in shared scenarios.

LANGUAGE ARTS: ENGLISH AS A FOREIGN LANGUAGE

Learning Materials
– Video clip
– Textbook
– Future scenario

Product/s
Future scenario

Assessment
Future scenario: is located in the future (far or near), one page long, mentions past, present and future, written in first person, has two additional characters, has a plot, creative, correct and relevant events, mentions processes, mentions connection between process, correct use of adjectives, comparatives and superlatives.

Modification for Special Needs Students
Mixed ability grouping, recording or filming instead of writing

Enrichment for Able and Gifted Students
Longer elaborated scenario, portraying more characters, events and use of English language correctly

6   Future Scenario

It is 7.7.2047. My name is Tom and today is a very special day for me and for my friend Jerry. We are best friends and we have both love extreme sports. We love surfing most of all. We are going to take part in a surfing competition today. We are very excited because we are going to use our new surfboards. The old surfboards were bigger and not that advanced. They were larger and could carry only one person. The new surfboards are smaller than the old one but they can carry 2 people. They also have wings on both sides. The wings are great, they can help us float on the highest waves and this can give us a chance to qualify for the finals. We both love our new surfing board, but we still remember the old one. The old one did not have all the improvements this one has. Part of it broke off when we practiced. The new one is much stronger because it is made of a special material that was invented recently and it cannot break. I still have the old one in my room. Jerry told me to throw it away, but I can't do it because I am attached to it. It reminds me of the good old days 25 or 30 years ago. Our dream is to design a new surfboard that plays music while surfing. The music will help us relax and will change with our moods. The surfboard will have sensors and will be able to detect dangers. It will also call an emergency number if something happens to us. In the meantime, we are enjoying our new surfboard and its beautiful red and green wings. Wish me luck, and please do not talk to me about the dangers because our parents have been doing it since I was a little child.

Note: The future scenario is a class product written with teacher's help.

Note

The unit was developed by Elsy Ghatas under the supervision of Hava Vidergor.

References

Abu-Rabia, S. (2003). Cognitive and social factors affecting Arab students learning English as a third language in Israel. *Educational Psychology, 23*(4), 347–360.

Gallagher, M. L. (2011). Using thinking maps to facilitate research writing in upper level undergraduate classes. *Journal of Family & Consumer Sciences Education, 29*(2), 53–56.

Glenday, C. (2016,). *Guinness book of world records.* Vancouver: Jim Pattison Group.

Holzman, S. (2004, April 4). *Thinking maps: Strategy-based learning for English language learners (and others).* In 13th Annual Administrator Conference: Closing the, Achievement Gap for Education Learner Student, Sonoma County Office of Education, California Department of Education, Sonoma County, CA.

Hyerle, D. N., & Alper, L. (2011). *Student successes with thinking maps: School-based research, results, and models for achievement using visual tools.* Thousand Oaks, CA: Corwin.

Hyerle, D. N., & Alper, L. (2014). *Pathways to thinking schools.* Thousand Oaks, CA: Corwin.

Israeli Ministry of Education. (2015). *Pedagogical secretariat, language department, pre-elementary and elementary education.* Retrieved July 15, 2017, from http://cms.education.gov.il/EducationCMS/Units/Tochniyot_Limudim/Chinuch_Leshoni/ChinuchLeshoni/maBatochnit.htm [in Hebrew]

Long, D., & Carlson, D. (2011). Mind the map: How thinking maps affect student achievement. *Networks, 13*(2), 1–7.

Shin, S. (2006). Learning to teach writing through tutoring and journal writing. *Teachers and Teaching: Theory and Practice, 12*(3), 325–345.

Zenkov, K., & Harmon, J. (2009). Picturing a writing process: Photovoice and teaching writing to urban youth. *Journal of Adolescent & Adult Literacy, 52*(7), 575–584.

Appendix: Worksheet (Lessons 4–5)

Worksheet

This is the coldest place on earth. This city is called Oymyakon. It's in Siberia, Russia. *Individually* – (a) How would you feel living in this place? Write at least 3 words or sentences. (b) Think of reasons for living in this place and then think about effects.

In groups – Share your opinion with your group and summarize the common points.

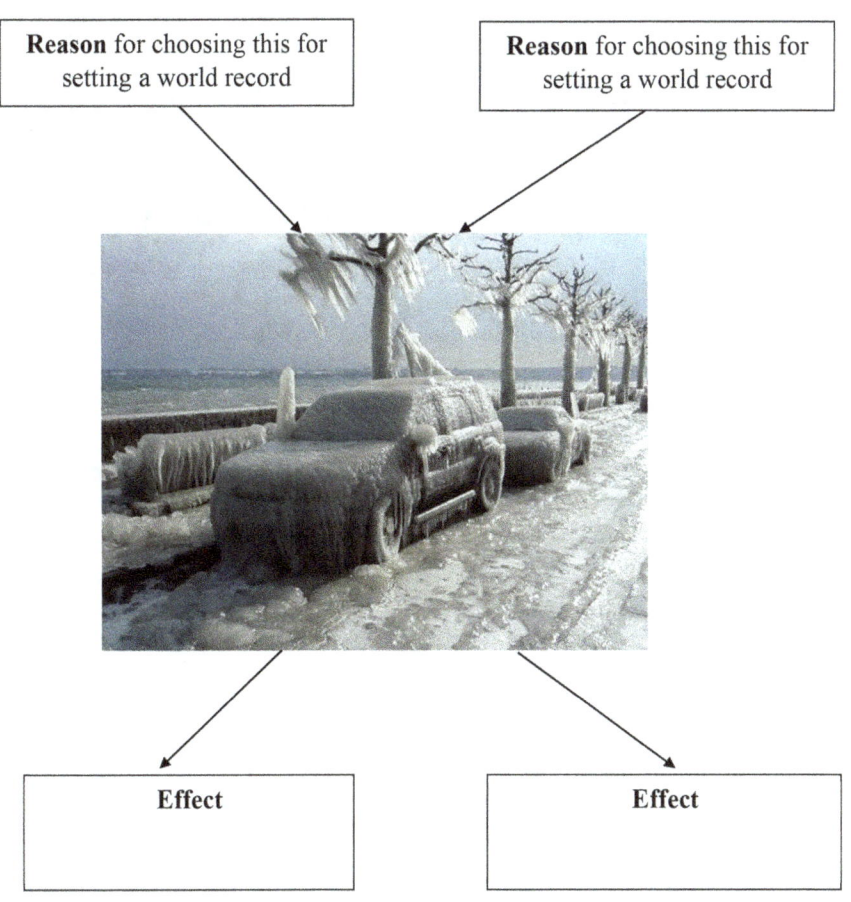

Reason for choosing this for setting a world record	**Reason** for choosing this for setting a world record

Effect	Effect

Group Members:

1. ....   2. ....   3. ....

4. ....   5. ....

Points in common:

1. _____
   _____

2. _____
   _____

3. _____
   _____

CHAPTER 6

Social Studies: Community Settlements

The subject of Homeland is part of social studies in Israeli schools. Within this subject we chose to focus on community settlements, as the students studying this unit live in one and the aim was to get acquainted with one's form of settlement during that school year. This chapter defines social studies and gives a brief explanation of the curriculum. It illustrates how the six thinking hats are incorporated into the unit developed based on MdCM, exemplifying the different stages and variety of ways the hats could be applied. It ends with a futuristic view of a community settlement fifty years from now.

1 Social Studies

Social studies in Israeli elementary schools, and specifically in fourth grade are focused on exploring the place students live in from many different aspects: historical, geographical, being a citizen etc. In Israel this subject of study is named Homeland. According to Sagi and Stern (2011) there are two meanings of Homeland – one is a person's primary home and the second is the political framework in which it exists. The establishment of Israel actualized the second, organizational aspect of returning to the homeland. The homeland is one's primary home, a place where one is born, where one's memories, culture, tastes, foods, smells, and overall orientation in the world are shaped. The significance of homeland as a primary home is expressed in different languages.

The Israeli social studies curriculum (Ministry of Education, 2003) focusing on homeland society and citizenship for 2nd to 4th grade students in elementary schools is modular and flexible, and allows for unique expression of diverse populations within Israeli society. The curriculum combines moral concepts (environmental-social-cultural-emotional- and historical) with concepts in citizenship. These are gradually constructed over the years, forming a foundation for further studies. The curriculum emphasizes the place of the individual and the relationship between individuals. The curriculum for 4th grade focuses on the place where the student lives. It could be a city, a town, a kibbutz, a community settlement (based on social cooperation that chooses its residents according to an ideology or desired lifestyle, without restricting them to an area of employment), or a moshav (a cooperative farming settlement). In our case it is a community settlement. The program deals with acquaintance with the settlement, lifestyle, stories, history and development of society. Students then are also exposed to other forms of settlements to get to know the "other" and form a common denominator of all Israeli students.

2   Thinking Hats

De Bono (1985) designed a very simple mode of metaphorically wearing different colored hats which can augment critical thinking if used correctly. The six hats cover the main modes of thinking. The wearing of a different colored hat each time, enables the wearer to bring a different perspective to thinking critically about an issue and to trying to find alternative solutions to any problem confronted. He distinguished six modes of thinking, each identified with one colored hat:

1. *Blue Hat* – control of the other hats, thinking about the thinking process, directs attention to other hats to facilitate "map-making" thinking.
2. *White Hat* – facts, figures, and objective information.
3. *Red Hat* – emotions, feelings, hunches, intuition.
4. *Black Hat* – logical negative thoughts, "devil's advocate," why something will not work.
5. *Yellow Hat* – logical constructive thoughts, positive aspects of why something will work.
6. *Green Hat* – creativity, generating new ideas, provocative thoughts, lateral thinking.

De Bono uses the "thinking hat" metaphor because of familiar expressions such as "put on your thinking cap (hat)." The hat is a tangible object that one can literally wear or that one can visualize putting on or taking off. "Putting on" a hat is a deliberate process that switches the thinker's attention exclusively to that mode, thus simplifying the thinking process; "switching" hats redirects thinking to another mode. The artificiality of the hats is their greatest value; they provide a formal and convenient way to request a certain type of thinking from oneself or others (de Bono, 1985). According to Carl (1996) the "Six Thinking Hats" model creates six artificial contexts for thinking, corresponding to the primary thought modes of objective, subjective, critical, and creative thinking within a comprehensive framework that allows the thinker to direct attention to the desired thinking mode (p. 1).

3 Three-Stage Application of Six Thinking Hats in MdCM

MdCM offers the opportunity to experience the six thinking hats in several stages:

1. Exposing students to thinking hats – demonstrating the solution of a dilemma using the different hats, each representing a different perspective.
2. Solving a dilemma using thinking hats when all members of the group wear the same hat.
3. Solving a dilemma using thinking hats when each group member chooses a different hat.

The teacher can decide whether the three stages are needed, or just ask students to select stage two or three. Stage two gives the opportunity to each student to experience all hats/thinking modes, while stage three is about each student selecting one hat (preferably not the one he or she tends to use in everyday life).

4 Example Unit and Lesson Plans: My Homeland

4.1 *Unit Description*

The unit illustrates the use of thinking hats in three stages (exposure to hats using a dilemma from school life, members of group relating to all hats in turn, and each member choosing one hat). The unit was designed for 4th grade students living in a community settlement in the Galilee region in the north of Israel.

The 14 lessons are divided into introduction to community settlements, personal perspective, and time perspective. The introduction includes a competitive game exploring the community settlement, getting acquainted with aspects of life and committees formed in order to preserve the lifestyle. Using the personal perspective, students review the community settlement and state what they like and dislike. Using the six thinking hats in stages, they trying to solve dilemmas such as: Do we need to organize a Friday night party only for teenagers of our settlement -Yes or No? or Do we stay and live in this community settlement or leave? Then they try to solve the ultimate problem of attracting young families to come and live there. These activities are followed by a simulation of a committee meeting and a pamphlet inviting people to join the settlement. Using the time perspective, they explore the past and present of the community settlement in general and based on that, write a future scenario (located in near or far future) imagining life on the community settlement from different aspects relating to past and present incorporating facts they have learnt.

5   Lesson Plans

Student Level
4th grade elementary school students living in a community settlement

The Chosen Perspectives
Personal and time perspectives

Unit Length and Lesson Length
14 lessons of 45 minutes each.

Lessons 1–2: My Community Settlement

Content
My community settlement

Aims
Student will get to know his/her community settlement

Thinking Processes Developed
Scientific thinking – inquiry

Thinking Strategies Developed
Gathering information

Learning Environment
– Outside – exploring the community settlement in groups for 60 minutes.
– Students will be accompanied by adult volunteers following them according to student instructions.

Opening/Exposure
– Introducing the silent map with 10 strategic places marked on the map without any words or explanations.
– Teacher will introduce the time limit (60 min.) and the adult accompanying each group.

- Teacher will announce a competition between groups. Teacher will explain students have information on each marked location. Students will have to use their phones to scan the barcode and read and summarize the information. The group which completes all ten locations will return to class. The first group to arrive will get a prize.

Teaching Strategies
Inquiry-based learning

Learning Activities and Grouping
In groups of 3–5, students will:

1. Explore the community settlement
2. Use their mobile phones to scan the barcode
3. Summarize the information

In plenary:
- Groups present the maps and the information on some of the places/locations visited.
- All the information is gathered to present the community settlement.

Learning Materials
- Scanned information on each location
- Silent map

Product/s
- Silent map and summarized information

Assessment
Silent map: at least 5 locations are mentioned on the map with a short explanation.

Modification for Special Needs Students
Fill in at least 5 locations on the map and videotape explanation

Enrichment for Able and Gifted Students
- Add extra locations that are not marked on the map, or
- Add extra information on each location marked on the map.

Lessons 3–4: Introduction to Community Settlements

Content
- Types of community settlements
- Characteristics of community settlements

Aims
- Student will recognize different types of community settlements.
- Student will be aware of the characteristics of community settlements.
- Student will be exposed to different aspects of community settlements (management, terms for admission, environmental planning, education, social services).

Thinking Processes Developed
Scientific thinking – inquiry

Thinking Strategies Developed
- Gathering and organizing information
- Graphic representation

Learning Environment
Classroom with personal laptops

Opening/exposure
Video clips presenting different types of community settlements. For example: https://www.youtube.com/watch?v=RJtfcnwuOr8
Introducing 2 thinking maps: The Circle Map and the Tree Map.

Teaching Strategies
Inquiry-based learning

Learning Activities and Grouping
1. Students watch the video clips on their personal laptops.
2. In pairs, students define the different aspects of living in a community settlement (management, terms for admission, environmental planning, education, social services).
3. Teacher designs information stations based on student aspects.
4. "Learning Coffee Shop": Students move from station to station spending approximately 7–10 minutes in each, and reading the information and

SOCIAL STUDIES: COMMUNITY SETTLEMENTS

writing what each station represents, and what it needs to include. Students can see what their peers wrote as they leave there notes at the station. Then they can add their ideas to what already exists at the station.
5 Students read the passage in the workbook related to community settlements.
6 Students summarize the information using 2 thinking maps. The *Circle Map* will be used to describe the different aspects/components of community settlements. The *Tree Map* will be used to describe the components and the suggested functions of each component.
7 Students write in their notebook the different components and what each one represents.

Learning Materials
– Video clips
– Workbook
– Thinking maps
– Information cards on aspects/components of community settlements

Product/s
– Thinking maps (Circle and Tree Map)
– Written summary in notebook

Assessment
– Thinking maps: (a) *Circle Map* has at least 4 aspects/components/areas. (b) *Tree Map* has at least 3 components/areas with description of at least 3 functions for each.
– Written summary: mentioning at least 3 components/areas. Description of each component in at least 3 sentences explaining committee work.

Modification for Special Needs Students
Templates of thinking maps with examples

Enrichment for Able and Gifted Students
Using the *Double Bubble Map* to compare the work of two committees

Lessons 5–7: Personal Perspective

Content
My connection to my community settlement

Aims
- Student will be aware of what he/she likes and dislikes in his settlement.
- Student will understand how he/she can influence a specific area in his settlement.
- Student will identify the different committees in his/her settlement.
- Student will use the thinking hats to solve a dilemma.
- Student will recognize the work of the different committees in dealing with everyday life on the community settlement.

Thinking Processes Developed
- Scientific thinking – inquiry
- Creative thinking

Thinking Strategies Developed
- Gathering and organizing information.
- Identifying perspectives.
- Walking in somebody else's shoes.

Learning Environment
Classroom with personal laptops

Opening/Exposure
- Invited guest telling the class about the function of one specific committee.
- Explaining the use of the six thinking hats using a dilemma from school life. (*First stage of using the six thinking hats*).

Teaching Strategies
Inquiry-based learning

Learning Activities and Grouping
Student/s will:

1 Choose one area he/she was introduced to earlier.
2 Write what he/she feels is good about living in the community settlement, what is wrong, and how it could be improved.
3 Form groups according to an area of interest.
4 Write in groups 6–8 questions starting with "How can I...?" that they are interested in investigating. For example: How can I solve the problem of the

SOCIAL STUDIES: COMMUNITY SETTLEMENTS

lack of activities for teenagers? Or, How can I influence the decisions made by the managing committee?
5. Investigate that area using information from the internet, the community settlement website, representatives of the different committees, and workbook "We are in Israel". Summarize information gathered.
6. Choose one question. Define a dilemma. For example: Do we need to organize a Friday night party only for teenagers in our settlement – Yes or No?
7. Use the six thinking hats to discuss and make a unanimous decision. *All group members use each hat in its turn.* Write down all comments. (*Second stage of using thinking hats*)
8. Present to class in the form of a simulation of a meeting of the selected committee discussing the issue.
9. In plenary: Students and teacher summarize what they have learned about the different committees, how they function, what they deal with, and how decisions are made concerning the major areas of life.
10. *HW assignment*: Interview parents and find out what made them choose to live on a community settlement, and why they chose this one in particular.

Learning Materials
– Meeting with committee member
– Six thinking hats
– Workbook "We are in Israel"
– Community settlement website

Product/s
Simulation of committee meeting discussing a relevant issue

Assessment
Simulation of committee meeting: all group members participated, the issue was relevant, at least 2 arguments were presented for and 2 against, decision was clear.

Modification for Special Needs Students
For dyslectic or weak students: use laptop for individual work, oral participation in group, participation in simulation based on ability.

Enrichment for Able and Gifted Students
– Interview a member of a different committee and write an article for the school newspaper.

- Attend one of the meetings of a selected committee (after obtaining permission from parents and committee members).

Lessons 8–10: Personal Perspective

Content
- Why do we need to live on a community settlement?
- How do we attract young families of quality to come and live here?

Aims
- Student will experience making a decision using the six thinking hats in a different way.
- Student will learn how to present data using a diagram.
- Student will recognize and experience the process of problem solving.

Thinking Processes Developed
Creative thinking – problem finding and problem solving

Thinking Strategies Developed
- Identifying perspectives
- Encountering different angles
- Walking in someone else's shoes
- Defining the problem
- Suggesting solutions
- Finding criteria
- Selecting best solution

Learning Environment
Classroom with personal laptops

Opening/Exposure

1. Present data using a diagram. Students gather information on the population of cities close to their community settlement in the Galilee area.
2. Students are introduced to the six stages of problem solving (PPT presentation), experiencing it using a problem connected to school life. For example: How can we stop violence at school?

Teaching Strategies
Problem-based learning

Social Studies: Community Settlements

Learning Activities and Grouping

Thinking hats – Third stage
In groups of 3–5, students will:

1 Use the six thinking hats (PDF). Each student picks a hat. The dilemma is: Do we stay and live in this community settlement or leave? A decision must be reached unanimously.
2 Present the process and decision in class.

- No matter what most of the class has decided (to leave or to stay) students and teacher define the main problem: How do we attract new young families of high quality to our settlement?
- Students can choose a different problem related to previous issues discussed such as: How can we help teenagers have more relevant and enjoyable activities in our settlement, so that they will not constantly need to be driven by parents elsewhere?

Problem solving
In groups of 3–5, students will:

1 Identify problems in community settlements.
2 Define the problem.
3 Suggest at least 5 solutions.
4 Find at least 4 criteria.
5 Select the best solution based on criteria.
6 Design an action plan based on the best solution.
7 Present the process and action plan in class.

Learning Materials
- Diagrams
- PPT presentation of problem solving stages
- Six thinking hats PDF
- Worksheet on the problem solving process

Product/s
Presentation of the problem solving process

Assessment
Presentation of the problem solving process: the worksheet is completed, all stages are presented orally, the problem is defined correctly, there are at least

5 solutions, there are 4 criteria, the table presenting the solution selection is filled, a solution was selected, the action plan is presented in stages, the action plan is presented in clear points.

Modification for Special Needs Students
Working in mixed ability groups. Recording stages of problem solving on computer

Enrichment for Able and Gifted Students
Create a pamphlet calling young families to join the community settlement

Lessons 11–12: Time Perspective

Content
The community settlement in the past and present

Aims
- Student will explore the development of community settlements in general.
- Student will explore his/her community settlement.
- Students will notice changes in his/her community settlement.
- Student will put in sequence (from past to present) events in the development of community settlements in general.
- Students will find connections between events.

Thinking Processes Developed
Future thinking – construction and analysis of concept

Thinking Strategies Developed
- Gathering and organizing information
- Classification and analysis
- Comparison
- Identifying connections

Learning Environment
Classroom with personal laptops

Opening/Exposure
- Video clip presenting the history of the community settlement
- Presenting the timeline

Teaching Strategies
Future-based learning

SOCIAL STUDIES: COMMUNITY SETTLEMENTS

Learning Activities and Grouping
In groups of 3–5, students will:

1 Find at least 10 events in the history of the development of community settlements in Israel.
2 Classify and analyze the events and put them in correct sequence.
3 Write 1–2 sentences to describe each event.
4 Compare the different events and look for a process.
5 Identify connections between events.
6 Present the timeline in class.

In plenary, discuss connection of events in the development of community settlements and other developments in the history of the country, technology etc.

Learning Materials
– Timeline template
– Community settlement websites
– Old newspapers
– Interview with people who founded community settlements

Product/s
Timeline

Assessment
– Timeline: has at least 10 events, the events are organized in the right sequence, there is a short explanation under each event, a process of development is mentioned.
– Bonus: a connection between mentioned events and other events is established.

Modification for Special Needs Students
Working in mixed ability groups, or receiving a template of timeline with a few events already marked. Instead of writing the description students could draw the timeline on the computer and give an oral explanation based on written keywords.

Enrichment for Able and Gifted Students
Design a timeline for a selected community settlement and compare and contrast with the general development of settlements to detect differences and similarities.

Lessons 13–14: Time Perspective

Content
My community settlement in the future

Aims
- Student will experience using future thinking skills.
- Student will understand how to predict the near or far future based on facts

Thinking Processes Developed
Future thinking

Thinking Strategies Developed
Predicting development

Learning Environment
Classroom

Opening/Exposure
- Introducing the future scenario.
- Mutually agreeing on the criteria for writing a good future scenario
  - Teacher will direct students and add criteria not mentioned.

Teaching Strategies
Future-based learning

Learning Activities and Grouping
In groups of 3–5, students will:

1 Write a future scenario
2 Present the future scenario

In plenary

3 Discuss connections between events of development of community settlements and other events in the development of the country.

Learning Materials
Future scenario criteria

Product/s
Future Scenario

Assessment
Future scenario: is located in the future (far or near), one page long, mentions past, present and future, written in first person, has two additional characters, has a plot, creative, correct and relevant events, mentions a process.

Modification for Special Needs Students
Videotaping the scenario as a first person narrative

Enrichment for Able and Gifted Students
Designing a model of the future community settlement

6   Future Scenario

6.1   *Our Community Settlement*
We are in 2057. We have a big swimming pool that cleans itself and renews the water so that it is fresh every day. The pool also has a machine that washes your hair and designs your hair according to latest fashion. Robots help children do their homework. A child who is having difficulties with his homework just needs to press a button and the application on his phone sends it to the robot, who then helps the child without giving him the answer. This is available only for the children of our settlement because it was developed by the startup company which belongs to our settlement. Later it will be available to other children in Israel and then the whole world. The robot also plays with the child when he is bored and can make him laugh.

We have a museum in our community settlement. The museum was built a few years ago. It is very modern. Everything is connected to the cloud, and there are holograms of people from the past who established our settlement. We can actually see them in their daily work, and hear how they got the idea of establishing the community settlement here. Everything is presented in 3D. Near the museum we also have a park called the 'season park'. It is divided into four seasons and when you go in you feel that you are in that season. In winter, it snows all the time, and the snow doesn't melt. There is also a big shopping mall and a play area for small and bigger children. Our website is more advanced now and presents information in 3D. Each house has a robot that cleans and does all the house chores. It also feeds the dogs and cats. We have virtual reality glasses and we use them at home and outside. We don't have roads anymore because we have flying cars. Each member of our community can lock his house using a code on his cellphone. Our kitchen prepares the food on its own. Everything is self-cleaned and controlled by the Galaxy SD13.

We know that many years ago people in our settlement people lived in regular houses, walked outside, and drove their cars that needed gasoline. People had to go through several stages to be accepted into our settlement, and it took time. Now every person who wants to live here is screened by the robot, who looks for information from several sources, sends it to the management and the decision is made on the same day.

Note

The unit was developed by Etti Mandel under the supervision of Hava Vidergor.

References

Carl, W. J. (1996). *Six thinking hats: Argumentativeness and response to thinking model*. Paper presented at the Annual Meeting of the Southern States Communication Association, Memphis, TN.
de Bono, E. (1985). *Six hat thinking*. Boston, MA: Little, Brown and Company.
Ministry of Education. (2003). *Homeland society and citizenship*. Jerusalem: Department of planning and Development of Curriculum. Retrieved September 19, 2017, from http://cms.education.gov.il/educationcms/units/tochniyot_limudim/moledet/tochniyhalimudim/tochnitlimudim.htm [in Hebrew]
Sagi, A., & Stern, Z. (2011). *Barefoot homeland Israeli thoughts*. Tel Aviv: Am Oved. [in Hebrew]

PART 3

Multidimensional Curriculum for Non-Core Domains

CHAPTER 7

The Bible: Leaders and Leadership

This chapter focuses on Bible studies and deals with leadership. It starts with the definitions and studies relating to creative thinking, problem solving and leadership. It goes on to explain leadership roles in the Bible. The example unit designed based on MdCM illustrates how secondary school students examine and relate to leadership in the Bible, in current times, and try to predict leadership in the future. A sample of future scenario writing is enclosed, as well as a template used for the problem-solving process.

1   Leadership, Creative Thinking, and Problem Solving

Leadership, creative thinking, and problem solving or decision making are definitely related. Scharmer (2009) described the single-person-centric concept of leadership as outdated and claimed that real leadership takes place through collective, systemic, and distributed action. Participants work through the ELIAS (Emerging Leaders Innovate Across Sectors) program and experience systems change beginning with a number of stages. The first stage Scharmer called *Downloading* and *Denial*, in which there is a focus on the past; this is followed by *Debate* in which the problem is viewed and blame is placed on others; then there is *Dialogue* in which multiple perspectives are viewed, including each person's part in creating the issue. This stage is followed by *Connecting to Source* in which there is an uncovering of common will and a shift from a "me" to a "we" focus. This stage is followed by *Envisioning*, in which there is a crystallizing of the vision and intention, and then *Enacting,* in which there is a prototyping of the "new" by linking head, heart, and hand; and finally *Embodying*, in which there is institutionalizing of the "new" in processes and practices. Throughout the ELIAS leadership experience, there is an emphasis on open mind, open heart, and open will. These situational conceptual theories and frameworks can add considerable meaning and relevance to the development of viable leadership programs for gifted students.

Sternberg (1999) claimed that good leadership is, in large part, a *decision-making process.*, Developing leadership, therefore, will involve guiding students who may be future leaders in developing the skills to ask the kind of questions they need to ask, and the decision-making skills they need to make wise, creative decisions. Sternberg and Lubart (1995) defined key creative decision-making skills as being able to redefine and analyze problems, sell solutions, realize the limitations of knowledge, take on sensible, principled tasks and overcome obstacles. Successful leaders propel followers from where they are to where the leader wants them to go (Sternberg, 1999). In addition, the leader will be successful to the extent that followers reach the destination willingly, with maximum positive and minimum negative outcomes for the leader-follower system (Sternberg, Kaufman, & Pretz, 2002). The WICS model of leadership has four components: wisdom, intelligence, creativity, synthesis. Sternberg (2005) said creative skills are needed to come up with functional ideas and to convince others of the values of the proposed ideas. Wisdom balances the effect of ideas on the individual, on others, and on institutions in both the short and long term. Leaders can be creatively intelligent, analytically intelligent and practically intelligent without being wise (Sternberg, 2005). Wisdom is especially important in today's world as a result of advances in technology, including destructive technology. This mismatch between the development and the lack of development of wisdom places the world at an enormous risk (Sternberg, 2005).

The model used for problem solving in this chapter, and the MdCM in general (Vidergor, 2015, 2017) originates from the Future Problem Solving Program International (FPSPI) which teaches students to solve problems located in the future using six steps. The steps are: (a) Identifying the problem; (b) Defining the problem; (c) Suggesting varied solutions; (d) Suggesting criteria for evaluation of the best solution; (e) Applying criteria to select the best solution; and (f) Designing an action plan (FPSPI, 2001).

2   Leadership in the Bible

Klein (2009) claims that leadership has presence in the Bible. The role of the leader is to be responsible for uniting the nation/tribe. The Bible describes leaders on two levels: The first, dealing with events relating to the generation in which the leader functions and his way of leading the people, while the second relates to the personal aspect of what the leader undergoes during his leadership period. Buber (1964) listed five main types of leadership in the Bible: (1) The nation ancestors – responsible for creating the nation from various tribes. (2) The various leaders chosen by God, whose mission was to set the nation free from slavery by enemies. (3) Judges – whose role was to draw people to believe in God and follow his ways. Most of their leadership was military. (4) Kings – Talmon (1975) explained that the king had two main roles:

military – organizing the army so that it would stand by him when needed; and economic – collecting taxes from crops. (5) Prophets – rising when monarchy fell, prophets often became the kings' adversaries, and suffered from the people as well. Prophets (Ahad Ha'am, 2011) had to be truthful, believe in ideals, and therefore also just.

3   Example Unit and Lesson Plans: Leadership in the Bible

3.1   *Unit Description*

This 13-lesson unit was implemented in 9th grade in a comprehensive high school, containing 28 students of medium SES. The lessons promoted different thinking processes, but the main focus of this unit was to develop the students' creative thinking in the form of problem finding and problem solving. The first four lessons were devoted to scientific thinking – inquiry from a personal perspective, and introduced students to thinking maps. Lessons 5 and 6 still dealt with the personal perspective, but promoted creative thinking using the Six Thinking Hats. Lessons 7–12 combined the global and time perspective, focusing on a broad view of leadership, designing a timeline, and using the problem-solving stages to solve past or current issues relating to leadership. The last lesson invited students to put everything together and project themselves into the future to practice future thinking based on information gathered.

4   Lesson Plans

Student Level
9th grade comprehensive high school

The Chosen Perspectives
Personal, global, and time

Unit and Lesson Length
13 lessons of 45 minutes each

Lesson 1: Introduction to Leadership

Content
Leaders and leadership

Aims
- Student will be exposed to the subject of leadership in general.
- Student will think about concepts connected to leadership.
- Student will define leadership.
- Student will understand the different definitions of leadership.

Thinking Processes Developed
Scientific thinking – inquiry

Thinking Strategies Developed
- Construction of a concept
- Analysis and classification

Learning Environment
- Classroom
- Using mobile phones

Opening/Exposure
- Children speak about leadership
  http://www.teamworkandleadership.com/2012/11/kids-and-leadership-what-makes-a-good-leader-inspiring-video.html
- Thinking maps – introducing the *Circle Map* and the *Bubble Map*.

Teaching Strategies
Inquiry-based learning

Learning Activities and Grouping
In pairs, students will:

1. Watch the video clip.
2. Fill in the Circle Map with association on leadership.
3. Look for other videos or information on leadership using mobile phones.
4. Use the Bubble Map to record as many characteristics of leaders as possible.
5. Define leadership.

In plenary, students will:

6. Present the definition of leadership.

7 Discuss definitions.
8 Form one class definition of leadership.

Learning Materials
- Video clip
- Thinking maps
- Mobile phone

Product/s
Definition of leadership

Assessment
Definition of leadership: includes at least two aspects (personal, cognitive, behavioral), has at least 5 characteristics

Modification for Special Needs Students
Watching video several times. Thinking map template partially filled in

Enrichment for Able and Gifted Students
Choose someone you consider a great leader and describe him/her. Keep in mind the definition agreed on in class

Lesson 2: Personal Perspective

Content
Leaders and leadership – main characteristics

Aims
- Student will develop awareness of personal characteristics as a leader.
- Student will identify the most important characteristics of a leader.

Thinking Processes Developed
Scientific thinking – inquiry

Thinking Strategies Developed
- Analysis and classification
- Comparison

Learning Environment
Classroom

Opening/Exposure
– Students are asked to think and write down individually: What are the 5 characteristics that I think a leader should have?
– Thinking maps – introducing the *Double Bubble Map*.

Teaching Strategies
Inquiry-based learning

Learning Activities and Grouping
In pairs students will:

1. Fill in the Double Bubble Map, comparing their characteristics with characteristics of a leader, showing similarities and differences.
2. Discuss similarities and choose 5 main characteristics that represent good leaders.
3. Grade characteristics from most to least important.
4. Write them on a page and post them on the board.

In plenary, students will:

5. Discuss suggestions posted on the board.
6. Vote for the top 5 characteristics that are important for current leaders.

Learning Materials
Thinking maps – The *Double Bubble Map*

Product/s
The Double Bubble Map

Assessment
The Double Bubble Map: has at least 4 different and 3 similar characteristics

Modification for Special Needs Students
The Double Bubble Map template will have one example of similarity and difference

Enrichment for Able and Gifted Students
Use the *Divergent Thinking Map* to describe the characteristics of a leader

Lessons 3–4: Personal Perspective

Content
Leaders in the Bible: David, Yoav and Absalom

Aims
- Student will be acquainted with leaders from the bible.
- Student will gather information on the selected leader.
- Student will draw conclusions about the leader's characteristics, based on his actions.

Thinking Processes Developed
Scientific thinking – inquiry

Thinking Strategies Developed
- Collecting information
- Organizing information
- Inferring

Learning Environment
- Classroom
- Mobile phones

Opening/Exposure
Presentation of the three leaders: David, Yoav, and Absalom using photos and attitudes

Teaching Strategies
Inquiry-based learning

Learning Activities and Grouping
In groups of 6, students will:

1 Select a leader.
   - Teacher could make sure that all leaders are selected, or divide the class in advance into six groups, where two groups choose one leader.
2 Look up information on that leader from the Bible and from the internet.
3 Design an identity card for the leader including: full name, pedigree, description, actions, and characteristics.

4 Write two characteristics they would like to possess.
5 Write two characteristics they would not like to possess.
6 Present the identity card on their desk.
7 Move around the class and read the identity cards.
    - Doing this in a computer room, students could leave the identity cards on the screen and circulate.
8 Write five facts that they have learned about each leader.

Learning Materials
- The Bible (Old Testament)
- Mobile phones

Product/s
Identity card

Assessment
Identity card: All items are completed, items are correct, at least 2 actions are mentioned, at least 2 characteristics are mentioned.

Modification for Special Needs Students
Instead of writing, students could record themselves presenting the leader

Enrichment for Able and Gifted Students
Role play an interview with the leader asking him about himself, his family, actions, and characteristics

Lessons 5–6: Personal Perspective

Content
Dilemmas relating to leaders and leadership

Aims
- Student will recognize the six thinking hats.
- Student will apply the six thinking hats to solve a dilemma.
- Student will define a dilemma that his/her selected leader encountered.
- Student will acquire teamwork skills.
- Student will put himself in the shoes of his selected leader.

Thinking Processes Developed
Creative thinking – dilemma solving

Thinking Strategies Developed
- Identifying perspectives
- Encountering different angles
- Experiencing being in the shoes of others

Learning Environment
Classroom

Opening/Exposure
- Introducing the six thinking hats.
- Review of main findings on the three leaders.

Teaching Strategies
Problem-based learning

Learning Activities and Grouping
In groups of 6, students will:

1. Define a dilemma their selected leader had.
   Optional – receive a card with a pre-prepared dilemma.
2. Use the six thinking hats to solve the dilemma.
   Options – either each student picks a different hat, or all hats are addressed by all group members.
3. Arrive at a unanimous decision. If they do not, they must continue the discussion to convince some group members to change their point of view.
4. Decide on a creative way of presenting their decision.
5. Present the decision in class.

Learning Materials
- The six thinking hats
- Dilemma cards (optional)

Product/s
Creative product illustrating the solution of the dilemma. Product could be one of the following: A song, poem, poster, petition, a Facebook page, a role play, etc.

Assessment
Creative product: clear decision, within time limit of 3 minutes, presenting the process, all group members participated

Modification for Special Needs Students
Working in mixed ability groups

Enrichment for Able and Gifted Students
Writing an article/story/fable about the dilemma and the decision

Lessons 7–8: Global and Time Perspectives

The global perspective will be used in these lessons to relate to the country.

Content
Leaders in Israel according to periods of time till the present

Aims
- Student will recognize the main periods of time in the history of Israel.
- Student will be acquainted with the leaders ruling the country from biblical times to the present day.
- Student will arrange information in sequence to create a timeline.

Thinking Processes Developed
Future thinking

Thinking Strategies Developed
- Collecting information
- Classification and analysis
- Organizing information
- Graphic representation
- Organizing in sequence
- Identifying connections

Learning Environment
- Classroom
- Mobile phones

Opening/Exposure
PPT introducing time periods in the history of Israel

Teaching Strategies
Future-based learning

Learning Activities and Grouping
In groups of 4, students will:

1. Receive a page illustrating the major periods of time in the history of Israel.
2. Select 2 leaders from each period of time.
3. Will look for information on these leaders including: name of leader, time of leadership, how he became a leader.
4. Design a timeline representing the development of leadership from biblical time to the present day.
5. Add information to the general timeline designed by the class.

In plenary, students will:

6. Explore the general timeline to find connections between the times and leaders.
7. Explore the timeline and look for connections between leaders and events and other events occurring in neighboring countries or globally.
8. Optional HW: Summarize what you have learnt about leaders in different times, look for a process, and connections between event within and outside of Israel.

Learning Materials
- A page illustrating the major periods of time in the history of Israel.
- Timeline template

Product/s
- Timeline
- Written summary

Assessment
Timeline: at least 12 dates of leadership and leader's names are mentioned, there is a short description of each leader, it stretches from biblical times to the present day, connections are indicated between the leader's views and actions.

Modification for Special Needs Students
The timeline template with three examples of leader's names, actions and characteristics already filled in. Students will fill in at least three additional names of leaders and describe their actions and characteristics using keywords only.

Enrichment for Able and Gifted Students
Students will add an extra leader to each period of time including required details. They will pinpoint connections between leaders' actions, as well as look for other global development that could have influenced leaders' actions.

Lessons 9–12: Global and Time Perspectives – Problem Solving

The global perspective will be used in these lessons to relate to the country.

Content
Leadership in Israel

Aims
- Student will recognize the problem-solving stages.
- Student will identify problems in leadership in biblical times.
- Student will be able to solve a defined problem and write an action plan.
- Student will apply the stages of problem solving to solve a current problem concerning leadership.

Thinking Processes Developed
Creative thinking – problem finding and problem solving

Thinking Strategies Developed
- Defining a problem
- Suggesting solutions
- Finding criteria
- Selecting the best solution

Learning Environment
Classroom

Opening/Exposure
Presentation of problem solving stages (PPT and worksheet, see Appendix)

Teaching Strategies
Problem-based learning

Learning Activities and Grouping
Stage 1: Practicing problem solving according to stages. (Lesson 1)

In plenary, teacher and students will choose a problem from the students' school environment (ways of preventing violence, ways of maintaining good health, ways of reacting to peer pressure etc.). Students will go through the stages following the worksheet.

Stage 2 (Lessons 2–3)
In groups of 5: Each group will choose one area they would like to deal with: the military, foreign relations, economics, education, religion, and leadership.

The teacher will explain that each committee is responsible for solving a problem in the selected area. The head or representative chosen by students will be responsible for presenting the process and action plan to the President/teacher at the special convention organized in Jerusalem at his residence.

Students can choose whether they would like to solve a problem related to leadership in biblical or current times. Examples of problems: How can we protect Israel from surrounding tribes/countries? How can we strengthen Israel from inside? How can we maintain good our relations with other influential tribes/nations? How can we preserve/change the practice of religion? How can we develop good leadership in Israel?

Students will:

1 Suggest problems.
2 Select one problem and define it.
3 Suggest at least 5 solutions.
4 Find at least 4 criteria for selecting the best solution.
5 Select best solution based on criteria.
6 Write an action plan.
7 As preparation for the convention at the President's residence, students review the process, choose a representative, and practice for the presentation at the convention.

Stage 3: Simulation (Lesson 4)
Simulation – convention at the President's residence

Teacher will explain that s/he, as the president of Israel is very concerned about its current situation and would like to hear the suggestions of representatives of the different committees on how to solve the problems they have raised.

8 Each representative has 5 minutes to present the problem, solutions, criteria, selected solution and action plan.

In plenary:

9 Students will discuss:

   a Similarities and differences between suggested action plans relating to biblical and current times.
   b Similarities and differences between suggested action plans in general.
   c Feasibility of action plan implementation.
   d Order of implementation of suggestions.

Summary:

10 Students will relate to the problem-solving process.

Learning Materials
– Timeline (from previous lesson)
– Worksheet (problem solving process)

Product/s
Process of problem solving and action plan as presented by group representative

Assessment
Presentation of process of problem solving: the problem, solutions, criteria, selected solution and action plan, was clear, within a 5-minute time limit, action plan was presented in stages and could be implemented.

Modification for Special Needs Students
Weak or dyslectic students will work in mixed ability groups

Enrichment for Able and Gifted Students
Students will suggest additional solutions and also add to the stages of implementing the action plan. They could volunteer to serve as group representatives.

Lesson 13: Time Perspective

Content
Future thinking about leadership in Israel

Aims
– Student will practice thinking about the future using collected data.

- Student will be able to predict the future based on facts from the past and present.

Thinking Processes Developed
Future thinking

Thinking Strategies Developed
Predicting development

Learning Environment
Classroom

Opening/Exposure
Exposing students to the future scenario and the criteria for writing

Teaching Strategies
Future-based learning

Learning Activities and Grouping
In groups of 4–5, students will write the future scenario using the pre-determined criteria

Learning Materials
- Future scenario
- All materials studied in this unit

Product/s
Future scenario

Assessment
Future scenario: is located in the far or near future, one page long, mentions past, present and future, is written in first person, has two additional characters, has a plot, creative, correct and relevant events, it mentions a process.

Modification for Special Needs Students
Oral or video presentation instead of written one.

Enrichment for Able and Gifted Students
Writing the future scenario in form of a rhymed poem

5   Future Scenario

The year is 2047. My name is Yossi and I am an Israeli citizen, 77 years old today. When I was a child 70 years ago, the leaders of the country were still the ones who had founded it, although they were getting old like Ben Gurion. Communication was only through radio and television. There was no internet and there were no computers. Then when the leadership changed, everything gradually changed. Leaders started caring only about themselves, and in the beginning of the 21st century till 2020some of them were sentenced to long periods of time in jail because they were very corrupt.

In the early days of the Bible, the nation was small, and when it settled in the land of Canaan, leaders like King David, Yoav and Absalom, who were brave and fought against other tribes, also fought against each other. Because of King David we have the capital of Jerusalem till today.

Over the years, leaders had to consider many aspects of life like military issues of defending the state of Israel from its enemies, economic issues, freedom of practice of religion, employment and housing, education and much more. From the beginning of the 21st century, leaders had access to social media, which got stronger. They appeared very often on television and had to look better and sound even better to be able to be elected. They learned how to get public sympathy sometimes saying things people wanted to hear, and not what they actually believed in.

Now in 2047, because of technology, there are no problems of air pollution and hunger that leaders need to worry about. My son is 37 years old now, and he would like to become the next prime minister of Israel. I am sure he has all the required characteristics, and wish him luck. It will be much easier to lead the country because of the latest technological developments compared to the past.

Note

The unit was developed by Meirav Biton under the supervision of Hava Vidergor.

References

Ahad Ha'am. (2011). Moses. In R. Gerber (Ed.), *Israeli humanism: Spiritual excellence for Israeli identity* (pp. 84–96). Tel Aviv: Mofet Institute. [in Hebrew]

Buber, M. M. (1964). Leadership in the bible. In M. M. Buber (Ed.), *Ways of the bible: Studies of style patterns in the bible* (pp. 123–134). Jerusalem: Bialik. [in Hebrew]

Future Problem Solving Program. (2001). *Future problem solving program coach's handbook.* Lexington, KY: Author.

Klein, S. (2009). *Introduction to the leaders and leadership in the bible.* Ramat Gan: The Higher Institute for Bible, Bar Ilan University. Retrieved July 23, 2017, from http://www.mgl.org.il/he/torah/view.asp?id=1385 [in Hebrew]

Scharmer, O. (2009). *Ten propositions on transforming the current leadership development paradigm.* Amherst, MA: Massachusetts Institute of Technology.

Sternberg, R. J. (1999). *Wisdom, intelligence, and creativity synthesized.* Cambridge: Cambridge University Press.

Sternberg, R. J. (2005). A model of educational leadership: Wisdom, intelligence, and creativity synthesized. *International Journal of Leadership in Education: Theory & Practice, 8,* 347–364.

Sternberg, R. J., Kaufman, J. C., & Pretz, J. E. (2002). *The creativity conundrum: A propulsion model of kinds of creative contributions.* New York, NY: Psychology Press.

Sternberg, R. J., & Lubert, T. I. (1995). *Defying the crowd: Cultivating creativity in a culture of conformity.* New York, NY: The Free Press.

Talmon, S. (1975). The king's trial. In A. Malmet (Ed.), *The beginning of Israeli monarchy* (pp. 16–27). Jerusalem: Zalman Shazar Center for the Study of the Jewish People, Israeli Historical Society. [in Hebrew]

Vidergor, H. E. (2015). The multidimensional curriculum model. In H. E. Vidergor & C. R. Harris (Eds.), *Applied practice for educators of gifted and able learners* (pp. 199–2014). Rotterdam, The Netherlands: Sense Publishers.

Vidergor, H. E. (2017). Effectiveness of the multidimensional curriculum model in developing high order thinking skills in elementary and secondary students. *The Curriculum Journal, 29*(1), 95–115. doi:10.1080/09585176.2017.1318771

Appendix: Problem Solving Process

Get into groups of 3–5

1 Identify the different areas.
2 Choose one area. (Each group will choose a different area).
3 Classify information in bullets relating to the whole story (Table 7.1). What do we know? What should we know? (that is not mentioned).
4 Define the problem. Start with "How can we...?"
5 Suggest at least 5 different solutions. Write them in Table 7.2.

6. Decide on at least 4 criteria for evaluating the solutions (i.e. cost). Write them in Table 7.2.
7. Select the best solution based on the criteria (Table 7.2). Give scores from 1–5 to each solution according to criteria.
8. Design an action plan to implement the selected idea.
9. Present the area, problem, criteria, selected solution and action plan in plenary. You will have 5 minutes.
10. Plenary will vote and select the best solution to be implemented first.

TABLE 7.1 *Classify information*

What do we know?	What should we know? (that is not mentioned)

TABLE 7.2 *Process of selecting the best solution*

Solutions	Criterion	Criterion	Criterion	Criterion	Sum
1.					
2.					
3.					
4.					
5.					

CHAPTER 8

Music: The Beatles

This chapter commences with the definition of music education outlining its cognitive, personal and social contribution. Then it introduces the Beatles as the topic for the unit designed based on MdCM. It illustrates how music could be taught in secondary school incorporating appreciation and understanding of this unique art form, using different thinking tools and perspectives. The Beatles were chosen as they represent an era, innovation in music, and are still known and loved today. The chapter closes with an example future scenario portraying the Beatles 50 years from now.

1   Music Education

Music is considered a tool of expression, a non-verbal and abstract international language. It has a major place in all cultures and ages, and its effect on human behavior is known and has been proven in research (Kuperwaser, 2017). Human beings have always been attracted to music. Dealing with this rich form of art creates great joy and improves self-expression and inter-personal communication among people of all ages (Portowitz, 2005).

Music education is one of the fields of art education and its many benefits can greatly contribute to children's education and development. Research indicates a correlation between music education and achievements in other school subjects (Scripp, 2002; Winner & Hetland, 2000). Music education can also improve learners' social skills and contribute to their general development (Weissblay, 2016).

Unfortunately, Music education is not included in the core curriculum of either elementary or secondary education in Israel. Middle schools can decide whether to allocate extra hours to an elective subject like music within arts education. The Ministry of Education recommends devoting three weekly hours over three years to music education (Weissblay, 2016). The music education curriculum was written in 1980, and on the Ministry of Education website (2017), music education relates only to elementary and high schools. The curriculum for music education in middle school suggests that students learn how to feel the music, express their feelings relating to it, decipher concepts studied, components, and ways of performing, including application via musical meetings, concerts and performances. The unit on the

Beatles described in this chapter was designed based on these principles and recommendations, making the most of the time and learning environment resources available at the specific school.

2   Cognitive Contribution

Costa-Giomi (2015) indicated that there are long-term effects of music education on children's cognitive abilities. Studies found that the brain of people who had been exposed to musical activities was different in certain significant characteristics compared to people less involved in music education, and a strong correlation was detected between exposure to music and the development of neural connections in the brain responsible for spatial intelligence and abstract thinking (Portowitz, Lichtenstein, Egorova, & Brand, 2009). Portowitz (2005) added that music studies improved spatial thinking including spatial orientation, which enables one to organize oneself in space and understand the relation between objects and events in terms of direction, sequence, order, and the proximity between them. Other studies confirmed the connection between music education and creativity, especially musical improvisation, and areas in which students are required to use their imagination (Weissblay, 2016).

3   Personal and Social Contribution

Many studies indicate that there is positive influence of music on the personal and social development of the learner. Personally, musical education was found to improve self-confidence, self-image, sense of achievement, independence and responsibility. Socially, music education indicated improvement in the ability to work in groups/teams, collaborate, communicate with others and acquire other social skills. Musical activity is important, as it sharpens and deepens social interaction skills within the group, and its ability to act well in coordination (Weisblay, 2016). Students perceive music as contributing to their social skills, influencing their self-esteem and satisfaction, influencing personal skills, and encouraging the development of self-achievement, self-confidence, and inner-motivation (Kokotaski & Hallam, 2000). An additional study showed that most students who participated in music lessons had positive perceptions of their participation, their rehearsals and preparations for performing before an audience (Sagi & Ezer, 2009).

4 The Beatles

The Beatles, with their unique style, constitute an important milestone in the history of light music (Heilbrunner, 2008). The appreciation and enthusiasm for the Beatles' music derived from their ability to assimilate and merge the different influences into a unique and private sound of their own, which combined the screaming and roughness of the rock 'n roll of the 1950s (the main source influencing the original writing) with the melodic emphasis and thoughtful construction of songs in the popular music industry style. The band's repertoire is considered the cornerstone of rock music for sound and emotional content, as well as the artistic prints, and social and cultural occurrences growing around it. The band wrote original songs, and its records contained mainly original materials (Regev, 1995).

There was an unprecedented phenomenon of admiration around the Beatles named Beatlemania, when many teenagers followed them everywhere, screamed and fainted at their concerts. The band members became major public figures and a focal interest for millions around the world, as well as a source of influence on musicians and artists in general (Regev, 1995). Heilbrunner (2008) determined that the band was an outstanding symbol of culture in the 1960s, and many saw them as the leaders of the generation. The vision behind the Beatles' culture called for freedom and liberation from negative feelings, slavery, oppression, poverty, and loneliness. The Beatles wanted to create a united and harmonious society, and their leader John Lennon, brought with him the message of belief and hope.

5 Example Unit and Lessons: The Beatles

5.1 *Unit Description*
The unit was designed for 7th grade students studying in middle school. It was taught over a period of two months. The unit about the Beatles introduced to students to the original songs and their unique characteristics, and their unique musical style as expressed in the songs' arrangements and use of musical instruments. The unit included an introduction dealing with the period the Beatles were active as a band and the biographies of its members. The students became acquainted with the tempos, types of arrangements, and repertoire of songs, and were more able to enjoy the music and understand it in depth. The Beatles' songs are well known and often heard online and on radio, and recognizing them could expand students' knowledge as cultural human beings possessing musical knowledge.

The first lesson dealt with introducing students to the biographical details of the band and its members. The focus of the lesson was students' feeling about the Beatles' songs and the construction of the inquiry process. Thinking strategies used included classification, comparison, and analysis, enabling students to identify the Beatles members, identify the musical instruments, and sing a chosen song.

Lessons 2–5 focused on the personal perspective, where students listened to the different Beatles' songs, related to them personally, and recounted a special experience reminding them of the specific song. The learning process included the use of the six thinking hats, and scientific thinking – inquiry to investigate different perspectives, and to graphically present student preferences of musical styles and bands.

Lessons 6–8 dealt with the time perspective. Lessons focused on solving problems which may have risen during the period when the Beatles were active as a band. It also deepened the understanding of the sequence of events in the history of the band, forming a timeline from the past to the present. This led to the ability to predict the future using the future scenario and criteria as a guide to project themselves into the shorter future span of 20 years, or the longer one of 50 years from now. This part of the unit developed creative thinking and future thinking skills.

6   Lesson Plans

Student Level
Middle School, 7th Grade

The Chosen Perspectives
Personal perspective and time perspective

Unit and Lesson Length
8 lessons of 80 minutes each

Lesson 1: Introduction

Content
Meeting the Beatles

Aims
– Student will recognize Beatles members

- Student will be exposed to Beatles songs.
- Student will recognize the musical instruments in songs.
- Student will be able to sing a selected Beatles song.

Thinking Processes Developed
Scientific thinking – inquiry

Thinking Strategies Developed
- Collecting information
- Classifying
- Analyzing
- Organizing information

Learning Environment
- Music room
- Mobile phones

Opening/Exposure
PPT presentation of the Beatles and some of their songs

Teaching Strategies
Inquiry-based learning

Learning Activities and Grouping
Students will get into groups of 3–4 and:

1 Look for information on the Beatles using cell phones.
2 Write at least 15 facts about the Beatles.
3 Present 5 selected facts in plenary without repeating facts mentioned by other groups.
4 Select one song and work on the following: The period in the band's history, the meaning of lyrics, melody, and musical instruments used.
5 Present to class.

Learning Materials
- PPT presenting the Beatles
- Websites and songs on the internet

Product/s
Presentation of selected song

Assessment
Presentation of selected song covered all aspects: the period in the band's history, the meaning of lyrics, melody, and musical instruments used.

Modification for Special Needs Students
Listening to the history of the Beatles, and recording some facts

Enrichment for Able and Gifted Students
Playing the selected Beatles song on a different musical instrument

Lesson 2: Personal Perspective

Content
– Personal connection to Beatles songs

Aims
– Student will recognize Beatles songs.
– Student will personally connect to one of the Beatles songs.
– Student will attach a personal experience to the selected song.

Thinking Processes Developed
Scientific thinking – inquiry

Thinking Strategies Developed
– Identifying
– Analyzing
– Identifying personal connections

Learning Environment
Music room

Opening/Exposure
– Listening to the song "Let it Be" and to the Israeli national song writer Naomi Shemer talking about her personal experience/connection to the song.
– Teacher telling about her experience/connection to one of the songs using the piano.

Teaching Strategies
Inquiry-based learning

MUSIC: THE BEATLES

Learning Activities and Grouping
In plenary:

1. Students suggest various criteria for selecting the song.
2. Students mutually agree on 5–6 criteria.

In pairs:

1. Listen to a variety of Beatles songs
2. Select the song they have the strongest connection to, using pre-determined criteria.
3. Define the meaning, musical structure, musical instruments, and musical characteristics.
4. Explain the personal experience/connection to the song.
5. Present to class.

Learning Materials
- YouTube videos
- PPT presentations
- Piano

Product/s
My personal connection to a Beatles song

Assessment
Presentation included: song meaning, musical structure, musical instruments, musical characteristics, and personal experience/connection

Modification for Special Needs Students
Choosing a song with translation to mother tongue

Enrichment for Able and Gifted Students
Presenting using rhymes, or using the melody of the selected song, or combining both

Lesson 3: Personal Perspective

Content
The history of the Beatles and their influence on the music world

Aims
- Student will recognize the history of the Beatles.
- Student will identify and recognize the Beatles' influence on the world of music.
- Student will experience a dilemma concerning the Beatles.

Thinking Processes Developed
- Scientific thinking – inquiry
- Creative thinking – decision making

Thinking Strategies Developed
- Collecting information
- Organizing information
- Identifying perspectives
- Encountering different angles
- Being in someone else's shoes (empathizing)

Learning Environment
- Music room
- Mobile phones

Opening/Exposure
- Short video on Beatlemania
- Exposure to the six thinking hats practicing using a dilemma from school life

Teaching Strategies
Problem-based learning – decision making

Learning Activities and Grouping
In groups of 6, students will:

1. Explore the Beatles' biography using their phones.
2. Create an identity card of the band including at least 10 facts.
3. Raise different dilemmas connected to the Beatles. For example: It is the year 1967. The Beatles are coming to Israel. Do I go to their concert or not? Another one could be: It is 1970 and almost the end of the Beatles' career. Am I for or against the Beatles breakup? It is 2017 now. The Beatles would like to be united for one concert. Am I for or against it?

4. Use the six thinking hats to solve the dilemma unanimously.
5. Present the process and solution using one of the Beatles melodies adding new lyrics.

Learning Materials
- Identity card template
- PPT presentation of the six thinking hats

Product/s
Dilemma solution using the six thinking hats

Assessment
- Identity card: has at least 10 facts, written correctly, in sequence, mentions all Beatles members, covers major events, presented aesthetically, has one extra interesting fact.
- Presentation of dilemma solution: use of one of Beatles melodies, clear decision, reflecting the process, all students participated.

Modification for Special Needs Students
Team work and mutual help

Enrichment for Able and Gifted Students
Student will serve as group leaders (blue hat), control and record the process

Lesson 4–5: Personal Perspective

Content
Student's current preferences in music

Aims
- Student will explore current preferences of music in class.
- Student will create a multiple choice questionnaire.
- Student will understand how to analyze the data in the questionnaire.
- Student will use graphic presentation.
- Student will draw conclusions from presented results.

Thinking Processes Developed
Scientific thinking

Thinking Strategies Developed
- Forming a research question
- Forming a hypothesis
- Collecting information
- Organizing information
- Graphic presentation
- Inferring

Learning Environment
Music room

Opening/Exposure
- Discussion on current musical preferences
- Introduction of the questionnaire: sample questions, number of questions, clarity

Teaching Strategies
Inquiry-based learning

Learning Activities and Grouping
In groups of 4, students will:

1. Decide on an area they want to explore. (For example: preference of music styles, admiration of bands or singers, imitation of famous singers, general information about certain popular bands etc.). Each group should choose a different area, so that students will not be required to answer the same questions.
2. Define the research question.
3. Write 7–8 multiple choice questions.
4. Administer the questionnaire to their class mates.
5. Analyze student replies.
6. Present student replies in graphs, distinguishing between boys' and girls' responses.
7. Draw conclusions from findings.
8. Present to class.

Learning Materials
- Questionnaire template
- Graphic presentation options

Product/s
- Questionnaire
- Graphic presentation of results

Assessment
- Questionnaire: Area is defined, research question is defined, At least 7 multiple choice questions, written correctly (according to template)
- Graphic presentation of results: Results are presented in at least one graph, differences between boys and girls are clear, drawn conclusions are correct

Modification for Special Needs Students
Recording the questions and/or answers

Enrichment for Able and Gifted Students
Using different forms of graphic representation

Lesson 6: Time Perspective

Content
Beatles history

Aims
- Student will explore the history of the Beatles.
- Student will organize information in a timeline.
- Student will be aware of the development of the Beatles.
- Student will look for connections between the development of the Beatles and other historical events.

Thinking Processes Developed
Future thinking – construction and analysis of concept

Thinking Strategies Developed
- Defining and identifying components
- Classification and analysis
- Organizing in sequence
- Comparison
- Identification of processes
- Identification of connections

Learning Environment
– Music room
– Mobile phones

Opening/Exposure
– Abby Road poster.
– Timeline template

Teaching Strategies
Future-based learning

Learning Activities and Grouping
In groups of 4, students will:

1 Explore the history of the Beatles up to the present day.
2 Put at least 20 major events on a timeline (year and short explanation).
3 Look for connections between events.
4 Look for a process of development.
5 Look for connection between Beatles development and major events in history.
6 Present the timeline to class.

Learning Materials
– Abby Road poster
– Timeline template
– Identity card

Product/s
Timeline

Assessment
Timeline: has at least 5 items, shows dates, shows a short explanation, is in the right sequence, identifies connections between events, identifies a process of development, identifies connection to other historical events, aesthetic, clearly written, colorful.

Modification for Special Needs Students
Use the timeline template and arrange the facts from the identity card using keywords for explanations.

Enrichment for Able and Gifted Students
Write an article/prepare a T.V. report/show/video about the Beatles history

Lesson 7: Time Perspective

Content
– Problems the Beatles faced

Aims
– Student will be introduced to (or reminded of) problem-solving steps.
– Student will apply these steps to solving a problem relating to the Beatles.
– Student will solve a problem relating to the Beatles.
– Student will design an action plan.

Thinking Processes Developed
Creative thinking – problem finding and problem solving

Thinking Strategies Developed
– Defining a problem
– Suggesting solutions
– Finding criteria
– Selecting the best solution

Learning Environment
Music room

Opening/Exposure
– Presenting problem-solving steps.
– Practicing problem solving on an area relating to school life

Teaching Strategies
Problem-based learning

Learning Activities and Grouping
In groups of 4, students will:

1 Brainstorm problem the Beatles may have encountered. For example: relationship between band members, band manager, fans, excessive travelling, writers' block, appearance etc.

2. Define a problem relating to the Beatles.
3. Suggest at least 5 solutions.
4. Suggest at least 4 criteria for selecting best solution.
5. Apply criteria to select the best solution.
6. Design an action plan to apply solution.
7. Present process pf problem solving and the action plan to class.

Learning Materials
Problem-solving steps

Product/s
Presentation of the problem-solving process and action plan

Assessment
Presentation of the problem-solving process and action plan

Modification for Special Needs Students
Working in mixed ability groups, students with special needs could participate orally and write keywords, or draw the suggestions for action

Enrichment for Able and Gifted Students
Role play of the application of the action plan

Lesson 8: Time Perspective

Content
The Beatles in the future

Aims
– Student will develop the ability to think about the future in music.
– Student will combine their knowledge to predict the future of the Beatles.

Thinking Processes Developed
Future thinking

Thinking Strategies Developed
Predicting development

Learning Environment
Music room

Opening/Exposure
A song with futuristic electronic arrangement
Introduction of future scenario and writing criteria

Teaching Strategies
Future-based learning

Learning Activities and Grouping
In groups of 4–5, students will:

1 Project themselves to the selected time span (10 years, 50 years from now)
2 Write a scenario about the Beatles, incorporating what they have learned.
3 Follow the criteria for writing the scenario.

In plenary:

4 Present the scenario to the class.
5 Discuss the similarities and differences between the scenarios presented in class.

Learning Materials
- Song with a futuristic arrangement
- Future scenario criteria
- Timeline

Product/s
Future scenario

Assessment
Future scenario: is located in the future (far or near), is one page long, mentions past, present and future, written in first person, has two additional characters, has a plot, creative, correct and relevant events, mentions a process.

Modification for Special Needs Students
Recording the scenario

Enrichment for Able and Gifted Students
Writing a futuristic Beatles song (lyrics and melody)

7   **Future Scenario**

The year is 2067 and we adore the Beatles. We are their greatest fans. The band has four members who control music systems that can change the lighting, back scenery and all other cool effects applied in big concerts. The golden ring moves during the performance. It moves upwards, and floats to the sides, which enables audience enjoy the performance much more. Lighting is created by multirotor drones, which creates a better view because there are no lighting posts which block your vision.

The first band of the Beatles became famous in the 1960s and they had iconic songs. They were so famous that whenever they performed, girls fainted. This was called "Beatlemania". John Lenon was murdered in 1980, 10 years after the Beatles broke up. But their songs were popular among people from all ages even at the beginning of the 21st century.

In 2021 the second version of the band, Beatles 2021, started performing. They performed on top of the highest building in the world. They created a unique way of inventing and writing songs everybody likes. They lived in a huge villa in England, where they had robot servants. They rehearsed in a special studio with robotic musical instruments. They did not have to fly to get to their concerts. They just projected themselves there, or sometimes used their holograms. Sometimes they played the old songs of the original Beatles.

In 2050 the band underwent a modernization stage, and now their videos are transmitted straight to our brains. They play special instruments which are directly connected to our brains (if we wish and approve) they are called the Taburosan and Mobiliturn. This has made them even more popular in our generation. Now we are 65 years old, and the Beatles 2021 band members are around 70, but still look young and energetic. Their next performance in 2068 is in New-Tel Aviv and we hope to buy tickets and be part of the Beatles 2021 experience.

Note

The unit was developed by Meirav Litani under the supervision of Hava Vidergor.

References

Costa-Giomi, E. (2015). The long-term effects of childhood music instruction on intelligence and general cognitive abilities. *Update: Applications of Research in Music Education, 33*(2), 20–26.

Heilbrunner, O. (2008). The beatles: A band for all the family or revolution leaders? *Note+: Music Art and Society, 11*, 54–59. [in Hebrew]

Kokotsaki, D., & Hallam, S. (2007). Higher education music students' perceptions of the benefits of participative music making. *Music Education Research, 9*(1), 93–109.

Kuperwasser, B. (2017). *Music inspector's welcome address: Inspectorate of music education.* Retrieved from http://cms.education.gov.il/educationcms/units/mazkirut_pedagogit/music/dvarhamafmar/dvar_hamafmar.htm [in Hebrew]

Ministry of Education. (2017). *Inspectorate of music education.* Retrieved from http://cms.education.gov.il/educationcms/units/mazkirut_pedagogit/music/dvarhamafmar/dvar_hamafmar.htm [in Hebrew]

Portowitz, A. (2005). Musical brains Jaffa project: Influence of guided music lessons on the development of elementary school at-risk students. *Note+: Music Art and Society, 6*, 61–67. [in Hebrew]

Portowitz, A., Lichtenstein, O., Egorova, L., & Brand, E. (2009). Underlying mechanisms linking music education and cognitive modifiability. *Research Studies in Music Education, 31*(2), 107–128.

Regev, M. (1995). *Rock music and culture.* Tel Aviv: Laor. [in Hebrew]

Sagi, R., & Yoezer, H. (2009). *Program "key" research evaluation report.* Tel Aviv: Levinsky Academic College of Education, Research Authority. [in Hebrew]

Scripp, L. (2002). Critical links: An overview of research on music and learning. In R. J. Deasy (Ed.), *Learning in the arts and student and academic development.* Washington, DC: Arts Education Partnership. Retrieved September 5, 2017, from http://www.aeparts.org/files/publications/CriticalLinks.pdf

Weissblay, E. (2016). *Conservatories and their place in musical education in the education system.* Jerusalem: Knesset Research and Information Center, Kiryat Ben Gurion. [in Hebrew]

Winner, E., & Hetland, L. (2000). The arts and academic achievement: What the evidence shows. *Journal of Aesthetic Education, 34*(3–4), 3–10

CHAPTER 9

Life Skills: Me Myself and I

Life skills and programs in school are presented and more specifically, the elaboration of the program designed for introducing life skills in first grade, followed by an example unit and lessons designed on the principles of MdCM. Two additional units on the topics of violence and accepting others are briefly described. Samples of student products include future scenarios written by 1st grade students projecting themselves five years into the future relating to the learned subject, as well as the use of different thinking maps.

1   Life Skills

Life skills is a program designed for students from 1st to 12th grade focusing on the development of social-emotional capabilities and strengthening their abilities to cope with different life situations. The World Health Organization (1997) defined education for life skills as the ability for adaptive and positive behavior enabling human beings to cope efficiently with the demands and challenges of everyday life. Life skills include: decision making, creative thinking, critical thinking, effective communication, personal relationships, self-awareness, empathy, and coping with feeling and stressful situations (Shefinet, 2017). The acquisition of life skills equips the children with a "toolkit" they acquire over the years, learning how to use these skills in many situations they have to cope with. The development of life skills, practicing the use of the different tools, and a sense of success in coping, enable the feeling of security. When children acquires tools and learn to select the suitable one for them, they develop a positive self-image which later becomes a component of their personal identity (Roseman, Frenkel, & Zaltzman, 1997).

The Israeli Ministry of Education (1996) developed a systematic, structured and developmental program from 1st grade to 12th grade named 'Life skills' which included topics dealing with development and prevention. Its uniqueness lies in the acquired skills and behaviors, extending the dialogue between teachers and students on topics relating to mental strength, and incorporating them into the different subjects. This elaboration of emotional, cognitive, and behavioral skills enables children to act effectively in events they cope with, through communication with others, their culture and their surroundings. According to Roseman, Frenkel, and Zaltzman (1997) the program seeks to develop among children mental strength based on the sense of self-control, self-value, a positive attitude to life, internal motivation, and a sense of humor, all enabling them to thrive in moments of distress and leading them to full realization of their potential.

The program is adapted to the age, level of development, and needs of students, and deals with mainly three areas of their lives: the individual, the family, and society. It is studied in three circles: personal, inter-personal, and systemic-social, where in each circle three components are addressed: the cognitive perspective – dealing with rational thinking and understanding of processes; the emotional perspective – dealing with emotional experience and self-confidence; and the behavioral perspective – dealing with the actual behavior in everyday life (Ministry of Education, 1996).

2   Life Skills in 1st Grade on the Topic of Self

According to the Israeli Ministry of Education (1996) entering 1st grade is a significant event in any child's life, involving numerous changes in his or her world. The child is expected to possess many developmental skills: focus on an assignment for a long period of time, take responsibility, acquire new skills and norms, behave according to accepted norms, fit in with society, and more. There are emotional changes, which are expressed in the perception of the child's self-image due to experienced changes. The 'Life skills' program defines three main conditions that are necessary for the proper development of students entering 1st grade. The teacher must:

1 Create an environment which supplies opportunities for learning at school and out of school in the family and the community; an environment that provides opportunities for self-expression, social-emotional, and artistic expression.
2 Help students with the acquisition of developmental skills by expressing interest, supporting student function, setting expectations of high achievements, and providing suitable experiences, recognizing the different ways students learn and providing feedback to help them progress, raising problems in students' lives as opportunities for problem solving, directing and supporting social activities within and out of school, and inviting parents' cooperation in values and procedures at school while respecting the different cultures in the community.
3 Provide mutual learning opportunities contributing to the cognitive development and recognition of differences among students while nurturing tolerance towards the other.

Studying the subject of Self in 1st grade focuses on three perspectives: the physical, the personal, and family perspectives. Its main aim is to make children recognize their personal inner-world, guide them to explore their inner experiences, while examining their feelings, thoughts, and behaviors; directing students to discover their uniqueness; encouraging them to develop their self-expression, increase the involvement of the significant characters in their lives, identify the negative themes in their perceptions and create positive ones; make children aware that perfection is impossible to achieve; teach children to recognize the boundaries between feelings and thoughts, develop imagination and humor, and encourage openness while preserving privacy (Ministry of Education, 1996).

3   Example Unit and Lessons: Me Myself and I

3.1   *Unit Description*

The topic was selected from the area of life skills dealing with "This Child is Me" and was named "Me Myself and I". It is focused on the thought that developing the "self" is one of the most important aims of human beings in their lives, and more so at the beginning of studies at school. Moving from kindergarten to school, the child is exposed to new norms and requirements, and faces new situations not previously encountered. Based on the core-curriculum taught in 1st grade, topics and concepts were selected according to their relevance to the students and their needs. The unit was designed using the MdCM and adapted to 1st grade students.

The unit consisted of 13 lessons, and was taught in a class of 22 children of medium to low SES from different backgrounds and cultures (Ethiopian, Russian, Moroccan, native Israeli). Unit aims were determined based on the three dimensions of thinking specified in the MdCM. Therefore, lessons 1–6 focused on scientific thinking and included inquiry and use of thinking maps. Lessons 7–10 aimed to develop creative thinking using the six thinking hats and problem solving, and lessons 11–12 focused on future thinking, including individual future scenario telling. Unit aims included: (1) developing abilities and thinking skills; (2) introducing students to various thinking tools (thinking maps, thinking hats, problem solving, future scenario); (3) strengthening the awareness and recognition of their characteristics and preferences as individual human beings; and (4) enabling students to experience learning in different frameworks to better understand themselves and their learning styles.

Lessons were taught during a one-month period as following: *Lesson 1* introduced students to the topic of "Me, Myself and I", as well as to the circle map. *Lessons 2–3* introduced the concept of "identity" and students prepared a personal identity card. *Lesson 4* was devoted to exploring their names and who they were named for in class and completing and presenting the project in class. *Lesson 5* focused on things student liked using the Divergent Thinking Map. *Lesson 6* was about describing personal characteristics using the Bubble Map. In *lessons 7–8*, the students were exposed to the six steps of problem solving, and were invited to solve different problems related to them in groups. In *lessons 9–10*, students learned to apply the six thinking hats using them for dilemmas relating to social relationships. In *lesson 11* the students learned to differentiate between wishes that could be attained and those that could not. In *lesson 12*, students learned the song "When I grow up" and individually worked on their future scenarios, projecting themselves into sixth grade using a five-year time span. All their products were collected in a personal portfolio and presented to parents in a special gathering devoted to the subject.

4 Lesson Plans

Student Level
1st grade students in elementary school

The Chosen Perspectives
Personal and time perspectives

Unit and Lesson Length
12 lessons of 45 minutes each.

Lesson 1: Personal Perspective – Exposure

Content
This child is me

Aims
- Student will write information about himself/herself.
- Student will tell how s/he feels about the subject.
- Student will become acquainted with the Circle Map.

Thinking Processes Developed
Scientific thinking

Thinking Strategies Developed
- Collecting information
- Organizing information

Learning Environment
Classroom

Opening/Exposure
Listening to "And This Child is Me" by Yehuda Atlas (in form of poem and song).
https://www.youtube.com/watch?v=tf7bs9Lc2vs (poem)
http://allfims.mobi/watch/t9Py-HdQzzA (song)
Guessing the subject of the unit/project.

Teaching Strategies
Inquiry-based learning

Learning Activities and Grouping
Individually:
1. Write 10 things about yourself on the worksheet.
2. In Plenary: Share with class mates. State how you feel about the poem.
3. Teacher exposes students to the Circle Map.

In small groups:

4. Think what areas they are connected to in their lives (family, friends, school etc.)
5. Write down the different areas with the help of the teacher.
6. Fill in the Circle Map writing "I" in the middle and different areas that are connected to me like: my name, my characteristics, things I like, my feelings etc.

Learning Materials
- The poem/song "And This Child is Me" by Yehuda Atlas
- Worksheet – 10 things about me
- Circle Map

Product/s
- Worksheet
- Circle Map

Assessment
- Worksheet: Writing at least 7 things about themselves, clear handwriting, correct spelling
- Circle Map: Mentioning at least four areas connected to themselves

Modification for Special Needs Students
Teacher mediation

Enrichment for Able and Gifted Students
Adding more details in the different areas

Lessons 2–3: Personal Perspective

Content
Information about myself

Aims
- Student will recognize personal information identifying him/her.
- Student will recognize the concept of "identity".

Thinking Processes Developed
Scientific thinking – inquiry

Thinking Strategies Developed
- Collecting information
- Organizing information
- Creating a graphic representation

Learning Environment
- Classroom and outdoor school space (hallway, yard)
- Two teachers in the class (homeroom teacher and art teacher)
- 6th grade students accompanying 1st grade students and helping them complete the different assignments

Opening/Exposure
- What is an identity card? Showing an authentic identity card
- Exploring the details presented in the identity card
- Using the word "identity".

Teaching Strategies
Inquiry-based learning

Learning Activities and Grouping
1. Teacher presents the four stations: Preparing my identity card, drawing my face, measuring myself, and my finger prints.
2. Students will circulate among different stations to complete at least three tasks.
3. Students will get help from two teachers (homeroom and art teacher) and 6th grade students.

Learning Materials
- Authentic identity card
- Stations:
    1. Identity card template
    2. Standing mirror for drawing student face
    3. Tape measure and table for writing measurements
    4. paint and paper for taking fingerprints.

Product/s
Multicategory product

Assessment
Completing at least three assignments in three different stations

Modification for Special Needs Students
Personal guidance by teachers and 6th grade students

Enrichment for Able and Gifted Students
Writing their feelings about the poem "I am lucky that I am me" by A. Hillel

Lesson 4: Personal Perspective

Content
My name

Aims
- Student will recognize the meaning of his/her name.
- Student will experience conducting an interview.
- Student will know how to collect information.
- Student will select a way to present the information.

Thinking Processes Developed
Scientific thinking

Thinking Strategies Developed
- Suggesting research question
- Collecting information
- Organizing information

Learning Environment
Classroom and home

Opening/Exposure
"Odd Names" by Shari Dash-Greenspan

Teaching Strategies
Inquiry-based learning

Learning Activities and Grouping

1. Discussion – Why were you given these names?
2. What would you like to know about your name?
3. Students suggest a research question.
4. Students create an inquiry/interview page with the teacher (Who chose my name? After whom or what am I named? Is my name rare/unique? How does it affect me? Do I have a nickname? Do people ever call me by offensive names? What is my favorite name? Would I change my name if I could?
5. Students think about ways of getting information about their name.
6. Students suggest criteria for evaluation of the process and product.

Teacher introduces the assignment to be done at home and explains that students can choose any way they feel appropriate to present the information collected about their names.
Students suggest ways of presentation.

Learning Materials
- Story – Odd names
- Inquiry/interview page

Product/s
- Inquiry/interview page
- Creative product

Assessment
- Inquiry/interview page: at least 3 questions are answered and there are explanations.

– Creative product – aesthetic, represents the name well, clear handwriting, no spelling mistakes.

Modification for Special Needs Students
Structures inquiry/interview page with some multiple choice answers

Enrichment for Able and Gifted Students
Adding questions to the interview

Lesson 5: Personal Perspective

Content
Things I like

Aims
- Student will identify things s/he likes in different areas.
- Student will classify the things s/he likes in different areas.
- Student will create a Divergent Thinking Map.

Thinking Processes Developed
Scientific thinking

Thinking Strategies Developed
- Collecting information
- Organizing information
- Creating a graphic representation

Learning Environment
Classroom

Opening/Exposure
- Song: I like chocolate/Jonathan Geffen
- Discussion: How can we describe/elaborate on the things we love?
- Introducing several types of Divergent Thinking Maps

Teaching Strategies
Inquiry-based learning

Learning Activities and Grouping
Individually students prepare a thinking map illustrating the things s/he loves (generalization and elaboration)

LIFE SKILLS: ME MYSELF AND I

Learning Materials
- Song and text: I like chocolate/Jonathan Geffen
- Divergent Thinking Maps

Product/s
Divergent Thinking Map

Assessment
Divergent Thinking Map: Relating to at least three areas (food, games, T.V. shows, animals, places, clothes, and books), writing at least two things in each category/area, correct spelling, colorful

Modification for Special Needs Students
Pre-prepared simple thinking map such as a Circle Map or Bubble Map with areas. Students will have to fill in what they like matching the item to the area

Enrichment for Able and Gifted Students
Encouraging students to add branches to the divergent map

Lesson 6: Personal Perspective

Content
My traits

Aims
- Student will recognize typical traits of human beings.
- Student will identify his/her own positive and negative traits.

Thinking Processes Developed
Scientific thinking

Thinking Strategies Developed
- Collecting information
- Drawing conclusions

Learning Environment
Classroom

Opening/Exposure
- Trait Game: Students sit on the floor in a circle. In turn, they pick a card with a specific trait, and explain how it relates to them.

– Discussion: What is a trait?

Teaching Strategies
Inquiry-based learning

Learning Activities and Grouping
Student fills in a worksheet choosing his/her traits and sticking them on to an image of a boy/girl drawn on the page

Learning Materials
– Trait cards
– Worksheet

Product/s
Worksheet

Assessment
Worksheet: Filling in all trait cards on the worksheet

Modification for Special Needs Students
Worksheet with illustrated traits. Students will color their own traits

Enrichment for Able and Gifted Students
– Preparing a thinking map of their positive and negative traits
– Preparing a crossword puzzle of traits

Lessons 7–8: Personal Perspective

Content
My feelings – dealing with anger

Aims
– Student will recognize pleasant and unpleasant feelings.
– Student will identify situations creating anger.
– Student will be aware of his/her style of dealing with anger.
– Student will be exposed to different solutions to dealing with anger.

Thinking Processes Developed
Creative thinking

LIFE SKILLS: ME MYSELF AND I 153

Thinking Strategies Developed
- Defining a problem
- Suggesting solutions
- Finding criteria for selecting the best solution

Learning Environment
Classroom

Opening/Exposure
- PPT presenting different sentences relating to feelings. Students have to guess which feeling is described.
- Teacher writes feelings and students sort them into positive and negative feelings.
- Discussion: Which feeling is easier for me to cope with? Which is more difficult? What make us angry (being disappointed, jealous, sad, lonely, frustrated, offended)?
- Reading the poem "Signs" by Shlomit Assif. Recognizing the sign indicating anger.
- Introducing the stages of problem solving.

Teaching Strategies
Problem-based learning

Learning Activities and Grouping
Students are divided into 4 groups. Each group receives one of the following four situations in which a child has to deal with a situation of anger:

1. At the end of the lesson Ben left his pencil box on his desk and went out for recess. When he came back, he discovered that his pencil box had disappeared. Ben was very angry.
2. John and Michael met after school at Michael's house. Michael was playing with a ball in his room and hit a building made of Lego that John had just built. The building collapsed. John was angry.
3. Yoni and Rami were playing marbles during recess. Yoni lost and was left with a single marble, while Rami had a box full of marbles. Yoni went back to class. He felt upset and angry.
4. The teacher invited Anna to participate in a game. Dana was angry that the lesson ended and she had not been invited to play.

In groups:

1. Discuss the situation.
2. Write down what you know.
3. How would you behave?
4. Write down a few solutions relating to how the students should have behaved.

In plenary:

1. Students think how they can decide which is the best solution.
2. Students suggest criteria for selecting the best solution.

Back in groups:

1. Students choose at least two criteria for selecting the best solution.
2. Students choose the best solution.

In plenary:

1. Students present the situation and their solution/suggestion for coping with the problem/situation in a role play.
2. Discussion of ways of reacting to situations triggering anger and violence.

Learning Materials
- PPT describing feelings
- Poem "Signs" by Shlomit Assif
- Four different situations
- Instruction for group work

Product/s
Oral presentation of solution in roleplay form

Assessment
Role play presents the situation, the solution is clear, it is based on at least two criteria

Modification for Special Needs Students
Worksheet – "When I am sad/When I am happy", writing about two feelings

Enrichment for Able and Gifted Students
- Completing sentences about feelings.
- Writing a new situation with two endings – one negative when students cannot control their anger; and one in which students cope with their anger in a positive manner.

Lessons 9–10: Personal Perspective

Content
Me in society

Aims
- Student will recognize a variety of ideas for activities with friends.
- Student will enrich the ability to create social contacts.
- Student will recognize different perspectives of thinking for coping with the creation of social contacts.

Thinking Processes Developed
Creative thinking

Thinking Strategies Developed
- Identifying perspectives
- Encountering different angles
- Experiencing being in another person's shoes

Learning Environment
Classroom

Opening/Exposure
- The teacher tells a story about a family thinking about adopting a dog from the SPCA (Society for the Prevention of Cruelty to Animals).
- Then the teacher introduces students to de Bono's the six thinking hats, showing actual hats in different colors. The teacher accompanies the explanation with a PPT presentation illustrating the different hats and their uses.
- Students raise different perspectives regarding the adoption of the dog "wearing" a different hat each time.
- Teacher presents a PPT with photos of children doing things together. Children share what they do with friends. They also try to answer questions

like: Why do we need friends? Do we sometimes meet friends and not manage to have fun together? Why does that happen? When does that happen?

Teaching Strategies
Problem-based learning – decision making about a dilemma

Learning Activities and Grouping
Teacher presents a dilemma: Do we need friends? Yes or no?
In groups:
 Class is divided into five groups, each representing one hat (not the blue one), and a hat in the selected color is placed on the desk.
 Students will:

1 Discuss the dilemma, with each student stating his/her opinion relating to the hat.
2 Unanimously decide on the solution to the dilemma.
3 Write the response relating to the chosen hat.
4 Add some activities showing how to make this decision happen (action plan).

In plenary:

– Teacher, acting as the blue hat, will invite students to present their decision to the class.
– Students will discuss the different perspectives and the final decision.
– Students will come up with a collective action plan.
– Teacher will invite students to relate orally to the process and what they have gained from it.

Learning Materials
– PPT six thinking hats
– PPT of children in different situations

Product/s
Oral and written decision and action plan

Assessment
Written decision and action plan fit the color of the hat (thinking perspective)

Modification for Special Needs Students
Guided questions for relating to each hat, and teacher's help, when needed

Enrichment for Able and Gifted Students
Relating to an additional selected hat

Lesson 11: Time Perspective

Content
Wishes and dreams

Aims
– Student will recognize the role of imagination as a tool for fulfilling wishes.
– Student will distinguish between wishes that can be attained and those that cannot be realized.

Thinking Processes Developed
Future thinking

Thinking Strategies Developed
Defining and identifying components

Learning Environment
Classroom

Opening/Exposure
– What does the word "magic" mean to you?
– What does a magic hat look like?
– Who wears a magic hat?
– Listening to the poem "The Magic Hat"/Lea Goldberg
– Discussion: Who is the poem about? (a little girl) What is she dreaming of? (owning a magic hat) What is special about this hat? (it obeys her and does everything she wants) What is her wish? (to be a grown up, to be big) How would you feel if you had a hat like that? What would you ask it to do?

Teaching Strategies
Future-based learning

Learning Activities and Grouping
Each student will:

1. Prepare a magic hat.
2. Complete the sentence "Magic hat, I want you to...", and decorate the hat.

Learning Materials
The poem "The Magic Hat"/Lea Goldberg

Product/s
A magic hat and a written wish

Assessment
Writing at least one wish

Modification for Special Needs Students
Teacher's help in writing the wish

Enrichment for Able and Gifted Students
– Adding a few lines to the poem
– Wring at least three wishes.

Lesson 12: Time Perspective

Content
I in the future

Aims
– Student will experience thinking about his/her future.
– Student will be encouraged to make a wish.

Thinking Processes Developed
Future thinking

Thinking Strategies Developed
Predicting development

Learning Environment
Classroom

LIFE SKILLS: ME MYSELF AND I

Opening/Exposure
- Reading the poem "When I am big"/Jonathan Geffen
- Students share what they would like to do or be when they are older

Teaching Strategies
Future-based learning

Learning Activities and Grouping
- Teacher introduces the future scenario: tell a story about yourself five years from now based on what you have learned in this unit. Start in the future and also mention today and when you were younger.
- Teacher explains criteria for writing and evaluation.

Learning Materials
- The poem "When I am big"/Jonathan Geffen
- Future scenario

Product/s
Future scenario

Assessment
Future scenario: Starting with the future, written in first person, there is at least one additional character, writing at least five sentences, there is a plot, relating to the present and past and future, creative, correct language

Modification for Special Needs Students
- Add another stanza to the poem "When I am big"/by Jonathan Geffen
- Dictate to the teacher the future scenario about yourself

Enrichment for Able and Gifted Students
Elaborate the future scenario writing more about yourself, adding a more complex plot and characters

5   **Future Scenario**

5.1   *Me, Myself and I*
I am almost 13 years old. I am in 6th Grade now and studying math, sciences and languages. I will have a Bar Mitzva soon. I will invite all my friends, and when the party is over I will give my friends presents because they came to celebrate with

me. I will give most of the money to my father. He will save the money for college. He will give me some money to buy a new mobile phone. When I was in 1st grade I found science very difficult, and I could not follow the teacher and spent a long time trying to find the right page in the book. Now we use only tablets, so it is much easier for me. In 3rd grade we started to use tablets and I started to understand science better because there were a lot of pictures and short explanations. I am in 6th grade now, I am not small, and I remember I always wanted to be in 1st grade. My uncle told me:" You have to study. You have to learn how to read well". Now I am in 6th Grade and I read many books and like it. I am the first born in my family, and I have a younger brother. I like being in charge and responsible for my brother. When he was five years old I used to take him home from kindergarten. Now he is in 1st Grade and we go to school together. My parents said that they knew I was smart and responsible from a very early age. They also said that I was a very sweet baby and was always in a good mood and made everybody laugh.

6 Additional Products and Units

My name

Emily: Leader, creative, power, determined, strong, good perception, pays attention to details, ambitious, honest and caring, strives for excellence, serves as an example to her environment and community, initiator.
My name fits me perfectly (100%)
©All rights reserved to father and mother.

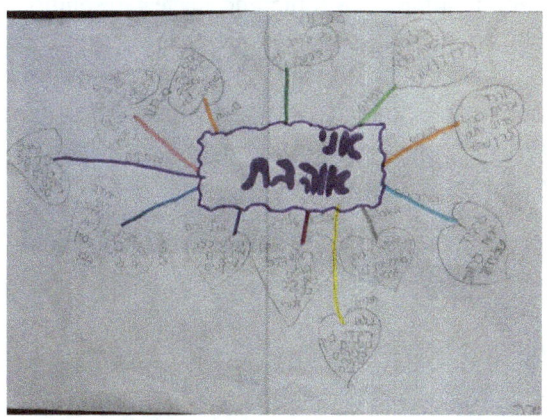

Things I like – using the Bubble Map

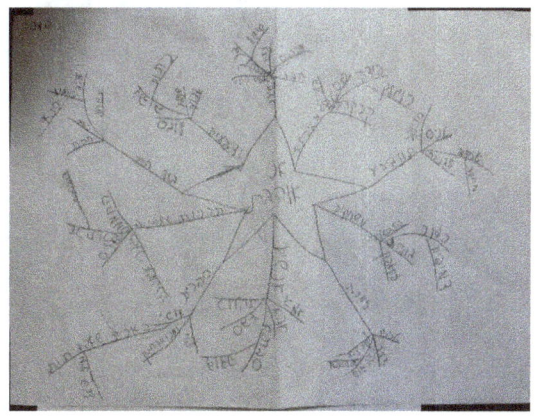

Things I like – using the Divergent Thinking Map

7 Unit on Accepting Others

Another unit developed for 1st grade students is "Accepting others". the unit commenced with the recognition and definition of accepting the other using the Bubble Map. In the lessons 3–4, the students discovered how openness and understanding of others in society helps, through a story. They used the Double Bubble Map to compare and contrast the traits of characters in the story. In the lessons 5–6, they were introduced to the six thinking hats and used them to solve a dilemma relating to accepting others at school. In the lessons 7–8, student raised different problems relating to the topic, and suggested solutions and action plans. In the lesson 9, they conducted an inquiry using photos from the past and present, and used the Double Bubble Map to compare the past with the present. In the lesson 10, the students were exposed to the future scenario and thought about their future 5 years from the present relating to the topic of accepting others.

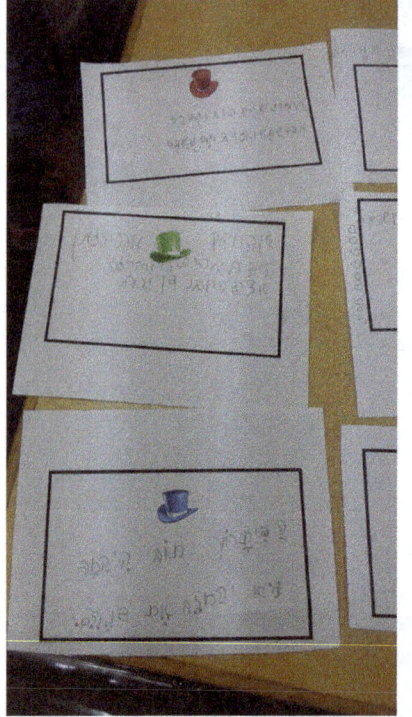 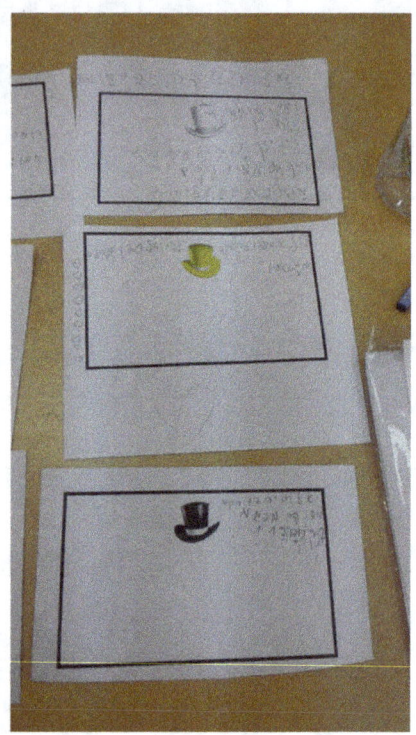

Decision-making process on "Accepting Others" using the Six Thinking Hats

8 Unit on Violence

Relevant subjects and concepts were chosen complying with student needs and life skills taught in 1st grade as part of the core curriculum. Ten lessons were designed, with stories and activities dealing with violence, incorporating thinking tools, and tools for preventing violence. Lessons 1–2 introduced students to the topic and to different types of violence. The product demonstrated the importance of the topic in the students' lives. Lessons 3–4 dealt with consideration and caring, preparing a group product reflecting the behavior they would like to stop. Lessons 5–6 dealt with the personal perspective of violence and introduced students to the Bubble Map. Lessons 7–8 continued the personal perspective, dealing with a dilemma and decision making using the six thinking hats. Lesson 9 dealt with the time perspective and focused on violence today and in the past in a selected area. Lesson 10 was devoted to writing a future scenario, which was dictated to the teachers, as students had not yet mastered the writing skill. The following example presents the future scenario written by a group dealing with violence in sports. Students projected themselves into the future, five years from their present.

9 Future Scenario

9.1 *Violence in Sports*

We are 6th grade students and we are big now. Some of the students in our class like soccer, and go to watch matches and also watch them on television. Once, when we were in 1st grade, many years ago, people came to the soccer field to watch matches and cursed and littered. We saw somebody eating sunflower seeds and spitting and throwing everything on the ground. He also left an empty bag of some kind of a snack. There was a lot of noise from their screaming and shouting. Then our parents banned the soccer matches, as the fans cursed and used improper words. Sometimes they also brought fire-crackers and would throw them on the players, and it was very dangerous.

In the future, it will be more difficult to misbehave. Robots will scan fans' bags and look for dangerous stuff. Whoever tries to throw a fire-cracker will be identified by the robot and it will spray him with paint. His seat will open and he will fall into a tunnel which will take him straight to the manager's office. The manager will throw him out, and he will never be able to come back to watch a match again. When somebody litters there will be a giant vacuum cleaner that will vacuum everything and the field will stay clean.

Now policemen drive cars that look like spaceships and they float above people's heads. They have cameras that are very special. All fans behave properly now, and there is no violence during soccer matches. Some of the fans know how to behave very well, because when they were in 1st grade their teacher, Miki, taught them what violence is and how to behave and not to hit other kids, and try to solve dilemmas and problems, so that we grow up to be non-violent people. And this is what we do. We come to the soccer field dressed properly, with the shirts that represent our favorite teams, and just watch the game and enjoy it without cursing or hitting. This is very nice and we feel like going very often.

Notes

The unit "Me Myself and I" was developed by Ronit Wolf under the supervision of Hava Vidergor.

The unit "Accepting Others" was developed by Maya Tikotsky under the supervision of Hava Vidergor.

The unit "Violence" developed by Miki Hazan under the supervision of Hava Vidergor.

References

Ministry of Education. (1996). *Core curriculum and series of activities and meetings for life skills education in first grade.* Jerusalem: Pedagogical Administration, Psychological Service, Ministry of Education. [in Hebrew]

Roseman, M., Frenkel, R., & Zaltsman, N. (1997). *Life skills: Developing personal identity in groups of children and adolescents.* Tel Aviv: Ramot Publishing. [in Hebrew]

Shadmi, H., & Zimmerman, S. (2008). *Core curriculum for life skills programs from first to twelfth grade.* Jerusalem: Pedagogical Administration, Psychological Service, Ministry of Education. [in Hebrew]

World Health Organization. (1997). *Life skills education for children and adolescents.* Retrieved October 8, 2017, from http://apps.who.int/iris/handle/10665/63552

PART 4

Multidimensional Curriculum Integrating Domains

CHAPTER 10

Energy: The Phenomenon-Based Approach

The current chapter illustrates the application of MdCM using a phenomenon-based approach focusing on teaching and learning about energy in high school. The phenomenon-based approach uses project- and problem-based learning to examine phenomena from multiple perspectives, breaking away from traditional subjects. MdCM offers thinking tools and processes, as well as an extra perspective of time, challenging students to think about the development and impact of the selected phenomenon in the future. Energy was selected as the phenomenon studied in high school examining energy transformation or conservation using a multi/transdisciplinary approach.

1   Phenomenon-Based Learning

The phenomenon-based approach to teaching and learning invites us to break the boundaries of traditional subject teaching and move toward interdisciplinary explorations of phenomena. Revealing and understanding the nature of a phenomenon from multiple perspectives is a complex process (Symeonidis & Schwarz, 2016). Finland has recently changed the school curriculum focusing on phenomenon-based learning and breaking away from the traditional school subjects. This was translated into seven transversal competence areas by defining the objectives and key content areas of the subjects:

1 Thinking and learning to learn;
2 Cultural competence, interaction and self-expression;
3 Taking care of oneself and managing daily life;
4 Multiliteracy;
5 Information and communications technology (ICT) competence;
6 Working life competence and entrepreneurship; and
7 Participation, involvement and building of a sustainable future (FNBE, 2016, section 3.3).

Silander (2015a) argued that holistic real-world phenomena help initiate learning, provided they "are studied as complete entities, in their real context, and the information and skills related to them are studied by crossing the boundaries between subjects" (p. 16).

A phenomenon is thus seen as:

- An authentic object of observation.
- A systemic framework for the things to be learned (systemic model).
- A metaphorical framework for the things to be learned (analogous model).

Examples of phenomena may include such topics as climate change, the European Union, media and technology, water, or energy (Silander, 2015a, p. 18).

Silander (2015b) suggested a phenomenon-based learning rubric consisting of five dimensions: Holisticity, authenticity, contextuality, problem-based inquiry learning and learning process. In its advanced level:

- *Holisticity* refers to the multidisciplinarity of phenomenon-based learning, focusing on a systematic, comprehensive exploration of current and actual events in the real world.
- *Authenticity* implies the use of authentic sources, materials, tools, and methods such as those that real experts and professionals use to solve problems.
- *Contextuality* refers to study of the phenomenon as a systemic entity, structuring it from different perspectives, observing the wider context, and combining aspects and topics.
- *Problem-based inquiry* learning is used to define questions and problems, and collaboratively construct knowledge by looking for answers and solutions.
- *Learning process* – in its advanced stage, it guides students to plan the learning process by creating their own learning tasks and tools, scaffolding learning to enable students to move beyond what they currently know toward what is to be known (Silander, 2015b).

2   Energy

Chen and associates (2014) explain that energy is one of the most important ideas and is useful for predicting and explaining phenomena within every science discipline. Yet, there are differences in the use of the concept across the disciplines. The physicist focuses more on conservation of energy, while the ecologist is more concerned with energy transfer. Students do not always connect the energy they learn about in physics lessons with the energy in biology, chemistry and geoscience. Chen and associates (2014) assert that students have to take a multidisciplinary approach to learning about energy that is found in biology, chemistry, physics, and earth and environmental sciences. They also must understand that the energy of the animate and inanimate is the same.

Ilomäki, Lakkala, Toom, and Muukkonen (2017) describe a set of three courses developed by a group of teachers in Finland integrating biology, chemistry and physics. The course, named "Energy in the Ecosystem", was designed as phenomenon-based learning (Francis, Breland, Østergaard, Lieblein, & Morse, 2013) and discussed energy in all three courses from different viewpoints. The aim was two-fold, to create a broader understanding about energy, as well as to impart some generic working skills. The courses lasted seven weeks, of which 2–3 weeks were devoted to a collaborative inquiry assignment on "energy in an ecosystem".

The following unit will illustrate the contribution of MdCM to the phenomenon-based approach, taking it one step further by adding the time perspective, challenging students to think about various uses of energy in the future.

3   Example Unit and Lesson Plans: Energy

3.1   *Unit Description*

The unit based on MdCM uses the broader concept or phenomenon of energy, and invites students to suggest projects they would like to research. Using project-based learning and creative problem solving as major teaching learning strategies helps students construct new knowledge on a sub-topic which interests them. Then, via the jigsaw method, students form larger groups where all types of conserved or transformed energy are represented, giving students a wider perspective of the phenomenon across many areas and disciplines. All three types of thinking processes are used, namely, scientific (research project), creative (problem solving), and time (predicting) as they write the future scenario related to energy, combining all aspects addressed in the different projects.

4   Lesson Plans

Student Level
11th Grade, comprehensive high school

The Chosen Perspectives
Personal, global, and time

Unit and Lesson Length
14 lessons of 45 minutes (7 weeks)

Lesson 1: Introduction

Content
- What is energy?
- Where can we find it in real life?

Aims
- Student will recognize the definition of energy.
- Student will identify different fields in which it is represented.
- Student will compare and contrast different sources of energy.

Thinking Processes Developed
Scientific thinking

Thinking Strategies Developed
- Defining and identifying components
- Classification and analysis
- Comparison

Learning Environment
Science lab + BYOD

Opening/Exposure
Is energy always conserved?
https://www.youtube.com/watch?v=GHCc9b2phn0

Teaching Strategies
Phenomenon-based learning

Learning Activities and Grouping
After watching the introductory video in groups of three students will:

1. Brainstorm different sources or types of energy.
2. Look for definitions of energy.
3. Divide the sources of energy to different fields of study.
4. List areas of life where conservation and transformation of energy are present.

ENERGY: THE PHENOMENON-BASED APPROACH 171

In plenary:

5 Present their definition of energy.
6 Present areas of life where conservation and transformation of energy are observed.

Learning Materials
– YouTube video
– Websites

Product/s
Areas of life where conservation and transformation of energy are observed

Assessment
Areas of life where conservation and transformation of energy are observed: Listing at least three areas under conservation and three under transformation, correct matching to field of study

Modification for Special Needs Students
Working in mixed ability groups

Enrichment for Gifted and Able Students
Naming five to six areas of conservation of energy and transformation of energy in different fields/disciplines.
   Note: Below are a few examples of energy representation in everyday life:

– *Energy transformation:* tornados and hurricanes (geoscience); food (biology, chemistry); wind and water (earth sciences); volcanos (geo sciences); roller coaster (entertainment); nuclear energy (physics, chemistry).
– *Energy conservation:* Solar panels (building, industry); green building (building); hybrid cars (transportation); electric cars (transportation); alternative fuels-biodiesel (industry) (see Appendix).

   Lessons 2–7

Content
Project work on selected area of conservation or transformation of energy

Aims
– Student will define the selected area.
– Student will describe how energy is transformed or conserved.

- Student will use graphic representation to demonstrate the process.
- Student will detect problems involved in conservation or transformation of energy relating to other fields/disciplines.

Thinking Processes Developed
Scientific and creative thinking

Thinking Strategies Developed
- Collecting information
- Organizing information
- Graphic presentation
- Identifying problems

Learning Environment
Classroom and/science lab + BYOD

Opening/Exposure
Students select an area and get into groups of three.
   Note: Teacher needs to make sure that there are at least 6 different topics relating to conservation of energy and 6 topics for transformation.

Teaching Strategies
Project-based learning

Learning Activities and Grouping
In groups of three students will:

1. explain why you have chosen this topic
2. collect information about the selected topic.
3. organize information according to a timeline (from past to present)
4. explain transformation or conservation of energy in past and present.
5. summarize new knowledge using graphic representation.
6. brainstorm and identify problems in conservation or transformation relating to the topic/selected area

Learning Materials
- Websites
- Textbook

Product/s
Short PPT or Prezi presentation

Assessment
Short PPT or Prezi presentation: Introduction explaining the selection of topic, defining the topic, explaining energy conservation or transformation, using graphic representation, raising problems.

Modification for Special Needs Students
Selecting a relevant and relatively easier topic like food or volcanos

Enrichment for Gifted and Able Students
Giving an elaborate explanation of conservation or transformation or energy using and describing physical terms and processes in depth

Lessons 8–9: Global Perspective

Global Perspective
- *Lesson 8*: Guest expert talk and demonstration on energy conservation using solar panels (30 min.)
- *Lesson 9*: Skype guest expert talk and demonstration on tornados and hurricanes (energy transformation) (30 min.)

Learning Activity

1. Students will listen to both guest experts.
2. During their talks students will write 5 new facts they learned from each expert.
3. After each short talk (about 30 min.) students will ask questions and pose problems.

Lessons 10–11: Global Perspective

Content
Looking at the phenomenon of energy from a wider perspective

Aims
- Student will share information with the group.
- Student will discuss differences and similarities between the different types of conservation or transformation of energy.
- Student will combine and summarize conservation or transformation of energy as manifested in the various topics.

Thinking Processes Developed
Scientific thinking

Thinking Strategies Developed
– Collecting information
– Organizing information
– Comparison
– Identifying connections
– Identifying processes

Learning Environment
Half the class in science lab, and half the class in classroom

Opening/Exposure
– Explaining the jigsaw process. Teacher will divide the 36 students in two groups according to conservation and transformation.
– Students form three groups of six, where each large group has one representative who is an expert on a researched sub-topic

Teaching Strategies
Project-based learning – jigsaw

Learning Activities and Grouping
In groups of six, students will:

1 Each present the selected research topic.
2 Find differences in conservation or transformation of energy.
3 Find similarities/connections in conservation or transformation of energy.
4 Identify the processes of conservation or transformation.
5 Summarize and create one PPT or Prezi presentation covering all topics.

Learning Materials
Information collected in small groups

Product/s
PPT or Prezi presentation

Assessment
PPT or Prezi presentation: Covers all six topics, explains differences and similarities, identifies processes and connections in energy transformation or conservation, clear, colorful, interesting, uses graphic representation/animation

Modification for Special Needs Students
Presenting information using visual aids and PPT presentation

Enrichment for Gifted and Able Students
Suggest additional areas of life/disciplines not mentioned earlier.

Lessons 12–13: Global Perspective

Content
Problem solving relating to energy

Aims
Student will solve a real-life problem related to conservation or transformation of energy

Thinking Processes Developed
Creative thinking – problem finding and problem solving

Thinking Strategies Developed
- Defining problems
- Suggesting solutions
- Finding criteria
- Selecting best solution according to criteria

Learning Environment
Classroom + BYOD

Opening/Exposure
Introducing the process of creative problem solving

Teaching Strategies
Project- and problem-based learning

Learning Activities and Grouping
In groups of six, students will:

1. Draw a table listing what they know about the case, and what is unknown
2. Define the problem, starting with: How can we…?
3. Suggest at least five solutions.
4. Identify at least four criteria for selecting the best solution.

5 Select the best solution based on the criteria.
6 Suggest an action plan.
7 Support their decision with at least two sources from the internet.
8 Present the process and action plan to the class.

Examples of problems: In what other innovative ways can we conserve energy?

How can we control the effects of a tornado/hurricane, or use the transformed energy?

Learning materials
– Accumulated information on the various topics relating to conservation or transformation of energy
– Stages of problem solving

Product/s
Process of problem solving and action plan

Assessment
Students presented the following (orally and in writing):

1 A table listing what they know about the case, and what is unknown.
2 A definition of the problem starting with: How can we...?
3 At least five solutions.
4 At least four criteria for selecting the best solution.
5 The best solution according to the criteria.
6 An action plan.

Modification for Special Needs Students
Working in mixed ability groups

Enrichment for Gifted and Able Students
Serving as group leader, recording the process, writing the suggested action plan, presenting in plenary

Lesson 14: Time Perspective – Future Scenario

Content
Energy in the future

Aims
- Student will think about life in the future relating to energy
- Student will predict life in the (near or far) future relating to energy

Thinking Processes Developed
Future thinking – construction and analysis of concept

Thinking Strategies Developed
Predicting development

Learning Environment
Science lab

Teaching Strategies
Future-based learning

Learning Activities and Grouping
In groups of six, students write a scenario illustrating how energy will influence human beings, guided by the following instructions:

1. Project yourself into the selected future time-span (medium – 10 years from now, or far – 50 years from now).
2. Write at least one page.
3. Write in first person.
4. Add two characters.
5. Relate to all three periods of time (past, present and future).
6. Try to be creative.
7. The plot has to show changes or development.
8. Mention processes.
9. Mention connection between processes.
10. Use appropriate register.
11. Present to the class.

Learning Materials
- Worksheet
- All information learnt in this unit

Product/s
Future scenario

Assessment
Ten criteria based on the instructions

Modification for Special Needs Students
Mixed ability grouping. Telling the story, without writing

Enrichment for Gifted and Able Students
Think about a "wild card" scenario which is unlikely to happen and write a scenario relating to energy.

References

Chen, R. F., Eisenkraft, A., Fortus, D., Krajcik, J., Neumann, K., Nordine, J. C., & Scheff, A. (Eds.). (2014). *Teaching and learning of energy in K-12 education*. Dordrecht: Springer Science & Business Media.

Finnish National Board of Education (FNBE). (2016). *National core curriculum for basic education 2014*. Helsinki: Finnish National Board of Education.

Francis, C., Breland, T. A., Østergaard, E., Lieblein, G., & Morse, S. (2013). Phenomenon-based learning in agroecology: A prerequisite for transdisciplinarity and responsible action. *Agroecology and Sustainable Food Systems, 37*(1), 60–75.

Ilomäki, L., Lakkala, M., Toom, A., & Muukkonen, H. (2017). Teacher learning within a multinational project in an upper secondary school. *Education Research International, 2017*, 1–13. Retrieved November 5, 2017, from https://doi.org/10.1155/2017/1614262

Silander, P. (2015a). Digital pedagogy. In P. Mattila & P. Silander (Eds.), *How to create the school of the future: Revolutionary thinking and design from Finland* (pp. 9–26). Oulu: University of Oulu, Center for Internet Excellence.

Silander, P. (2015b). *Rubric for phenomenon-based learning*. Retrieved November 5, 2017, from http://nebula.wsimg.com/c58399e5d05e6a656d6e74f40b9e0c09?AccessKeyId=3209BE92A5393B603C75&disposition=0&alloworigin=1

Symeonidis, V., & Schwarz, J. F. (2016). Phenomenon-based teaching and learning through the pedagogical lenses of phenomenology: The recent curriculum reform in Finland. *Forum Oświatowe, 28*(2), 31–47. Retrieved from http://forumoswiatowe.pl/index.php/czasopismo/article/view/458

Enrichment Activity

Roller coaster worksheet and simulation
https://advlabs.aapt.org/document/ServeFile.cfm?ID=8228&DocID=154

ENERGY: THE PHENOMENON-BASED APPROACH 179

Appendix

Energy Transformation

Energy Conservation (for environmental preservation)

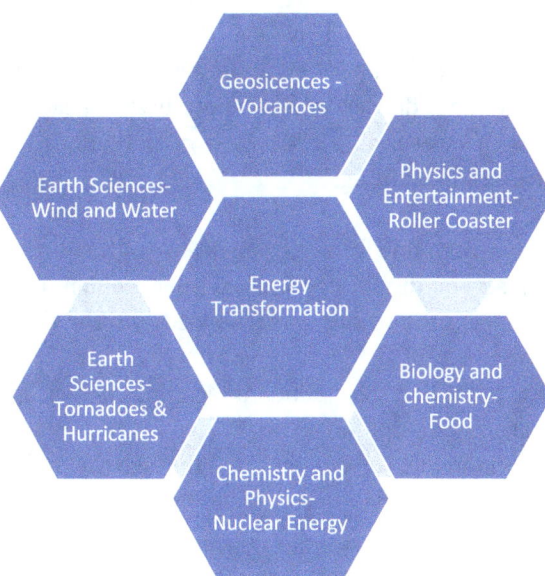

CHAPTER 11

Jerusalem: The Transdisciplinary Perspective

The unit designed and presented in this chapter based on MdCM involves studying Israel culture and heritage using a multidisciplinary and transdisciplinary approach, as this unique school subject integrates disciplines from social studies as well as other disciplines. The topic of Jerusalem invites students to investigate and learn the different aspects connected to this cosmopolitan city, experiencing interdisciplinary and transdisciplinary engagement in the subject.

With Israel culture and heritage and the topic of Jerusalem being a mere example, this chapter illustrates how any large topic could be taught and learned starting from an interdisciplinary approach and moving to a transdisciplinary view of the issue or topic, trying to solve an authentic problem. Its added value of experiencing future thinking based on a transdisciplinary perspective helps students acquire skills that are much required nowadays.

1   Interdisciplinarity and Transdisiplinarity Teaching and Learning

The term transdisciplinarity was first coined in 1972 by Erich Jantsch and Jean Piaget (Nicolescu, 2014). Transdisciplinarity is an innovative educational approach that can inform, develop, deliver, and promote best educational practices beyond disciplines (Nicolesu, 2010). Meeth (1978) describes four levels of approaches to teaching and learning:

Crossdisciplinary – viewing one discipline from the perspective of the other.
Multidisciplinary – involving several disciplines focused on a problem or an isuue, where each discipline contributes its own knowledge to the theme with no intent of integration.
Interdisciplinary – Starting with one discipline, integrating knowledge/contributions from several other disciplines.
Transdiciplinary – starting with the issue or problem, and through the process of problem solving using the knowledge from the different disciplines to solve the problem.

Interdisciplinary teaching and learning motivates students to broaden their concepts about the world and about themselves, create connections between different fields or disciplines, investigating connections, acquire knowledge and use it in authentic and natural ways, while thinking about goals and resources. It invites students to make changes, design tools, process new ideas, use mutually agreed upon graphic representation of tools, and transfer interdisciplinary knowledge among the different disciplines (Brand & Triplett, 2012).

Mishra, Kohler, and Henriksen (2010) explain that "although the overall goals of 21st century learning skills (analysis, creativity, collaboration, communication and use of new technologies) are commendable, we must focus on ways to interpret them in cross-disciplinary terms. We argue that higher order thinking skills such as creativity cannot be taught in a vacuum. Creativity emerges from 8 habits of mind that cross disciplinary boundaries. What we need is a trans-disciplinary approach that both values the disciplines and looks across them for common patterns and strategies. Only this can lead to true transformational learning" (pp. 7–8). Transdisciplinarity fosters collaboration across and beyond disciplines and allows for creative emergence. Indeed, it transcends disciplines in order to create new meanings, which have the potential to reconcile seemingly paradoxical positions and to create possible solutions for super-complex and multidimensional problems – the so called 'wicked problems'" (Brown, Harris, & Russell, 2010).

2 Israel's Culture and Heritage and the City of Jerusalem

Israel's Culture and Heritage is a multidisciplinary subject comprised of various bodies of knowledge including sources of information, values, cultural creation, expriences and lifestyles, symbols and more (Ish Shalom, 2011). Rubinstein (2003) explains that the Shenhar Committee report from 1994 indicated that this provides students with opportunities for encountering selected Jewish creations, while exminining their content and understanding their social, historical, and cultural connections. In addition, it enables the exmination and clarification of personal and social values originating in universal perspectives, the Zionist ethos, and Jewish heritage. These were meant to develop among students a moral and humanistic perception and contribute to the forming of an Israeli-Jewish identity and establishing a personal and collective identity. The subject "Israel's culture and heritage" is not a body of knowledge, but a discipline evoking questions dealing with Jewish-Israeli identity, using a constructivist approach connecting between knowledge and formation of identity (Leon, 2014).

Jerusalem was considered the center of the world and for many generations the subject of longing and yearning (Elon, 1991). The Holy Temple was situated there and it was a place of pilgrimage. When it passed from one reign to the other, it still existed in the hearts of people as the capital of Israel. The topic of "Jerusalem" studied in the subject "Israel's Culture and Heritage" deals with the boundary between the real city and the one the Jewish people longed for across the centuries. The main aims are: recognition of Jerusalem's place in Jewish culture, making acquaintance with its present-day characteristics, and recognition of its characteristics as a capital. They are also exposed to the various names Jerusalem has had, and its culture including songs, stories and liturgical poems (Shai, 2014). Therefore, it is only natural that the teaching and learning about Jerusalem should use a multidisciplinary approach.

The uniqueness of this unit is the incorporation of thinking tools based on MdCM and more specifically, creative problem solving, which enabled expanding students' views using the transdisciplinary approach integrating knowledge from different disciplines to solve an authentic up-to-date problem.

3 Example Unit and Lessons: Jerusalem

3.1 *Unit Description*

The unit was designed based on MdCM and was adapted to the curriculum of the subject named "Israel's Culture and Heritage", for 5th grade students dealing with the topic of Jerusalem. The unit contained fifteen lessons divided into three parts.

The first part invited students to investigate and prepare an individual PPT presentation revealing their personal interest in the topic of Jerusalem. Students practiced collecting and organizing information, focused and relevant writing, using computer skills, and peer learning. This part aimed to introduce students to the topic of Jerusalem.

The second part led students to investigate the topic of Jerusalem from the personal point of view/perspective. Students were encouraged to raise questions of personal interest, and were then divided into groups based on fields/issues. In their groups, they chose one question they wanted to focus on. Within the specific issue or field, such as architecture they tried to solve the dilemma of 'preservation for or against' using the six thinking hats. Other issues suggested by students were: transportation, religions, rule/government, and culture. Students also designed and administered a multiple choice questionnaire integrating the different issues/fields and analyzed and presented their findings. Starting with the issue, they integrated knowledge/contributions from several disciplines, thereby applying a multidisciplinary approach or view of Jerusalem.

The transdisciplinary view was developed in *the third part* of this unit, enabling students to start with a problem, and through the process of problem solving use the knowledge from the different disciplines to solve it. Problems were connected to the future development of Jerusalem after investigating the past and present and presenting them in a timeline. The product named "future scenario" invited students to project themselves into the future, selecting the preferred time span, and write a scenario of all aspects of Jerusalem, irelating to the past and present as well as the future. This unit had an additional product which creatively summarized the knowledge accumulated by students while learning about Jerusalem, focusing on a transdiciplinary view of the topic.

The unit focused on a transdisciplinary view of Jerusalem incorporating scientific thinking, creative thinking – problem solving, and future thinking, enabling students to bring their personal perspectives and interests, discuss, and experience construction of concepts, inquiry, decision making, problem solving and future thinking. Individual, group and class products reflected the multi- and transdisciplinary approach integrating content, process, and concepts learned in a creative, varied, and interesting manner, incorporating pre-determined and mutually agreed upon criteria which resulted in high-quality products.

4   Lesson Plans

Student Level
5th grade elementary school students

The Chosen Perspectives
Personal and time perspectives

Unit and Lesson Length
15 lesson of 45 minutes each

Lessons 1–2: Introduction to Jerusalem

Content
My Jerusalem

Aims
- Student will relate personally to Jerusalem.
- Student will recognize his/her connection to Jerusalem.
- Student will prepare a presentation on his/her personal experience.

Thinking Processes Developed
Scientific thinking

Thinking Strategies Developed
Collecting and organizing information

Learning Environment
- Computer room
- Classroom – Smart Board

Opening/Exposure
- Introduction of topic
- Song "My Jerusalem" https://www.youtube.com/watch?v=vigzQJLOx4g

In the song people from different neighborhoods describe their experiences, sounds, flavors, sites that make Jerusalem theirs.

Teaching Strategies
Inquiry-based learning

Learning Activities and Grouping
Individual assignment:

1. Talk about experiences and feelings connected to Jerusalem.
2. Investigate different sites and/or concepts raised online.
3. Prepare a PPT presentation about your connection/memories from a visit to Jerusalem. (Students who have never been in Jerusalem will select a site they would like to visit.)
4. Present the PPT to class.

Learning Materials
Internet websites

Product/s
PPT presentation

Assessment
PPT presentation: Relevance, at least 2 memories/experiences are mentioned, accompanied by short explanation, photos, attached music or song, correct language. Selected site: two reasons for selecting the site, photos, music or song, short explanation, correct language

Modification for Special Needs Students
Working in pairs and helping each other with inquiry, preparation of PPT, and presentation

Enrichment for Able and Gifted Students
Elaborate on the different sites, add information, photos and songs

Lessons 3–4: Personal Perspective

Content
Different perspectives and dilemmas regarding Jerusalem

Aims
- Student will raise different questions about Jerusalem.
- Student will select one question and turn it into a dilemma.
- Student will be introduced to different perspective of decision making using the six thinking hats
- Student will be able to work in small groups.
- Student will develop verbal communication skills.
- Student will present the dilemma creatively.

Thinking Processes Developed
Creative thinking – decision making

Thinking Strategies Developed
- Identifying perspectives
- Encountering different angles
- Experiencing being in the shoes of others

Learning Environment
Classroom

Opening/Exposure
- Introducing assignment

- Introducing students to the six thinking hats. Practicing decision making on the topic of 'school uniform, yes or no?'

Teaching Strategies
Problem-based learning – decision making

Learning Activities and Grouping
Individually, students will:

1 Raise questions that interest them about Jerusalem.

In groups of 6 students will:

2 Present their questions.
3 Select the question they want to deal with.

For example: How can we preserve the old buildings in Jerusalem?

4 Turn the question into a dilemma. For example: Should we preserve the old building in Jerusalem – yes or no?
5 Use the six thinking hats to arrive at a mutual decision.
6 Prepare a creative presentation (no longer than 3 minutes) illustrating the topic, process, and final decision.
7 Present the creative product to class.

Learning Materials
– six thinking hats
– cardboards in the six colors of hats

Product/s
Creative presentation of decision

Assessment
Creative presentation of decision: Clear dilemma, clear decision, mention of process, creative, interesting, within a 3-minute time limit, all students participated

Modification for Special Needs Students
Oral participation in a mixed ability group

Enrichment for Able and Gifted Students
Assigned as group leader, or blue hat, recording and managing the process

Lessons 5–6: Personal Perspective

Content
Our class and Jerusalem

Aims
- Student will understand how to build a multiple choice question.
- Student will phrase several multiple choice questions about a selected topic.
- Student will analyze replies and present them to class.
- Student will form an understanding of the class perspective on Jerusalem.

Thinking Processes Developed
Scientific thinking – inquiry

Thinking Strategies Developed
- Organizing information
- Graphic representation
- Inferring

Learning Environment
Computer room/lab

Opening/Exposure
- Eliciting different field of interest such as: religion, transportation, architecture, sites/attractions, songs, stories, etc.
- Introducing students to the formation of multiple choice questions in one of the fields/areas.

Teaching Strategies
Inquiry-based learning

Learning Activities and Grouping
In groups of five, students will:

1. Suggest three multiple choice questions in a selected area.
2. Form a shared document incorporating all questions.
3. Answer the questionnaire (individually) on the computer.
4. Analyze the replies to questions relating to selected field/area.

In plenary:

5 Present results to the class using graphics.
6 Discuss class perspective on Jerusalem as shown from the results of the questionnaire.

Learning Materials
Computer programs for designing a questionnaire and graphic representation of the results.

Product/s
– Class questionnaire – shared document
– Presentation of results

Assessment
Presentation of results: graphic representation is clear, differences are indicated by color, graph is suitable for the question

Modification for Special Needs Students
– Worksheet with examples of multiple choice questions
– Working in mixed-ability groups

Enrichment for Able and Gifted Students
In writing – Summarizing the results and drawing conclusions on the class perception of Jerusalem

Lessons 7–9: Time Perspective

(Leading to Transdisciplinary View of Jerusalem)

Content
The history of Jerusalem in the past 200 years

Aims
– Student will recognize the main events in the history of Jerusalem in the past 200 years.
– Student will organize the events in a sequence forming a timeline.
– Student will be aware of connections between events.
– Students will look for processes of development.

Thinking Processes Developed
Future thinking

Thinking Strategies Developed
– Defining and identifying components
– Classification and analysis
– Organizing in sequence
– Comparison
– Identification of connections
– Identification of processes

Learning Environment
Computer lab

Opening/Exposure
– The history of Jerusalem
  https://www.youtube.com/watch?v=DNhBLakTGtk
– Illustrating a timeline from biblical times up to 1820

Teaching Strategies
– Future-based learning
– Inquiry-based learning

Learning Activities and Grouping
In groups of five, students will:

1 Look for information on Jerusalem in the past 200 years in at least 3 different areas.
2 Classify and organize the information.
3 Integrate information from the different areas in sequence to create a timeline.
4 Look for connections between events.
5 Look for process of development od Jerusalem.

In plenary:

6 Present the timeline to the class.
7 Form one joint timeline representing the different areas investigated.
8 Discuss connections between the different areas and how they affected the development of Jerusalem.

Learning Materials
- The history of Jerusalem – YouTube video
- A timeline template
- Websites on Jerusalem

Product/s
Timeline

Assessment
Timeline: Relates to 3 different areas/fields, presents at least 7 major events in each area, shows at least 20 events in the last 200 years, indicates the year it took place correctly, describes the event in 2–3 short sentences, events are showed in correct sequence, connection between areas is established, connection between events is mentioned, process of development is indicated

Modification for Special Needs Students
- Working in mixed ability groups
- Looking for photos relating to each event

Enrichment for Able and Gifted Students
- Integrating the timelines prepared by the various groups into one class timeline
- Looking for connections and processes across areas/fields/disciplines

Lessons 10–11: Time Perspective

(*Transdisciplinary view* – through the process of problem solving using the knowledge from the different disciplines to solve a problem.)

Content
Current and future problems Jerusalem faces

Aims
- Student will be exposed to the problem-solving process and stages.
- Student will suggest current and future problems Jerusalem faces.
- Student will select one problem.
- Student will suggest solutions drawing on the different areas/disciplines.
- Student will write an action plan explaining the application of the solution.

Thinking Processes Developed
Creative thinking – problem finding and problem solving

Thinking Strategies Developed
- Suggesting transdisciplinary problems
- Defining a problem
- Suggesting solutions
- Finding criteria
- Selecting the best solution
- Suggesting a transdisciplinary action plan

Learning Environment
- Classroom
- Outside classroom: Open space between classes and in the yard

Opening/Exposure
- Introducing the six steps of the problem-solving process
- Eliciting current and future problems Jerusalem faces

Example of problems:

- How can Jerusalem maintain its status as an international (cosmopolitan) city? (Politics, religion, population, arts, urban planning, transportation.)
- How can Jerusalem preserve its historic character in the future? (History, geography, architecture/urban planning, culture, religion, arts, archaeology.)
- How can Jerusalem welcome people from all religions to live in peace in the city? (Politics, religion, culture, demographics/population, urban planning.)

Teaching Strategies
Transdisciplinary problem-based learning

Learning Activities and Grouping
In groups of five, students will:

1 Review problem-solving process and stages.
2 Suggest current and future problems Jerusalem faces.
3 Select one problem.
4 Suggest solutions:
   a Drawing on the shared timeline.
   b Relating to different areas/disciplines.

5   Write an action plan explaining application of solution.

In plenary:

6   Present the process and action plan.
7   Discuss the different problems and solutions.

Learning Materials
– Problem solving process and stages
– Shared class timeline representing a variety of areas and disciplines

Product/s
Problem solving process and action plan

Assessment
Problem solving process and action plan: Representing the different stages of problem solving, used different areas/disciplines for solving the problem, focused, presents an action plan involving stages of application, action plan relates to at least 3 areas/disciplines, correct language, teamwork

Modification for Special Needs Students
Simplified problem-solving stages with examples

Enrichment for Able and Gifted Students
Integrate the different problems and suggestions for solutions presented in action plans and write a summary on Jerusalem. Present the summary in class

Lesson 12: Time Perspective

Content
Jerusalem in the future

Aims
– Student will be exposed to future thinking.
– Student will practice future thinking on the topic of Jerusalem.
– Student will predict developments in different areas.

Thinking Processes Developed
Future thinking

Thinking Strategies Developed
Predicting development

Learning Environment
Classroom

Opening/Exposure
Future scenario writing

Teaching Strategies
Future-based learning

Learning Activities and Grouping
In groups of 3–4, students will:

1 Write a future scenario of the development of Jerusalem in the selected time span relating to different fields/areas/disciplines.

In plenary:

2 Present the written future scenarios in class.
3 Discuss similarities and differences between the future scenarios.

Learning Materials
Future scenario writing criteria

Product/s
Future scenario

Assessment
Future scenario writing criteria: it is located in the far or near future, one page long, mentions past, present and future, is written in first person, has two additional characters, has a plot, creative, correct and relevant events, it mentions a process

Modification for Special Needs Students
Future scenario template

Enrichment for Able and Gifted Students
Students will suggest criteria for comparison of future scenarios, write a summary of analysis and present it in class

Lessons 13–15: Transdisciplinary Perspective

Content
Jerusalem – summary of learning

Aims
– Student will reflect on learning about Jerusalem.
– Student will gather information from different lessons and products illustrating learning about Jerusalem.
– Student will creatively present a summary of the learning.

Thinking Processes Developed
Creative thinking

Thinking Strategies Developed
Encountering different angles

Learning Environment
– Classroom
– Computer lab
– Outdoor space

Opening/Exposure
– Introducing assignment
– Eliciting examples of creative products

Teaching Strategies
Project-based learning

Learning Activities and Grouping
In groups of five, students will:

1 Reflect on learning about Jerusalem.
2 Gather information from different lessons and products illustrating learning about Jerusalem.

In plenary (during third lesson):

3 Present a summary of the learning.

Learning Materials
All materials, processes and products of current unit

Product/s
Creative presentation of learning (digital book/booklet, TV show – Jerusalem this is your life, play, video clip, Facebook page, puppet show, art/photo exhibition, children's book/story, radio program, poem, advertising campaign, website, stand-up-comedy, rap song, PPT presentation etc.)

Assessment
Creative presentation criteria: interesting, creative, covers material, relates to at least three areas/disciplines, reflects different assignments, accurate, correct language (spoken and/or written), all members participated, within a time limit of 10 minutes

Modification for Special Needs Students
Mixed ability grouping

Enrichment for Able and Gifted Students
Relating to two more areas or disciplines while creating the final product

5   Future Scenario

The year is 2022 and we are in Grade 10. The virtual teacher gave us a new assignment. The assignment was to write our group summaries on Jerusalem. We remember studying about Jerusalem in fifth grade. Uri's father suggested we go to the time machine that he invented in 2021. This machine cannot yet take you to other periods of time, but can show you holograms and you feel that you are actually there. You need to wear special suits and you feel as if you are actually travelling through time. This was a great idea, and also a bit scary, because till then children were not allowed to enter the machine. We think that in five years from now we will be able to travel through time.

We went to the time machine and decided to investigate Jerusalem from three different but connected aspects: religion, transportation and city planning. In the past, Jerusalem was conquered by many kings and changed many hands, this affected the religion and culture. Each time a new king governed Jerusalem, all other religions were banned. They also built big buildings to show their power. In 2017 the situation was different, people from different religions were living in Jerusalem, but there still was a great dispute between the Orthodox Jews and non-religious Jews concerning many issues like: opening stores on Shabbat, using the same buses, showing ads portraying women in public and more. The orthodox Jews lived in their own neighborhoods, but wanted to dominate and dictate to everybody how they should live and behave.

Now the situation is different. After the big clash in 2020, everybody realized that they needed to find a common ground if they wanted to stay and live in Jerusalem. All the buildings from 1950s and even earlier, built from special Jerusalem stones, having special ornaments, were now beautifully preserved. When we went on a trip to Jerusalem in 2017 (in fifth grade) they looked very old and neglected.

Transportation to the city was now much easier as electric cars could fly above the ground. City planning improved and there are more roads and bridges for religious people who think they are not supposed to fly in Jerusalem. A consensus was reached regarding the display of women's photos, and now sensors detect who the person is, and show the ads according to his or her religion.

In 2021 the city became the center of the world again, combining modern and ancient, high tech and low tech, serving as a true capital. It has many different kinds of restaurants offering food from all over the world, and museums showing the history using very cool and high-tech techniques, but also new up-to-date places for young people to hang out. It welcomes all religions and has a place for everybody. There is no more fighting between religious grouos, and city planning and architecture are done by robots who know how to combine the old and new.

Note

The unit was developed by Hagar Shapira under the supervision of Hava Vidergor.

References

Brand, B. R., & Triplett, C. F. (2012). Interdisciplinary curriculum: An abandoned concept? *Teachers and Teaching, 18*(3), 381–393.

Brown, V. A., Harris, J. A., & Russell, J. Y. (2010). *Tackling wicked problems through the transdisciplinary imagination*. London: Earthscan Ltd.

Elon, A. (1991). *Jerusalem: Madness for the thing*. Jerusalem: Domino. [in Hebrew]

Ish Shalom, B. (2011). *Israel's culture and heritage: Rationale and program framework for elementary and middle schools in public education in the Jewish sector.* Jerusalem: Ministry of Education. [in Hebrew]

Leon, H. (2014). The never-ending story: The multidisciplinary department for Israeli culture and heritage. *Circles of Research and Creation, 4,* 41–42. Retrieved September 19, 2017, from http://www.dyellin.ac.il [in Hebrew]

Meeth, L. R. (1978). Interdisciplinary studies: Integration of knowledge and experience. *Change, 10,* 6–9.

Mishra, P., Koehler, M. J., & Henriksen, D. (2010). The 7 transdisciplinary habits of mind: Extending the TPACK framework towards 21st-century learning. *Educational Technology, 51*(2), 22–28.

Nicolescu, B. (2010). Methodology of transdisciplinarity: Levels of reality, logic of the included middle and complexity. *Transdisciplinary Journal of Engineering and Science, 1,* 17–32.

Nicolescu, B. (2014). Methodology of transdisciplinarity. *World Futures, 70*(3–4), 186–199.

Rubinstein, I. (2003). *Interdisciplinarity and multidisciplinarity in education.* Beer Sheba: Beit Yatziv. [in Hebrew]

Shai, Y. (2014). Israel culture in poems and songs: Suggestion for interdisciplinary teaching. In *Teacher's guide on Israel culture and music.* Jerusalem: Ministry of Education. [in Hebrew]

CHAPTER 12

Human Rights: Moral Ethical Social Medical and Legal Aspects

This chapter focuses on the issue of human rights from different aspects investigating children's, women's and refugees' rights, as well as medical and judicial aspects regarding moral and ethical issues related to violation of privacy using a biometric database, and use of embryo stem cells. Based on MdCM, it exposes students to all three perspectives: personal, global, and time. The uniqueness of the designed unit is three-fold: (1) It illustrates the use of the different thinking processes (scientific, creative and future thinking) translated into group activities involving students in decision making, problem solving, and presenting a mock trial. (2) It applies the flipped classroom technique (which is part of the blended learning environment), requiring students to watch short videos at home, which serve as the basis for their classwork. (3) It exposes students to the topic of human rights in different relevant areas, which, when combined, offer a broad perspective for practicing future thinking on this important and authentic issue.

1   Blended Learning

Christensen, Horn, and Staker (2013) explain that school, as we know it today, has to change its physical and organizational structure (schedule/timetable) to fit the learning needs of the students and comply with the latest strategies. Blended learning is described as a learning approach that combines different delivery methods and styles of learning. The blend could be between any form of instructional technology (e.g., videotape, CAI, web-based learning) with classroom teaching (Wu, Tennyson, & Hsia, 2010).

Creating a blended, flexible, learning environment involves project-based learning (Bell, 2010; Grant, 2002; Gultekin, 2005; Partnership for 21st Century Skills, 2008) and problem-based learning (Isaksen & Treffinger, 2004; OECD, 2015; Savery, 2006, 2015), enhances the use of technology and authentic use of language, and deals with relevant issues (Christensen, Horn, & Staker, 2013). Within blended learning environments students can use mobile phones as part of Bring Your Own Device (BYOD), game-like apps, tablets, learning apps (An, 2014), and MOOCS (Brahimi & Sarirete, 2015), rotate between the classroom and computer room, flip learning, and work on selected personal projects with mentor teachers in specific time slots and designed spaces.

2   Designing Blended Learning Environments

Christensen, Horn, and Staker (2013) reviewed several models of blended learning environments that have been developed: (1) The Rotation Model involving: station rotation, lab rotation, flipped classroom and individual rotation; (2) The Flex Model; (3) The 'A La Carte' Model; and (4) The Enriched Virtual Model. They defined the models as follows: Station Rotation occurs within a contained classroom; Lab Rotation occurs between a classroom and a learning lab for online learning; the Flipped Classroom Model rotation occurs between the school (face-to-face working on projects) and the home for online content and instruction; the Individual Rotation Model occurs when individual students are based on an individualized 'playlist', not necessarily going through all stations. The Flex Model occurs online and sometimes directs students to offline activities. Students move along an individually customized, fluid schedule among learning modalities, and the teacher is on-site. The 'A La Carte' Model involves studying in the traditional classroom and taking one or more courses entirely online with an online teacher at the same time on-site or off-site; and the Enriched Virtual Model divides time between attending a traditional classroom and distance learning within each course.

Magen-Nagar and Steinberger (2017) examined how Israeli students perceived 10 characteristics of their classroom learning environment: student cohesiveness, teacher support, involvement, task orientation, investigation, cooperation, equity, differentiation, computer usage, and young adult ethos. Participants were 1022 students in 33 classes from 12 computerized elementary and middle schools in Israel. Results indicated a gap between the actual and the preferred states for all characteristics, although the scope of these gaps differed between elementary and middle school students for certain characteristics. Nine characteristics of the innovative environment in both actual and preferred states were related to cooperation, with these relations being primarily direct, with the exception of teacher support and differentiation, which had an indirect influence. Teacher support was mediated through student cohesiveness, involvement, equity and young adult ethos, whereas differentiation was mediated through investigation.

3 Flipped Classroom

The flipped classroom is based on the premise that students watch videos at home, which means we're not just bridging the digital divide at school, we are also doing it at home (LaFee, 2013). He explains that "with lectures out of the classroom, teachers are free to use time during the school day for more individualized instruction, labs, and projects to promote and motivate deeper learning. In the parlance of flipped-learning advocates, teachers become "guides on the side," shepherding students in charge of their own learning" (LaFee, 2013, p. 14).

The idea of teachers converting lectures and lessons to videos to be watched as homework strikes some as problematic for various reasons. Among them: How do you do it if you've never done it before? Where do you get the training, the technical tools, the time? Bergman and Sams (2012, cited in LaFee, 2013, p. 18) believe flipped learning is built on four main pillars:

– *A flexible learning environment* in which teachers redesign their class to make best use of increased face-to face, individual instruction. It gives more freedom for activities such as project-based learning.
– *A revamped learning culture in the classroom.* "Students take responsibility for their own learning. I think every kid should have an individualized education program. Not the paperwork, but the personalization. We need to move away a bit from standardization."
– *Intentional content.* "This means creating quality videos and other materials to support learning in the classroom. It's best if teachers produce them, but it's not necessary."
– *Professional educators.* "Thus far, flipped learning has been mostly a grassroots effort. It needs to professionalize. We need to identify and disseminate best practices, share ideas, and get people connected."

Bergmann and Sams (2012) do not describe flipped learning as pedagogical reform, but as a tool, or a new way for doing, reaching students in different ways, and being more inventive with the help of technology.

Millard (2012) stated five advantages of the flipped classroom technique: (1) Increases student engagement; (2) Strengthens team-based skills; (3) Offers personalized student guidance; (4) Focuses classroom discussion; (5) Provides faculty freedom. Neilsen, (2012) on the other hand, identified the following five reasons to implement the flipped classroom with caution: (1) Many students don't have computers at home; (2) Flipped homework is still homework; (3) Flipping instruction might end up doing more memorization and regurgitation that just do not work. (4) Flipping allows for grouping students by interest and multi-age learning, which is often overlooked; (5) The flipped classroom is built on a traditional model of teaching and learning: The teacher lectures (at home) and student learns (at home and in class).

Schmidt and Ralph (2016) report a case of a high school social science teacher who used both online and offline resources in her flipped classroom. She had students read the textbook for homework. Whenever textbook readings were assigned, the teacher required students to complete a task while reading the text. These activities could be a graphic organizer, sentence frames, or open-ended questions. The teacher often had the students write down what questions they had or clarifications they needed. She then had them submit them to her in one of three ways: (1) Hand in when they arrive at class the next day; (2) Email them to her the night before; (3) Write them in a blog or online discussion board the night before. The teacher then uses these questions to guide her lesson and assure the students have a full grasp of the material.

Song and Kapur (2017) coined the term "productive failure-based flipped classroom". They reported on a variation of flipped classroom for a 2-week curricular unit on polynomials in a Hong Kong secondary school. Different from the flipped classroom, where students are provided with video clips with new concepts and associated procedures to review at home before solving problems in class, the "productive failure" pedagogical design in the flipped classroom worked the other way around. Supported by mobile technologies, students explored, discussed and solved problems related to the new concepts first in class even though they might come across failures, followed by consolidating the concepts and associated procedures using video clips at home. The study was carried out in two Grade 7 classes: one with "traditional flipped classroom" and one with the "productive failure-based flipped classroom". Findings showed that both classes had significant improvement in procedural knowledge. However, regarding conceptual knowledge, students in the "productive failure" variation performed better than those in traditional flipped classroom. This suggests that the "productive failure-based flipped classroom" pedagogical design may be better able to improve students' problem solving skills.

4   Example Unit and Lessons: Human Rights

4.1   *Unit Description*
The unit focuses on human rights from different aspects. It utilized the flipped classroom technique to expose students to authentic and relevant topics

by carefully selected videos. Students using this technique for the first time need to be gradually introduced to it, and understand that they still have a homework assignment, but it is different. In this case they use short videos to learn and prepare for class work; sometimes being allowed to select from among a longer list suggested by the teacher.

Human rights are addressed in five major areas: UN History and Human Rights Council; children's rights, women's rights; refugees' rights, human rights in medicine; and human rights in law.

The first part introduced human rights in general, the different area, and great leaders who fought for human rights. It also introduced students to a guest visitor sharing personal experiences of being an activist fighting for human rights. Students learned about the human rights council in the UN and thought about the existing areas of violation of human rights.

The second part focused on studying the selected areas, each time focusing on a different area. Studying at home involved watching two videos and summarizing. In class students worked in groups, helped each other with the material and carried out activities promoting higher order thinking skills. On the topic of children's rights, they first investigated their rights and whether they had been granted or violated (using the personal perspective). Then, they used the thinking hats to determine if children's rights were respected in their country (global perspective). Regarding women's and refugees' rights, they were allowed to select the topic which was more appealing to them forming two groups. Within these groups they were challenged to debate the following issues: (1) Women should be considered equal, and are entitled to all rights men possess; and (2) All infiltrators living currently in Israel should be granted refugee rights (global perspective). Human rights in law invited student to explore the violation of privacy through a simulation on using a biometric database, following the problem solving steps (global perspective). And on the last topic of human rights in medicine, students focused on organ transplants, stem cells, and embryo stem cells, and organized a mock trial prosecuting a scientist (global perspective).

The third part focused on the history of human rights, designing a timeline and writing a future scenario, incorporating everything studied, and predicting the near or far future regarding the preservation or violation of human rights in different areas (time perspective).

5   Lesson Plans

Student Level
10th grade heterogeneous class, medium SES

Chosen Perspectives
Personal, global, and time

Unit and Lesson Length
15 lessons of 45 minutes each

Lesson 1: Introduction

Content
- Introduction to human rights
- What are basic human rights?
- In what areas are human rights are expressed?
- Leaders who fought for human rights (Mahatma Gandhi, Martin Luther King, Nelson Mandela, Mother Teresa)

Aims
- Student will watch videos at home and summarize main points.
- Student will define human rights.
- Student will identify areas in which human rights are represented.

Thinking Processes Developed
Construction and analysis of concept

Thinking Strategies Developed
- Defining and identifying components
- Classification and analysis

Learning Environment
Classroom + BYOD

Opening/Exposure
The story of human rights
https://www.youtube.com/watch?v=oh3BbLk5UIQ

- The teacher will explain that students will watch videos at home as preparation for classes.
- The teacher can use the Google Classroom App, or other applications, and create a classroom platform for sharing videos and products.

Google classroom App

https://play.google.com/store/apps/details?id=com.google.android.apps.classroom&hl=en

Teaching Strategies
Inquiry-based learning

Learning Activities and Grouping
In groups of 4–5, students will:

1. Watch the following videos
   – *Universal declaration of human rights*
     https://www.youtube.com/watch?v=YUdxBRxEXEc
   – *30 articles of human rights*
     https://www.youtube.com/watch?v=hyVJHpiHO8I
2. Make a list of the most important rights in their opinion.
3. Explain why they chose each one.
4. Select a great leader who fought for human rights and design an identity card.

In plenary:

5. Present the chosen rights and reasons.
6. Present the selected leader.

Learning Materials
– Videos
– Websites

Product/s
– List of human rights
– Identity card

Assessment
– List of human rights: Selected at least five human rights, explanations are relevant and clear.
– Identity card: Enclosed photo of the leader, mentions at least ten important facts, provides dates, focuses on the leader's contribution to human rights, one page long.

Modification for Special Needs Students
Drawing or videotaping the identity card

Enrichment for Gifted and Able Students
Elaborating on the selected leader, explaining in greater detail how his actions changed human rights.

Lesson 2: Guest Lecturer

- Students will meet a human rights activist.
- They will listen to a short talk and ask questions.

Lesson 3: Global Perspective

Content
UN Human Rights Council

Aims
- Student will watch videos at home to prepare for the lesson.
- Student will learn how the council works.
- Student will identify the areas of concern.
- Student will discuss violation of human right in the region.
- Student will report on a country and its votes regarding human rights violations.

Thinking Processes Developed
Scientific thinking

Strategies Developed
- Defining and identifying components
- Classification and analysis
- Identifying processes

Learning Environment
- Home (flipped learning – watching videos and summarizing)
- Classroom + BYOD

Opening/Exposure
UN Human Rights Council – short revision of videos

Teaching Strategies
Inquiry-based learning

Learning Activities and Grouping
At home: Videos to be viewed prior to lesson, summarizing the history and mechanisms (how it actually works) in points or graphic organizers (thinking maps) and writing questions about issues that were unclear.

In Class, In groups of 4–5, students will:

1. Write how the council works.
2. List the main issues the council has been concerned with in recent years.
3. Discuss where in our region there are violations of human rights.
4. Select one country and check how it voted regarding different issues.
5. Report to the class.

Learning Materials
https://www.youtube.com/watch?v=Qp5KLCQUKlc
https://www.youtube.com/watch?v=MdkTOCFaQVg
– Websites

Product/s
Report on a selected country

Assessment
Report on a selected country: mentioning at least five cases in three different areas, including dates

Modification for Special Needs Students
Select two cases and present them orally

Enrichment for Gifted and Able Students
Explain the selected country's voting on detected issues in a larger context, connected to processes within and outside the country

Lessons 4–5: Personal and Global Perspective

Content
– Children's rights
– What are my basic rights?
– Are children's right respected in my country?

Aims
- Student will recognize the rights of children.
- Student will analyze his/her individual rights.
- Student will identify perspectives regarding the respect of children's rights in the country.
- Student will conclude and suggest ways of improving children's rights in the country.

Thinking Processes Developed
Creative thinking

Thinking Strategies Developed
- Identifying perspectives
- Encountering different angles

Classroom Learning Environment

Opening/Exposure
- Introducing the six thinking hats
- Introducing the topic: Children's rights are respected in my country

Teaching Strategies
Problem solving – decision making

Learning Activities and Grouping
At home, students:

1. Select and watch 3 out of 4 videos.
2. Summarize new information in brief. Summarize in points or graphic organizers (thinking maps) and write questions about issues that were unclear.

In Class, In groups of six, students will:

3. Discuss: What rights do I have? What rights are violated? What rights are missing?
4. Discuss the issue: Children's rights are respected in my country.
5. Follow the six thinking hats process to determine whether they agree or disagree with the statement.

In plenary:

6 Report to the class on the decision and process.
7 Discuss in what ways children's rights are violated/not met.
8 Suggest ways to influence and improve children's rights in the country.

Learning Materials
Children's rights (to be watched at home prior to lessons)
https://www.youtube.com/watch?v=TFMqTDIYI2U
https://www.youtube.com/watch?v=5KQGz-toMnk
https://www.youtube.com/watch?v=qTiCCyfgroE
https://www.youtube.com/watch?v=3rNhZu3ttIU

Product/s
Decision regarding children's right in this country

Assessment
Decision regarding children's right in this country: Presenting the unanimous decision, presenting the process of working on the six thinking hats

Modification for Special Needs Students
Work in mixed ability groups

Enrichment for Gifted and Able Students

– Performing as group leader, taking notes of the process of working on the thinking hats.
– Write an e-mail to a children's rights activist regarding violation of rights and suggestions for improvement.
– Write a short speech about children's rights in this country.

Note: Teacher introduces the next two topics, and based on student interest, divides the class into two large groups. One group will deal with women's rights, and the other with refugee's rights. As preparation for next lesson, students will view the videos relating to their selected topic.

Lessons 6–7: Global Perspective

Content
– Women's rights, or

– Refugee's rights

Aims
– Student will identify violations relating to women's or refugee's rights.
– Student will define key components.
– Student will identify perspectives and arguments.
– Student will encounter different angles of the topic.
– Student will experience working in teams.
– Student will improve oral language skills.

Thinking Processes Developed
Creative thinking – decision making

Thinking Strategies Developed
– Defining and identifying components
– Identifying perspectives
– Encountering different angles

Learning Environment
– Home
– Classroom

Opening/Exposure
The art of debating
https://www.youtube.com/watch?v=yi6Im-Sb6Vw

Teaching Strategies
Problem-based learning – decision making

Learning Activities and Grouping
– Videos to be viewed at home prior to lesson. Summarize in points or graphic organizers (thinking maps) and write questions about issues that were unclear.

Based on students' selected topic, students will work in groups to prepare for a debate on the following issues:

1 Women should be considered equal, and are entitled to all rights men possess.
2 All infiltrators living currently in Israel should be granted refugee rights.

Debating process:
Two teams of students will debate each topic. One will be the affirmative team and the other the negative team.

1. *The first speaker from the affirmative team will:* define keywords; introduce arguments; begin the debate.
2. *The first speaker from the negative team* will: define keywords; introduce arguments; rebuts points made by the other team.
3. *Second speakers* of both teams present more arguments and rebuttals.
4. *Third speakers:* Summarize and address the audience.
5. *The teacher will keep time:* A limit of three minutes per speaker.
6. *Judicators* (three selected students): Based on predetermined criteria, they will decide which team won. A class vote can also be used to determine the winning team.

Learning Materials
Video on debating

- Women's rights
  https://www.youtube.com/watch?v=gkjW9PZBRfk
  https://www.youtube.com/watch?v=6CbDeaqBA7c
- Suffragettes fighting for the right to vote (Part one and two)
  https://www.youtube.com/watch?v=FUP-pGcmb4s
  https://www.youtube.com/watch?v=n38NkE-Dd6E
- Refugee Crisis
  https://www.youtube.com/watch?v=KVV6_1Sef9M
  https://www.youtube.com/watch?v=rIolTbJ_K5U
- Refugees' rights
  https://www.youtube.com/watch?v=wIWAo9tedLY

Product/s
Debate

Assessment
Debate criteria: presentation skills, staying within time limit, presentation of relevant arguments, and most convincing arguments (winning team)

Modification for Special Needs Students
Students will serve as judicators

Enrichment for Gifted and Able Students
Students will serve as team leaders

Lessons 8–10

Content
Human rights in law – The right to privacy and the biometric database

Aims
- Student will be exposed to a current issue relating to human rights dealing with the biometric database and potential violation of privacy.
- Student will recognize and experience the process of problem solving.
- Student will define the problem.
- Student will suggest solutions.
- Student will suggest criteria for selecting the best solution.
- Student will suggest an action plan for applying the best solution.
- Student will work in teams.
- Student will develop oral and writing skills.

Thinking Processes Developed
Creative thinking – problem finding and problem solving

Thinking Strategies Developed
- Defining the problem
- Suggesting solutions
- Finding criteria
- Selecting best solution

Learning Environment
Classroom + BYOD

Opening/Exposure
Human rights in law

Teaching Strategies
Problem-based learning

Learning Activities and Grouping
Select three out of the four videos and watch them prior to lesson. Summarize in points or graphic organizers (thinking maps) and write questions about issues that were unclear.

In groups of 4–5, students will:

1. Read the simulation (see Appendix).
2. Identify problems in relating to the simulation on the biometric database.
3. Define the problem.
4. Suggest at least 5 solutions.
5. Find at least 4 criteria.
6. Select the best solution based on the criteria.
7. Design an action plan based on the best solution.
8. Present the process and action plan in class.

Learning Materials
- Human Rights and law
- Human right to privacy (obligatory)
  https://www.equalityhumanrights.com/en/human-rights-act/article-8-respect-your-private-and-family-life
- Information privacy law – Biometrics
  https://www.youtube.com/watch?v=3yRTuEqkA-I
- Privacy of medical information
  https://www.youtube.com/watch?v=H7bKoiINwbk
- Biometric database in Israel (obligatory)
  https://www.youtube.com/watch?v=ESxpAowXZho
  https://www.youtube.com/watch?v=SWJPOloPeMg

Product/s
Problem solving process and action plan

Assessment
Problem solving process and action plan: the worksheet is completed, all stages are presented orally, the problem is defined correctly, there are at least 5 solutions, there are 4 criteria, the table presenting the solution selection is filled, a solution was selected, the action plan is presented in stages, the action plan is presented in clear points

Modification for Special Needs Students
Mixed ability grouping

Enrichment for Gifted and Able Students
Create an ad or a video describing the solution and action plan. Write an e-mail to an MP relating to the biometric database

Lessons 11–14: Global Perspective

Content
- Human rights in medicine
- Organ transplants
- Stem cells and embryo stem cells

Aims
- Student will recognize the connection between human rights and medicine.
- Student will use information about organ transplants and stem cells and apply it to the presented case.
- Student will develop creative and critical thinking.
- Student will understand the judicial system.
- Student will practice public speaking.

Thinking Processes Developed
Inquiry-based learning, creative and critical thinking

Thinking Strategies Developed
- Collecting information
- Organizing information
- Encountering different angles
- Identifying perspectives and arguments
- Identifying connections

Learning Environment
Classroom and auditorium

Opening/Exposure
An example of a mock trial
https://www.youtube.com/watch?v=fllnvzmdJck

Teaching Strategies
Project-based learning

Learning Activities and Grouping
Summarize in points or graphic organizers (thinking maps) and write questions about issues that were unclear

The following case is presented to students: A scientist used embryonic stem cells in a procedure he offered one of his patients in order to grow an organ that was cut off his body. The state is prosecuting him for the use of these stem cells.

Students are divided into groups: Prosecution, defense attorneys, witnesses, and judges.

Prosecution and defense attorneys will:

1 Review the data relating to embryo stem cells.
2 Prepare an opening statement.
3 Perform direct examination of witnesses.
4 Perform a cross-examination of opposing witnesses.
5 Prepare a closing statement.

Witnesses need to act out the story as if they were part of the procedure, as doctors, or family members.

Judges need to be familiarized with the case and the law regarding the use of embryonic stem cells.

Jury: The audience will serve as the jury determining whether the defender is guilty or acquitted.

Learning Materials
– Videos to be viewed at home prior to lesson.
– Human rights in medicine – Donation and transplantation of organs
  https://www.youtube.com/watch?v=HuKx2a5HkIM
– How do stem cells work?
  www.youtube.com/watch?v=cEB8656TCIE
– For and against stem cell research
  http://www.foxnews.com/story/2001/08/09/cases-for-and-against-stem-cell-research.html
– Embryo ethics
  http://www.nejm.org/doi/full/10.1056/NEJMp048145%20#t=article

Product/s
Mock trial

Assessment
Mock trial criteria: All roles performed well, speeches were fluent, relevant, witnesses added new information, the defendant presented

his case well, the judge was aware of the law regarding use of embryonic stem cells, the jury considered all information presented and decided objectively

Modification for Special Needs Students
Will serve as witnesses or will be part of the jury

Enrichment for Gifted and Able Students
How do the three monotheistic religions relate to the issue of using embryonic stem cells?

Lessons 15: Time Perspective

Content
History of human rights – timeline

Aims
- Student will explore the development of human rights in general.
- Students will notice changes and developments in human rights.
- Student will put in sequence (from past to present) events in the development of community settlements in general.
- Students will detect processes.
- Students will find connections between events.

Thinking Processes Developed
Future thinking – construction and analysis of concept

Thinking Strategies Developed
- Gathering and organizing information
- Classification and analysis
- Comparison
- Identifying processes
- Identifying connections

Learning Environment
Classroom + BYOD

Opening/Exposure
Human rights history

http://www.humanrights.com/what-are-human-rights/brief-history/

Teaching Strategies
Future-based learning

Learning Activities and Grouping
In groups of 4–5, students will:

1. Find at least 10 events in the history of the development of human rights in Israel.
2. Classify and analyze the events and put them in correct sequence.
3. Write 1–2 sentences to describe each event.
4. Compare the different events and look for a process.
5. Identify connections between events.
6. Present the timeline in class.

In plenary:

7. Discuss connection of events to the development of human rights and other developments occurring at certain times.

Learning Materials
Human rights history
http://www.humanrights.com/what-are-human-rights/brief-history/

Product/s
Timeline

Assessment
Timeline: has at least 15 events, the events are organized in the right sequence, there is a short explanation under each event, a process of development is mentioned

Modification for Special Needs Students
Receiving a template of timeline with a few events already marked

Enrichment for Gifted and Able Students
Add 5 extra events and justify their importance relating to human rights

Lesson 16: Time Perspective

Content
The future of human rights

Aims
- Student will experience using future thinking skills.
- Student will understand how to predict the near or far future based on facts.

Thinking Processes Developed
Future thinking

Thinking Strategies Developed
Predicting development

Learning Environment
Classroom

Opening/Exposure
- Introducing the future scenario.
- Mutually agreeing on the criteria for writing a good future scenario

Teaching Strategies
Future-based learning

Learning Activities and Grouping
In groups of 4–5, students will:

1 Decide on the future time span (10, 30, 50 years from now).
2 Write a future scenario.

In plenary:
3 Present the future scenario.
4 Discuss connections between events in the development of human rights and other events in the development of the world.
5 Discuss similarities and differences between the perceptions of human rights presented in the future scenarios.

Learning Materials
- Future scenario criteria

– All information collected in this unit of study

Product/s
Future scenario

Assessment
Future scenario: The scenario is located in the far or near future, it is one page long, it mentions past, present and future, is written in first person, has two additional characters, has a plot, is creative, correct and mentions relevant events and a process

Modification for Special Needs Students
Videotaping the scenario as a first-person narrative

Enrichment for Gifted and Able Students
You are a social activist fighting for children's rights in the year 2067. Write an entry in your intergalactic blog

Note

The problem solving simulation was developed by Moran Chen Verman-Harel under the supervision of Hava Vidergor.

References

An, H. (Ed.). (2014). *Tablets in K-12 education: Integrated experiences and implications.* Hershey, PA: IGI Global.

Bell, S. (2010). Project based learning for the 12st century: Skills for the future. *The Clearinghouse, 83,* 39–43.

Bergmann, J., & Sams, A. (2012). *Flip your classroom: Reach every student in every class every day.* Washington, DC: International Society for Technology in Education.

Brahimi, T., & Sarirete, A. (2015). Learning outside the classroom through MOOCs. *Computers in Human Behavior, 51,* 604–609.

Christensen, C. M., Horn, M. B., & Staker, H. (2013). *Is K-12 blended learning disruptive? An introduction of the theory of hybrids.* San Mateo, CA: Clayton Christensen Institute. Retrieved February 18, 2016, from http://www.christenseninstitute.org

Grant, M. M. (2002). Getting a grip on project-based learning: Theory, cases and recommendations. *Meridian: A Middle School Computer Technologies Journal, 5*, 1–17. Retrieved February 19, 2017, from http://www.ncsu.edu/meridian/win2002/514/project-based.pdf

Gultekin, M. (2005). The effect of project based learning on learning outcomes in the 5th grade social studies course in primary education. *Educational Sciences: Theory and Practice, 5*(2), 548–556.

Isaksen, S. G., & Treffinger, D. J. (2004). Celebrating 50 years of reflective practice: Versions of creative problem solving. *Journal of Creative Behavior, 38*, 75–101.

Magen-Nagar, N., & Steinberger, P. (2017). Characteristics of an innovative learning environment according to students' perceptions: Actual versus preferred. *Learning Environments Research, 20*(3), 307–323.

Partnership for 21st Century Skills. (2008). Retrieved February 1, 2017, from http://www.21stcenturyskills.org

OECD. (2015). *Draft pisa 2015 collaborative problem solving framework*. Retrieved January 10, 2017, from http://www.oecd.org/pisa/pisaproducts/pisa2015draftframeworks.htm

Savery, J. R. (2006). Overview of problem-based learning: Definitions and distinctions. *The Interdisciplinary Journal of Problem-Based Learning, 1*(1), 9–20.

Savery, J. R. (2015). Overview of problem-based learning: Definitions and distinctions. In A. Walker, H. Leary, C. Hmelo-Silver, & P. A. Ertmer (Eds.), *Essential readings in problem-based learning: Exploring and extending the legacy of Howard S. Barrows* (pp. 5–15). Lafayette, IN: Purdue University Press.

Schmidt, S. M., & Ralph, D. L. (2016). The flipped classroom: A twist on teaching. *Contemporary Issues in Education Research (Online), 9*(1), 1.

Song, Y., & Kapur, M. (2017). How to flip the classroom: "Productive failure or traditional flipped classroom" pedagogical design? *Journal of Educational Technology & Society, 20*(1), 292–305.

Wu, J. H., Tennyson, R. D., & Hsia, T. L. (2010). A study of student satisfaction in a blended e-learning system environment. *Computers & Education, 55*(1), 155–164.

Appendix: Problem Solving Simulation

The Biometric Database

In the state of Seahaven there was a school named Apple. One day a parent arrived in school as he was invited to meet with the school counselor and the management staff, regarding the behavior problems exhibited recently by his son. The meeting turned into a loud argument during which the parent drew a gun and shot all the members of the management staff. While fleeing from the building, he shot and killed two students and a seeing-eye dog. As a result of this case, and other violent acts occurring recently, the state decided to convene an emergency committee to make some decisions concerning the necessary steps to be taken in order to control the upsurge of violence.

After a long meeting, the committee decided that all adult state residents would deposit their identity cards at the nearest police station. The citizens had to promise that without any objection, they would provide fingerprints, facial photos, and tissue samples, when required. It was decided that manned police stations would be in charge of these procedures. Moreover, anyone who was not present oneself when summoned, would be jailed, and would undergo the tests, where reasonable force by the authorities could be applied. When all tests were completed, each citizen would receive a chip serving as an electronic identity card that would will carry all the data, including fingerprints, DNA, and facial features. All electronic chips would be kept by the state and deposited in the hands of a few very reliable people. It was also promised that the database would be secured, and no one could hack it.

Human rights organizations were astonished at the acts of the authorities, and two human rights activists, one named Yuman and the other named Rite, protested and called for a coup against the electronic identity cards and the biometric database, and against the regime. Activists claimed that the biometric database constituted a real danger to the state, the citizens, and the humanity as a whole.

Instructions
Get into groups of 3–4

1 Identify the different areas.
2 Choose one area.
3 Classify information in bullets relating to the whole story (in the form of a table). What do we know? What should we know? (that is not mentioned)
4 Define the problem. Start with In what way/ways or how can we.......?
5 Suggest at least 5 different solutions.
6 Decide on at least 4 criteria for evaluating the solutions. (i.e. cost)
7 Select the best solution based on the criteria.
8 Design an action plan to implement the selected idea.
   Focus on the following questions:
   a What are the goals?
   b What is the process to achieve the goals?
   c What will be considered as success?
   d How should achievements be assessed?

9 Present the area, problem, criteria, selected solution and action plan in plenary.
   You have 5 minutes.
10 Plenary will vote and select the best solution to be implemented first.
   – *Extension/Enrichment activity:* You are a group of citizens who support the foundation of the biometric database and are interested in promoting it. Write a document addressed to the authorities and state the advantages of having this database.

CHAPTER 13

Language Arts and Sciences: The Cell Phone

This chapter introduces a unit designed and developed based on MdCM for high school students studying English as a foreign language (EFL) combined with physics, using a relevant subject like the cell phone. It shows how to develop higher order thinking skills such as melioration and creation by challenging students to solve problems, improve a product or invent a new one. Students are exposed to different formats of writing in English in blended learning environments, design, plan and develop improved or new cell phones using a 3D desktop printer, considered state-of-the-art technology. It illustrates the process of developing student's future thinking literacy throughout the unit, ending with the writing of a future scenario asking students to project themselves into the future, and based on accumulated knowledge about the past and present, imagine how will life will be using cell phones 20 years from now.

1   Inventive Thinking and Technology: Melioration Creation and Use of 3D Printers

Johansen and Schanke (2013) stated that in Europe, and more specifically in Norway, entrepreneurship has become a hot topic, and is organized as a separate subject or a topic in other subjects, or is integrated in various subjects through projects. Moberg (2014) analyzed the influence of two different approaches to entrepreneurship education in middle school: the influence of education *for* entrepreneurship and education *through* entrepreneurship on pupils' level of school engagement. Moberg reported that education *for* entrepreneurship, which focuses on content and cognitive entrepreneurial skills, had a positive influence on pupils' entrepreneurial intentions but a negative influence on their level of school engagement. On the other hand, education *through* entrepreneurship had a more pedagogical orientation and focused on fostering non-cognitive entrepreneurial skills. This chapter and the unit developed focus on the latter.

Barak (2002) explored nurturing creativity in the high-tech industry and in modern organizations, particularly in the context of problem solving and product development, and examined the potential implications for technology education. He reported on Systematic Inventive Thinking (SIT) which resulted in the development of a range of new original and successful products. The experience indicated that people can learn efficient techniques for solving a problem, or developing a new product, by breaking it down to its basic components and by 'playing' systematically with ideas in order to achieve new results. Similarly, the stages of S.C.A.M.P.E.R. developed by Eberle (1996) stand for seven techniques; (S) substitute, (C) combine, (A) adapt, (M) modify, (P) put to another use, (E) eliminate and (R) reverse. These keywords represent the necessary questions addressed during the creative thinking process. Tran, Ho, and Hurle (2016) explain that in order to enhance student creativity, teachers should be fully aware of creativity and of teaching for creativity, be required to develop and assess student creativity and trained to use creative tools.

Developing student creativity and innovation require higher order thinking skills. Anderson, Krathwohl, and associates (2001) revised Bloom's taxonomy and added another dimension to the cognitive process, naming it creation, defining it as generating/hypothesizing, planning/designing and producing/constructing a new product or idea. Passig (2007) elaborated on the new taxonomy by adding a middle phase between evaluating and creating called melioration. This dimension of thinking involves the competence to borrow a concept from a field of knowledge supposedly far removed from his or her domain, and adapt it to a pressing challenge in an area of personal knowledge or interest. One stage before actual creation, this competence improves an existing concept or object to solve a need or a problem.

Using 3D desktop printers in the regular classroom, and not for STEM is still uncommon. Chamberlain and Meyers (2015) indicated that since the invention of the desktop 3D printer in 2001, this technology has become less and less expensive and more available to the general public. They added that different methods for the use of 3D printers and other manufacturing technologies in educational settings were developed to further familiarize the engineers of tomorrow about this useful technology, incorporating it into STEM curricula. In this unit, the 3D printer is used to enhance thinking processes and enable students to apply their knowledge to produce an actual model of the improved or new product they have designed. All this is strongly connected and carefully combined with writing in different formats in EFL for authentic purposes.

2   Writing in English as a Foreign Language

Writing involves expressing emotions, thoughts, facts, desires and dreams in a written format (Çer, 2017). It has three important aspects, namely: planning, transition and reviewing. Effective writing is a complex process requiring the coordination of several cognitive skills like planning, drafting, evaluating, revising and editing; that can be learned through practices and structured feedback, and enable higher order thinking (Çer, 2017). Mahmoudi (2017) argues that the majority of learners think writing is boring and as a result they are quite reluctant to produce written texts. She adds that writing consists of complex processes where the learner has to give and receive clear information. Thus, more attention in EFL classrooms should be devoted to it.

According to Brilliant (2005) the act of writing involves three aspects: cognitive, affective, and interpersonal. These cognitive aspects of writing include "having ideas, being able to present those ideas in written language, and being able to organize them sufficiently to be understood" (p. 505). Nevertheless, Shin (2006) asserted that writing of EFL learners often presents difficulties that are different from those found in the writing of native English-speaking students. Thus, teachers often find it difficult to provide feedback on EFL writing. They are confused whether to start correcting all errors, or to leave the errors untouched because there are simply too many of them. Zenkov and Harmon (2009) argue that the act of writing is itself a complicated practice that draws on visual and action modes. Therefore, students are more willing to engage in a writing task about a topic, if teachers use images as starting points, and an ongoing focus. They explain that consequently, teachers should use various strategies to promote students' writing skills.

3 Teaching Physics

Huffman (1997) investigated the effect of explicit problem-solving instruction on high school students' conceptual understanding of physics. Results indicated that the explicit strategy improved the quality and completeness of students' physics representations more than the textbook strategy, but there was no difference between the two strategies for matching equations with representations, organization, or mathematical execution. In terms of conceptual understanding, there was no overall difference between the two groups. The explicit strategy appeared to benefit female students, while the textbook strategy appeared to benefit male students.

Bell (2015) reported using a "flipped classroom" method with three high school classes in the US during seven periods, while the other four were taught using a "traditional" method of instruction of physics, based on inquiry. The flipped classes watched video lectures at home to learn the majority of the content, then did what is traditionally known as "homework" in class with the teacher present to help. She found no statistically or practically significant difference in mean test scores for the first three units. Student responses showed no difference in attitudes towards the classroom environment in either instructional method. Nevertheless, this unit will present embedding several physics lessons on waves, explaining how cell phones work, using the flipped classroom method, in a unit focused on teaching writing in EFL on the topic of the cell phone.

4 Example Unit and Lesson Plans: The Cell Phone

Student Level
10th Grade

The Chosen Perspectives
Personal, global, and time perspectives

Unit and Lesson Length
20 lessons of 45 minutes each (some of which are optional)

4.1 Unit Description

The unit was aimed to develop thinking skills in foreign language learning in high school using the cell phone to teach writing in an authentic whole language approach.

It focused on creative thinking, challenging students to meliorate and create new products, as well as work in blended learning environments to practice different forms of writing. It also incorporated physics lessons in a flipped classroom model illustrating how students need to be acquainted with a relevant topic from different angles, learn individually at home, and practice at school combining the two subjects and better understanding how the cell phone works.

The unit consisted of 20 lessons, where the first was an introductory lesson and other lessons were taught in different lesson periods ranging from of 45 to 135 minutes. The unit dealt with different aspects of the cell phone focusing on the acquisition of writing skills, combined with speaking and reading in EFL, reinforced by physics lessons and terms learned in both English and the home language.

The first lesson was devoted to an introduction to the cell phone, writing facts about inventors of the phone and cell phone, and how landline and cell phones work. Lessons 2–4 related to the personal perspective, focusing on scientific thinking and challenged students to write a shared multiple choice questionnaire and present results using graphic representation. Lessons 5–6 were devoted to understanding how the cell phone works and dealing with electromagnetic waves and spectrum. In these lessons, cooperation was required between the English teacher and the physics teacher. Lessons 7–8 focused on the personal perspective and writing in EFL in blended learning – station rotation, in which students practiced connectors in various situations, until they felt they had mastered them. Lessons 9–10 continued dealing with the personal perspective and practiced creative thinking, using the six thinking hats for decision making regarding the dilemma whether or not to buy the latest version of the cell phone. This was followed by writing an essay stating arguments for and against the issue.

Lesson 11, which was optional, introduced the global perspective, dealing with teenage addiction to cell phones, and challenged students to participate and report on an experiment of not using the cell phone for a whole day. Lessons 12–13 focused on the time perspective, developing future thinking and asking students to review the history of the development of the cell phone designing a timeline, looking for connections and processes. Lessons 14–16, aimed at developing creative thinking by solving problems in different areas connected to the use of cell phones.

The highlight of this unit was lessons 17–19, which focused on improving a cell phone or and inventing a new one. It developed creative or inventive thinking while using the latest technology of 3D desktop printing. The use of the S.C.A.M.P.E.R. technique was documented by writing a review, or describing the features of the model of the new phone. The last lesson was devoted to future thinking, summarizing the learning throughout the unit by writing a future scenario in groups. Students projected themselves 20 years into the future and imagined life using cell phones, based on accumulated knowledge about the past and present, problems involved, understanding of its operation from the physics point of view, using enhanced writing skills in EFL.

5   Lesson Plans

Student Level
10th high school students

The Chosen Perspectives
Personal, global, and time perspectives

Unit length and Lesson Length
20 lessons of 45 minutes each

Lesson 1: Introduction

Content
Getting to know the phone and its inventors

Aims
- Student will collect information on the landline phone and cell phone.
- Student will summarize information in ten sentences.
- Student will analyze information on a selected topic.
- Student will create new knowledge on the cell phone.
- Student will develop writing skills in English.

Thinking Processes Developed
Scientific thinking

Thinking Strategies Developed
- Collecting information
- Organizing information
- Classification and analysis

Learning Environment
Classroom

Opening/Exposure
YouTube Video on the cell phone
https://www.youtube.com/watch?v=DMbGrakUHc4
Introducing the topics:

1. Martin Cooper
2. Alexander Graham Bell
3. How the landline phone works
4. How the cell phone works
5. Types of cell phones

Teaching Strategies
Inquiry-based learning

Learning Activities and Grouping
In groups of 4–5, students will:

1. Choose a topic.
2. Look up information using their cell phone.
3. Write ten facts about the topic.
4. Leave the information on their desk.

Individually:

5. Circulate and read the information on the other topics.
6. Write three new facts that they have learned.

In plenary:

7. Present the new facts they have learned in class.

Learning Materials
Examples of websites:
   https://en.wikipedia.org/wiki/Cell_phone
   http://www.cellular.co.za/cellphone_inventor.htm
   http://www.techpin.com/who-invented-the-cell-phone/
   http://www.youtube.com/watch?v=SUIuXoZs7hU
   http://en.wikipedia.org/wiki/Alexander_Graham_Bell
   http://www.howstuffworks.com/cell-phone.htm
   http://wirelessguide.org/types/index.php
   http://edition.cnn.com/2010/TECH/cell/07/09/cooper.cell.phone.inventor/index.html

Product/s
– In groups: Summary of facts about a selected topic
– Individual: Three new facts

Assessment
Summary of facts about a selected topic: Used appropriate terms/words, selected ten most important facts, clear, correct

Modification for Special Needs Students
The three new facts can be presented orally, through drawing, or animation, using the cell phone

Enrichment for Gifted and Able Students
Find at least one new fact attributed to each topic

Lessons 2–4: Personal Perspective

Content
The cell phone and I

Aims
- Student will develop awareness of personal uses of cell phone.
- Student will learn to write multiple choice questions.
- Student will use technology to create a questionnaire/shared document.
- Student will analyze the replies.
- Student will present results using graphic organizers.
- Student will compare and contrast results and draw conclusions.

Thinking Processes Developed
Scientific thinking

Thinking Strategies Developed
- Collecting information
- Organizing information
- Graphic representation
- Inferring/drawing conclusions

Learning Environment
Classroom + BYOD

Opening/Exposure
Forming multiple choice questions + examples

Teaching Strategies
Inquiry-based learning

Learning Activities and Grouping
Individually, student will:

1 Brain storm associations relating to the cell phone.
2 Write 5–7 questions of interest.
 (How will I manage without my cell phone foe a day/week? How do I treat my cell phone? What do I use it for? What would I do if my parents took it away? What apps would I like it to have? etc.)

In groups of 4–5, students will:

3 Share associations.
4 Share questions.
5 Select one question and discuss it.

In plenary:

6 Present the question and points discussed.

In groups:

7 Write 3 multiple choice questions on one of the following topics:
   a Current use of cell phone
   b Parents' attitudes
   c Types of cell phones owned by classmates
   d Needs and requirements (currently unavailable)
8 Upload the questions to Google Docs to create one questionnaire.

Individually:

9 Fill in the questionnaire.

In groups:

10 Analyze the data relating to the questions written by the group.
11 Select appropriate graphic representation.

In plenary:

12 Present results to the class.
13 Discuss results.

Learning Materials
– Examples of multiple choice questions
– Questionnaire on Google Docs

Product/s
– Questionnaire
– Results and conclusions relating to 3–4 questions (presented orally and in writing),

Assessment
- Questionnaire: three to four questions relating to one area, following multiple choice question design, use of appropriate concepts/terms, correct English, uploaded to Google docs
- Results: Broken down into categories, using suitable graphic representation, followed by oral explanation, conclusions match results, within time limit of 5–7 minutes, clear, colorful

Modification for Special Needs Students
Working in mixed ability groups, students could suggest one question, upload all questions to the shared document, *and/or* present results orally using one graph

Enrichment for Gifted and Able Students
Summarize orally and in writing the findings and conclusions relating to the whole questionnaire focusing on personal uses and preferences regarding the cell phone

Lesson 5–6: Personal Perspective

Note: Physics lessons are taught by physics teacher with the cooperation of the English teacher.

Content
Electromagnetic waves and spectrum

Aims
- Student will watch videos on electromagnetic waves at home as many times as needed.
- Student will summarize information on electromagnetic waves.
- Student will define terms in Hebrew and use their English wording.
- Student will share information with peers.
- Student will develop his/her oral ability.
- Student will suggest experiments on electromagnetic waves.
- Student will connect electromagnetic waves with cell phone operation.

Thinking Processes Developed
Scientific thinking

Thinking Strategies Developed
- Collecting information

- Organizing information
- Defining and identifying components
- Classification and analysis
- Identifying connection

Learning Environment
- Home (computer/tablet/cell phone)
- Science lab + BYOD

Opening/Exposure
Tutorial on waves
http://www.physicsclassroom.com/class/waves

Teaching Strategies
Flipped classroom

Learning Activities and Grouping
Individually:

1 Student will watch several videos in English or mother tongue introducing electromagnetic waves.
2 Student will summarize the information and use the correct terms in English.

In class in groups of four, students will:

3 Share the information collected from the videos.
4 Clarify/define concepts and give their English meaning.
5 Suggest an experiment.
6 Conduct the experiment with the help of the teacher.
7 Draw conclusions.

In plenary, students will:

8 Discuss how electromagnetic waves are related to cell phones.

Learning Materials
http://study.com/academy/lesson/electromagnetic-spectrum-and-waves-definition-categories.html
https://www.khanacademy.org/science/physics/light-waves/introduction-to-light-waves/a/light-and-the-electromagnetic-spectrum

Product/s
Definition of terms/concepts

Assessment
Definition of terms/concepts

Modification for Special Needs Students
Write two to three new concepts or terms they have learned in English and explain in simple words in Hebrew

Enrichment for Gifted and Able Students
Watch the elaborate explanation on electromagnetic waves and write at least five terms/concepts and describe them in English
https://www.khanacademy.org/science/physics/light-waves/introduction-to-light-waves/v/electromagnetic-waves-and-the-electromagnetic-spectrum

Lessons 7–8: Personal Perspective

Content
Using connectors in writing

Aims
- Student will recognize the different connectors.
- Student will identify connectors in a reading passage.
- Student will create authentic/relevant, oral and written situations relating to cell phones.
- Student will practice writing using connectors on the topic of cell phones.

Thinking Processes Developed
- Scientific thinking
- Creative thinking

Thinking Strategies Developed
- Remembering
- Understanding
- Applying
- Analyzing
- Creating

Learning Environment
Classroom – Station rotation

Opening/Exposure
Introducing station rotation and the different stations

Teaching Strategies
Blended learning – station rotation

Learning Activities and Grouping
Station rotation: Students can rotate between corners till they feel they have mastered the use of connectors:

1. *Tablet corner:* Language exercises on using connectors (according to level of difficulty).
2. *Writing and performing corner:* Role play and writing in pairs – Role playing the situation in pairs. Writing a letter to parents asking for the latest model of cellphone, using connectors.
3. *Group writing corner:* Writing a serenade to my cell phone using connectors (singing is optional).
4. *Challenge corner:* Writing a wiki entry on the cell phone in pairs.
5. *Individual practice corner:* Write a paragraph of 7–8 sentences about your cell phone using as many connectors as possible.
6. *Teacher's corner* (one-on-one or small group): Explanation and practice of connectors.

Learning Materials
Worksheet presenting all common connectors and their uses

Product/s
Depending on student needs and interests

Assessment
Self-evaluation test on tablet

Modification for Special Needs Students
Teacher's corner: One-on-one teacher explanation, tablet corner: lower level exercises; and role play without writing, or with help from peers

Enrichment for Gifted and Able Students
Challenge corner

Lessons 9–10: *Personal Perspective*

Content
Decision making: Whether or not to buy the latest version of the cell phone

Aims
– Student will be exposed to the six thinking hats.
– Student will use the six thinking hats for decision making.
– Student will present his/her decision in class.
– Student will write an essay using arguments for and against buying the latest version of the cell phone.

Thinking Processes Developed
Creative thinking – decision making

Thinking Strategies Developed
– Identifying perspectives
– Encountering different angles
– Being in the shoes of others – empathy

Learning Environment
Classroom

Opening/Exposure
– Exposure to the six thinking hats and practicing using a dilemma from the students' life
– Writing a short essay, presenting arguments for and against an issue

Teaching Strategies
Problem-based learning

Learning Activities and Grouping
In groups of six, students will:

1 Read the scenario.
2 Select a thinking hat.
3 Discuss the scenario using the thinking hats.

4 Reach a unanimous decision.
5 Work on presenting the decision creatively.
6 Present the decision to the class.

Individually:

7 Write a short essay, presenting arguments for and against buying the latest version of a cell phone, including ideas raised in the decision-making process and using the six thinking hats.

Learning Materials
- PDF and website on the six thinking hats
  http://www.debonogroup.com/six_thinking_hats.php
- Guidelines for writing an essay for or against a topic/issue.

Product/s
- Creative presentation of decision
- Written summary

Assessment
- Creative presentation of decision: Clear decision, presenting different angles (according to hats), all group members participated, interesting, creative, within three minute time limit, correct use of language, fluent
- Written summary: Follows the guidelines of writing for and against, presented relevant arguments, written in paragraphs, correct spelling, correct use of grammar

Modification for Special Needs Students
Special needs students can use less English while discussing the issue using the thinking hats.

They can write or record two arguments for and two arguments against, instead of writing the essay.

Enrichment for Gifted and Able Students
Gifted or able students will be in charge of the process and serve as the blue hat. They will document the process in English. They will write at least three arguments for and three against, elaborating on the issue.

Note: For the next lesson student are asked to take part in an experiment of not using their cell phone for a whole day and documenting the experience.

Lesson 11: Global and Personal Perspective (Optional)

Content
- Teenage addiction to cell phone
- Report on an experiment of not using the cell phone for a whole day

Aims
- Student will raise awareness of teenage use of cell phones around the world.
- Student will experience not using the cell phone for a whole day.
- Student will notice and document feelings, thoughts, and actions during the day.
- Student will analyze the experience.
- Student will evaluate the experience.
- Student will suggest creative ways of coping with reduced/controlled use of cell phone.
- Student will summarize the experience in written form.

Thinking Processes Developed
Scientific and creative thinking

Thinking Strategies Developed
- Classification and analysis
- Identifying connections
- Identifying processes
- Evaluation
- Inferring/drawing conclusions
- Encountering different angles

Learning Environment
- Home (experiment)
- Classroom

Opening/Exposure
Teenage addiction to cell phone
http://edition.cnn.com/2016/05/03/health/teens-cell-phone-addiction-parents/index.html

Teaching Strategies
Experiential learning

Learning Activities and Grouping
Students will:

1. Be encouraged to join an experiment of not using their cell phone for a whole day.
2. Document during the day (by writing or video):
   a. Their actions
   b. Their feelings
   c. Their thoughts
3. Summarize the experience in writing noticing connections and processes.
4. Write their opinion on the issue.
5. Suggest new ways of coping with reduced use of cell phone.

Summary of lesson

Teenagers giving up their cell phones (report on an experiment in USA) https://www.today.com/parents/9-teens-gave-their-phones-week-here-s-what-happened-t105539

Learning Materials
Guidelines for writing an opinion essay

Product/s
Opinion essay

Assessment
Opinion essay: Following guidelines, expressing opinion, describing emotions, actions and thoughts, summarizing the experience, and suggesting new ways of coping based on experience

Modification for Special Needs Students
– Film themselves and speak instead of writing.
– Write short sentences or use keywords to describe feelings, behaviors and thoughts.

Enrichment for Gifted and Able Students
Write a more elaborate essay suggesting creative ways of coping, as well as using the cell phone in new ways that will reduce exposure time

Lessons 12–13: Time Perspective

Content
The history of the cell phone

Aims
- Student will collect information on the cell phone.
- Student will organize events in sequence to form a timeline.
- Student will detect connections between events.
- Student will identify processes and outside events that influenced progress.

Thinking Processes Developed
Future thinking – construction and analysis of a concept

Thinking Strategies Developed
- Identifying components
- Classification
- Analysis
- Organizing in sequence
- Comparison
- Identifying connections
- Identifying processes

Learning Environment
Classroom + BYOD

Opening/Exposure
Introducing the timeline and instructions

Teaching Strategies
Future-based learning

Learning Activities and Grouping
In groups of five, students will:

1. Collect information on significant events.
2. Select ten dates and organize them in sequence.
3. Write a short description under each date.
4. Find connections between events.
5. Look for processes.

In plenary:

6 Present the significant events detected on their timeline. (One group will present, and other groups will add significant dates).
7 Discuss connections between events and detected processes.

Learning Materials
– Timeline template
– Relevant websites

Product/s
Timeline

Assessment
Timeline: At least ten dates, short explanation for each date, presented in the right sequence, oral explanation includes observation of connections between events, relating to the development of the cell phone

Modification for Special Needs Students
Working in mixed ability groups

Enrichment for Gifted and Able Students
Try to find external events that triggered the development of the cell phone

Lessons 14–16: Time Perspective

Content
– Teenage addiction to cell phone
– Report on an experiment of not using the cell phone for a whole day

Aims
– Student will recognize problem-solving process and stages.
– Student will suggest problems caused by the use of cell phones.
– Student will select one problem.
– Student will suggest solutions in the selected area.
– Student will write an action plan explaining the application of the solution.

Thinking Processes Developed
Creative thinking– problem finding and problem solving

Thinking Strategies Developed
- Suggesting problems
- Defining problem
- Suggesting solutions
- Finding criteria
- Selecting best solution
- Suggesting action plan

Learning Environment
Classroom + BYOD

Opening/Exposure
- Introducing the six steps of the problem-solving process
- Eliciting problems faced by cell phone users
- Defining areas – health, economics, language, social interaction, etc

Teaching Strategies
Problem-based learning

Learning Activities and Grouping
In groups, students will:

1. Review the problem-solving process and stages.
2. Select one area.
3. Suggest problems faced by cell phone users.
4. Select one problem and define it. Starting with: How can we…?
5. Suggest at least 5 solutions
6. Suggest 4 criteria for selecting the best solution.
7. Use criteria to select the best solution.
8. Write an action plan explaining the application of the solution.

In plenary:

9. Present the process and action plan.
10. Discuss the different problems and solutions presented in class.

Learning Materials
- Creative problem solving process and stages
- Relevant websites

Product/s
- Process of problem solving
- Action plan

Assessment
- Process of problem solving: Presents the different stages of problem solving, uses one area for solving the problem, focused
- Action plan: Presents stages of application, relates to the selected area, correct language, teamwork

Modification for Special Needs Students
- Working in mixed ability groups.
- Simplified problem-solving stages with examples.

Enrichment for Gifted and Able Students
Gifted and able students could work in a separate group and use the process of problem solving integrating areas (transdisciplinary approach) to look for a solution that will cover as many fields as possible

Lessons 17–19: Time Perspective

Content
Designing a model of the future cell phone

Aims
- Student will identify cell phone components needing improvement.
- Student will design an improved model using the S.C.A.M.P.E.R. technique.
- Student will create a new model of the future cell phone.
- Student will use a 3D printer to print a model of the cell phone.
- Student will describe the features of the new cell phone orally and in writing.

Thinking Processes Developed
Inventive/Creative thinking and entrepreneurship

Thinking Strategies Developed
- Melioration
- Creation

Learning Environment
- Computer lab + 3D printer

– Classroom

Opening/Exposure
The future phone 2020
https://www.youtube.com/watch?v=82bgLliQOHs

Teaching Strategies
Project-based learning

Learning Activities and Grouping
In groups of 4, students will:

1. Follow the stages of S.C.A.M.P.E.R.:
   Substitute – Replace one thing with another. Change parts, materials, processes, rules.
   Combine – Add or put things together. Add features, ideas, resources.
   Adapt – Meet other needs.
   Modify – Change the look or quality. Make bigger or smaller, add extra features.
   Put to another use – Use it in a different way.
   Eliminate – Take away characteristics (simplify, take out parts, split).
   Reverse/rearrange – Turn around, change order, reorganize, swap features.
2. Design a model of the future cell phone.
3. Print a model of the future cell phone using a 3D printer.
4. Describe the features of the future cell phone in writing/in an advertisement.

In plenary, students will:

5. Present the printed model and describe its features

Learning Materials
– S.C.A.M.P.E.R. worksheet and website
  http://www.brainstorming.co.uk/tutorials/scampertutorial.html
– Operating the 3D printer
– Description of a new invention – keywords

Product/s
– A future model of the cell phone printed by a 3D printer

- An advertisement of the latest model describing its main features

Assessment
- Development of the cell phone model followed S.C.A.M.P.E.R. steps.
- The cell phone is:
  a an improved version of an existing model, or
  b a new model of phone
- The 3D printed model matches the description in the advertisement.
- Keywords are used to describe the model.
- Connectors are used to combine sentences.

Modification for Special Needs Students
Designing and printing the cell phone. Sticking keywords on the product to describe its features. Use of two connectors to describe the product orally/or in written form

Enrichment for Gifted and Able Students
Written description of the new model in form of a professional review of a new product released to the market, or: presentation of future cell phone to an authentic audience

Lesson 20: Time Perspective

Content
Writing a future scenario – The cell phone 10/20/50 years from now

Aims
- Student will practice future thinking on the topic of cell phones.
- Student will combine the new knowledge and draw conclusions about future developments.
- Student will develop oral skills.
- Student will develop writing skills.
- Student will develop collaboration/teamwork skills.

Thinking Processes Developed
Future thinking

Thinking Strategies Developed
Predicting development

LANGUAGE ARTS AND SCIENCES: THE CELL PHONE 245

Learning Environment
Classroom

Opening/Exposure
Future scenario writing: guidelines and criteria

Teaching Strategies
Future-based learning

Learning Activities and Grouping
In groups of 3–4, students will:

1 Write a future scenario about the cell phone, in the selected time span (10/20/50 years from now).

In plenary:

2 Present the written future scenario in class.
3 Discuss similarities and differences between presented future scenarios.

Learning Materials
– Future scenario writing: Guidelines and criteria
– Knowledge accumulated throughout the unit

Product/s
Future scenario

Assessment
Future scenario writing criteria: Starting with the future, written in first person, there is at least one additional character, there is a plot, relating to the present, past and future, creative, correct English, at least one page long, correct use of terms/concepts

Modification for Special Needs Students
Future scenario template and keywords

Enrichment for Gifted and Able Student
Students will summarize in writing future scenarios presented by peers, and suggest similarities and differences. Students will draw conclusions regarding the class perspective on the future development of the cell phone

6 Future Scenario

The year is 2037. I woke up this morning and hooked up to my school-phone. A math lesson was just about to start, so I took part in it. Then, Rami invited me to play soccer with him on the phone. We played against two robots. We won because Rami's phone was recently upgraded and had extra features, and one of the robots had a bug in its program.

At noon, I spilled some water on the school-phone, and because it was not waterproof I could not use it till it dried. So, I had to use my sister's old iPhone 20. She has been using it as a toy, but it actually worked. This reminded me of past times we had learned about, when the first cell phone was invented by Martin Cooper in 1973. Then they had first, second, third and fourth generation cell phones. The smartphone, which was invented in 2007, combined the features of a palm device and a computer. This seems so old-fashioned now. Then in 2017, they had a more advanced cell phone with many features like a good camera, but unlike today the phones, were heavy and thick. Now most people have a phone with a foldable screen, while very rich people have chips implanted in their wrists.

After school, I met with some friends at a net-party. I was thirsty, so I ordered a coke with my credit card and a hologram immediately popped out of my phone with the cold drink. In the afternoon I put my virtual creature to sleep online, and went to play on my new FIFA 2037 for several hours. I ordered Chinese food directly from China, and it arrived a few minutes later. I pressed my cell phone and a fork and knife automatically appeared because now the phone has an improved smell detector. I spoke with my parents, who are currently in Antarctica, and they told me about their work and travel. Although they were so far away, it felt as if they were actually in the room, because their holograms came out of the screen and they stood right in front of me.

I lay down in bed and the music-phone started playing my favorite songs. I plugged-in to the charger and went to sleep. Sweet dreams...

References

Anderson, L. W., Krathwohl, D. R., Airasian, P. W., Cruikshank, K. A., Mayer, R. E., Pintrich, P. R., Raths, J., & Wittrock, M. C. (2001). *A taxonomy for learning, teaching and assessing: A revision of Bloom's taxonomy.* New York, NY. Longman Publishing.

Bell, M. R. (2015). *An investigation of the impact of a flipped classroom instructional approach on high school students' content knowledge and attitudes toward the learning environment*. Provo, UT: Brigham Young University, School of Technology.

Brilliant, J. (2005). Writing as an act of courage: The inner experience of developmental writers. *Community College Journal of Research and Practice, 29*(7), 505–516.

Çer, E. E. (2017). The effects of creative drama on developing primary school pupils' writing skills. *Education & Science, 42*(190), 379–400.

Chamberlain, S., & Meyers, M. (2015). *Incorporation of 3D printing in STEM curricula.* Worcester, MA: Worcester Polytechnic Institute Publishing.

Eberle, B. (1996). *Scamper on: Games for imagination development.* Waco, TX: Prufrock Press Inc.

Huffman, D. (1997). Effect of explicit problem-solving instruction on high school students' problem-solving performance and conceptual understanding of physics. *Journal of Research in Science Teaching, 34*(6), 551–570.

Johansen, V., & Schanke, T. (2013). Entrepreneurship education in secondary education and training. *Scandinavian Journal of Educational Research, 57*(4), 357–368.

Mahmoudi, A. (2017). Effect of planning on Iranian intermediate EFL learners' mastery of writing skill. *Theory & Practice in Language Studies, 7*(3), 219–226.

Moberg, K. (2014). Two approaches to entrepreneurship education: The different effects of education for and through entrepreneurship at the lower secondary level. *The International Journal of Management Education, 12*(3), 512–528.

Passig, D. (2007). Melioration as a higher thinking skill to enhance intelligence. *Teachers College Record, 109*(1), 24–50.

Shin, S. (2006). Learning to teach writing through tutoring and journal writing. *Teachers and Teaching: Theory and Practice, 12*(3), 325–345.

Tran, L. T. B., Ho, N. T., & Hurle, R. J. (2016). Teaching for creativity development: Lessons learned from a preliminary study of Vietnamese and international upper (high) secondary school teachers' perceptions and lesson plans. *Creative Education, 7*(07), 1024–1043.

Zenkov, K., & Harmon, J. (2009). Picturing a writing process: Photovoice and teaching writing to urban youth. *Journal of Adolescent & Adult Literacy, 52*(7), 575–584.

CHAPTER 14

Women's Status and Rights: Bible and Social Studies

This chapter focusing on women's status and rights from biblical times to the present day first introduces the topic explaining that the few women in the Bible who were presented as powerful were also very submissive, as men were in power and decided on everything, including women's status and rights. The unique teaching strategy interwoven into the MdCM-based unit design is debating. Following the principles of public speaking and debating, the developed unit illustrates how debate could be used to encourage students to present an opinion clearly to listeners. In addition to the benefits of self-confidence, development of oral speech, and forming an opinion on an important issue, the students gain a tool they can use in everyday life in varied situations. The chapter progresses with the description of the unit and the actual lessons taught in secondary school.

1   Women's Status in the Bible

Catz (2006) claimed that women's status presents the place of the woman and her influence in society. Itzhak-Amiram (2011) explained that there are few women in biblical stories, and when they are mentioned, it is only to indicate their status. Most central characters in the Bible are men, and women are portrayed next to them, or in their shadow. Ashman (2008) added that women were given to men and moved in with them, while their main role was to produce male heirs to keep the dynasty going and be responsible for the land and other possessions. While the man's role was to feed and protect his wife, Catz (2006) and Bruner (2007) mention a few of the women's jobs such as weaving, decorating, bringing presents and donations, and mourning the dead. They also served as cooks, bakers, and pharmacists, but could not take on the role of priest (Cohen). Itzhak-Amiram (2011) added that women were considered as the man's property, similar to gold and silver, and could be driven out. According to Brunner (2007), a woman who could not bear children was considered cursed. Another difference between men and women she mentioned related to inheritance: in the Bible, a woman was not allowed to inherit land or other possessions, so when a man had only daughters he was concerned as to who would be his successor. Granot (1982) elaborated on deportation, claiming that a woman who was sent away did not need to be compensated, but she could not inflict the same act on her husband. The only place she could flee to is her father's house. De Buboire (2001) stated that women were expected to be virgins on the day of their marriage, and if not, they faced severe punishment. If a woman betrayed her husband she would be punished by stoning, and when her husband died she was given to his brother.

Granot (1982) pointed out that in biblical law, a woman was seen as a human being and not as the man's possession. She possessed virtues such as wisdom and passion, as well as deviousness, and hatred. Itzhak-Amiram (2011) indicated that contrary to what was described earlier, there are stories in the Bible of women who possessed power and fought for their status and rights, and showed the ability to make changes in their lives. Catz (2006) explained that women who fought for their status and acquired power were socially involved, sometimes more educated, and also owned property, which allowed them to become prophets and judges.

The three women characters focused on in this unit of study are very different and faced different life circumstances. The first is Michal, the daughter of King Saul, Sometimes she is portrayed as very passive and does what her father and her husband, David order her to do, and sometimes very active and brave, when helping David to escape from her father, Saul (Steinsaltz, 1983). The second woman is Bathsheba, who was Uriah the Hittite's wife. Uriah was one of David's heroes, but after David makes sure he dies in battle, he marries Bat-Sheba. Shraga Ben-Ein (2005) explains that Bat-Sheba was very confident and independent, and it showed by David addressing her by her name, and also by putting her son Salomon on the thrown. Using her prominent status, she manages to make David do as she wishes. Ashman (2008) added that women in the Bible usually did what they were instructed to do by their husbands, and accepted their authority. Tamar, the third woman in this unit, was an exception. Tamar, Absalom's sister was raped by Amnon. She fought and tried to prevent him from raping her. As women were considered male's possessions, and they were not supposed to be active sexually and seduce men. Itzhak-Amiram (2011) explained that the Bible considered the abuse and rape of women less severe than other sexual acts.

2   Public Speaking – Debate

Mazor (2011) claimed that mastery of articulate speaking has become an important asset and skill in the democratic society that supports freedom of speech. Barak (2013) explained that debate neutralizes the wrappings and focuses on content and logics; rather than placing importance on 'dressing', it focuses on a person's arguments. A survey conducted by the Union of Colleges and Employers (2012) found public speaking as the most important skill employers look for when hiring employees. Palmer (2014) explained that the development of writing skills is important, but nowadays, students need to master speaking in public incorporated in teaching-learning activities which summon its practice. Hammond and Nessel (2011) found that the use of public speaking in class had a positive effect on teaching-learning processes, increasing understanding, as well as recall. Gallili (2016) detected that project-based learning and inquiry involve the use of alternative assessment. In other words, instead of a test, students get a grade for a project, or paper they have prepared. When presenting the final product, evaluation is partly determined by the level of oral presentation, which requires the teaching of rhetoric.

In 2015, the Israeli Ministry of Education declared the practice of public speaking as an important goal of students' preparation for real life. The principles set by the Ministry are as follows: Each student will experience two events of public speaking every year throughout his/her school education; experiences will be suitable for student level, and age; at younger ages work should be carried out in pairs or small groups; no importance is placed on arena, discipline, or topic; the audience could be varied in number, age, status: classmates, parents, school community, external communities in the country and national platforms; student will have the opportunity to select the topic and arena; debating will be incorporated in the discipline, combining knowledge and skills of preparing the presentation, standing before the audience, speaking, listening, and giving respectful feedback; each practice will be followed by oral or written feedback, addressing strengths and weaknesses for future learning/practice; and finally, teachers will create a safe space for practice and improvement of the speaking skills of students who encounter difficulties (shyness, anxiety, stuttering, hearing difficulties etc.) designing a program with the help of professional staff in order to enable students to advance their capabilities.

Dialogue differs from debate in many aspects. While dialogue is collaborative, makes a person examine his/her thoughts and beliefs and sometimes change them, debate is about trying to prove others wrong, finding flaws, defending opinions, presenting arguments, looking for differences, eliminating feelings, and seeking to draw conclusions. Mazor (2011) explained that the use of public speaking varies from person to person, according to traits, skills, and values. He drew an outline of presentation of information for the purpose of persuasion indicating three main parts: opening, body and summation. The body of the speech should include a varied presentation of facts, definition of the issue being debated, and a set of logical arguments. The opening and summation will usually include an emotional address or attempt to establish speaker credibility. He noted that the basic principles and rules of speaking in public developed by the Greek and Romans are still valid and relevant today.

The following unit based on MdCM will illustrate how a version of debate could be used in the important topic of women's status and rights.

3 Example Unit and Lessons: Women's Status and Rights

3.1 *Unit Description*

The current unit focused on topics from the Bible studies curriculum. The topic of women's status in the Bible was chosen due to its relevance to students' lives, as women's status in society is and authentic issue still encountered in everyday life. As the 9th-grade curriculum deals with a few women in biblical times, we combined and enabled students to investigate the similarities and differences between them, in the hope that they would be able to transfer their learning to our era, change their perspectives, and even act upon them to create change.

The 9th-grade students studied thirteen lessons on the topic of women's status. Lessons 1–3 focused on scientific thinking and students experienced collecting, organizing and presenting information using thinking hats. Lessons 5–9 focused on creative thinking using thinking hats to solve a dilemma, and problem solving. Lessons 10–11 focused on debating the topic of women's rights in current society, and lesson 12 was devoted to writing a future scenario asking students to project themselves into the future and imagine what women's status will be like 50 years from now.

During the *first lesson* the students were exposed to the topic of women's status in general. Students encountered the Circle Map and were instructed to work in pairs and write down concepts/words related to women's status. By the end of the lesson the class formed a mutually agreed on definition.

In the *second lesson* the students worked individually and in pairs and wrote what interested them about this topic. They used the double bubble to compare and find differences and similarities in their interests. Selecting one interest, they looked for five main facts and presented them to the class.

Lessons 3–4 presented three characters of women in the Bible. Students were asked to create an identity card for their chosen character, and choose two traits they would like to possess, and two they would not like to have.

Lessons 5–6 introduced students to different dilemmas faced by the women in the Bible. In groups, they used the six thinking hats to present the dilemma from different perspectives and reach a consensus. In plenary, they creatively presented the process of decision making and the solution.

In *lessons 7–8* students were introduced to different periods in history and women's status and rights, from biblical times to the present. Students were asked to get into groups and select one period, within which they looked for events indicating the opening of doors/a change in status and put them in sequence to create a timeline. When all timelines were united, students could envision the status of women and women's rights throughout history.

In *lessons 9–10*, students defined a problem identified in the timeline relating to women's rights and followed the six steps of problem solving to reach the best solution. The solution was turned into an applicable action plan presented to the class.

Lessons 11–12 were devoted to practicing debate and public speaking, based on group discussion and preparation. Students prepared a three-minute speech presenting a point of view (for or against), while another student from a different group presented an opposing view. Both students had to follow the principles and instructions of debate focusing on presentation of topic and stance, arguments for or against (based on student's role, and not necessarily on student's own opinion), creating eye-contact, clear and convincing speech, and roviding a focused response to the opposing arguments. Listeners then were welcomed to vote following pre-determined criteria, on who of the two students was more convincing.

Lesson 13 was devoted to predicting the future, writing a future scenario relating to women's status thirty years from now, based on the knowledge accumulated.

4   Lesson Plans

Student Level
30 middle school 9th-grade students

The Chosen Perspectives
Personal and time perspectives

Unit Length and Lesson Length
13 lessons of 45 minutes each

Lesson 1: Introduction

Content
Women's status in general

Aims
- Student will be introduced to women's status in general.
- Student will think about concepts related to women's status.
- Student will define women's status.
- Student will recognize the definition of women's status.

Thinking Processes Developed
Scientific thinking – inquiry

Thinking Strategies Developed
- Construction of concept
- Classification and analysis

Learning Environment
Classroom

Opening/Exposure
- Video on women's status
  https://www.youtube.com/watch?v = N3HIW797GFw
- Exposure to thinking maps – Circle Map

Teaching Strategies
Inquiry-based learning

Learning Activities and Grouping
In plenary:

1. Students will suggest criteria for filling in the Circle Map.

In pairs students will:

2. Watch the video again.
3. Fill in the Circle Map looking for all the concepts, areas, adjectives, etc. related to women's status
4. Define women's status based on the items in the Circle Map.

In plenary:

5 Present the definition.
6 Discuss the definitions and reach one agreed upon definition.
7 The teacher will present the definition adding to students' knowledge.

Learning Materials
- Video clip on women's status
- Thinking maps

Product/s
Circle Map

Assessment
Circle Map: Not more than 3 names of women, at least 10 associations

Modification for Special Needs Students
Template of map with a few items. Adding 5 items

Enrichment for Able and Gifted Students
Adding at least 15 items from various fields of life

Lesson 2: Personal Perspective

Content
Women's status in general

Aims
- Student will recognize their personal interest in women's status.
- Student will compare and contrast issues relating to women's status.
- Student will compare and contrast interest using a Double Bubble Map.
- Student will represent information using a Brace Map.

Thinking Processes Developed
Scientific thinking – inquiry

Thinking Strategies Developed
- Collecting information
- Classification and analysis

– Comparison

Learning Environment
Classroom

Opening/Exposure
– Connecting the topic to students' personal lives by telling a story.
– Exposure to the Double Bubble Map and the Brace Map.

Teaching Strategies
Inquiry-based learning

Learning Activities and Grouping
Individually student will:

1 Write what interests him/her about women's status.
2 Choose topics.

In pairs, students will:

3 Compare and contrast their interests.
4 Present the comparison using a Double Bubble Map.
5 Choose a topic and research it.
6 Write 5 facts about it.

In plenary students will:

7 Report on selected topic
8 Fill in a Brace Map representing the topic mentioned by classmates (first copying from the board, and then completing the map individually).

Learning Materials
– Personal story on women's status.
– Double Bubble Map
– Brace Map
– Internet websites

Product/s
– Double Bubble Map

- Brace Map

Assessment
- Double Bubble Map: presenting at least 2 similar and 2 different topics of interest
- Brace Map: copying correctly from the board, adding at least 3 topics and subtopics

Modification for Special Needs Students
Working with templates of maps partially filled in. Adding 2 topics to each

Enrichment for Able and Gifted Students
Brace Map: adding five topics, each divided into at least 2 sub-topics

Lessons 3–4: Personal Perspective

Content
Characters of women in the Bible: Michal, Bathsheba and Tamar

Aims
- Student will be exposed to three characters of women in the Bible.
- Student will collect information on the women.
- Student will draw conclusions regarding their traits.

Thinking Processes Developed
Scientific thinking – inquiry

Thinking Strategies Developed
- Collecting information
- Organizing information
- Drawing conclusions

Learning Environment
- Classroom
- Computer room

Opening/Exposure
Presenting the three female characters: Michal, Bathsheba and Tamar

Teaching Strategies
Inquiry-based learning

Learning Activities and Grouping

Students will be divided into six groups. Each group will select one female character. The teacher will make sure all characters are represented. Another option is that each two groups will select one character.

In groups of 5, students will:

1. Look for information on the selected female character using the Bible and the internet.
2. Prepare an identity card for the selected character including: name, pedigreesocial status, description, two main acts, at least two traits evident from each act.
3. Write two traits that they would personally want to possess and explain why.
4. Write two traits that they would definitely *not* want to possess and explain why.
5. Place the identity card on the desk.
6. Circulate the classroom and read the identity cards.
7. Add information on the female character based on other group/s' cards.
8. Write 5 facts about each of the other two female characters.

Note: Another version could be working in the computer room and leaving identity cards on the screen. A more advanced option would be creating a Facebook page for each female character.

Learning Materials
Worksheet – Identity card

Product/s
Identity card

Assessment
Identity card – Filling in all details. Writing two main actions, and two traits for each action

Modification for Special Needs Students
Working in mixed ability groups

Enrichment for Able and Gifted Students
Adding at least one action and several traits

Lessons 5–6: Personal Perspective

Content
Dilemmas in the lives of the biblical female characters

Aims
- Student will be exposed to the dilemmas in the lives of the biblical female characters.
- Student will use different perspectives.
- Student will make a decision on how to act, identifying with the female character.
- Student will develop verbal skills.

Thinking Processes Developed
Creative thinking – decision making

Thinking Strategies Developed
- Identifying perspectives
- Encountering different angles
- Being in another person's shoes – empathy

Learning Environment
Classroom

Opening/Exposure
- Review of information collected on the three female characters in previous lessons.
- Explanation about decision making and dilemmas.
- Introducing the six thinking hats.
- Practicing the six thinking hats in plenary on a topic related to school life.
- Explaining the assignment and determining criteria for the evaluation of the creative product.

Teaching Strategies
Problem-based learning

Learning Activities and Grouping
In groups of 6, students will:

1. Select a female character.
2. Define a dilemma in her life.
3. Use the six thinking hats to present the different perspectives of the dilemma.
4. Reach a consensus on the solution to the dilemma.
5. Prepare a creative 3-minute presentation of the process and the solution.

In plenary:

6. Present the creative product.

Learning Materials
Six thinking hats

Product/s
Creative presentation of the process and final decision (see the dilemma and creative product at the end of this chapter)

Assessment
Creative presentation: defining the dilemma, relating to the process, clear decision, interesting, all students participated, within time limit of three minutes

Modification for Special Needs Students
Working in mixed ability groups

Enrichment for Able and Gifted Students
Serving as group leader (blue hat) organizing the process. Delegating the assignment of recording the process

Lessons 7–8: Time Perspective

Content
The development of women's status and rights from biblical times to the present day

Aims
- Student will recognize different periods in history.
- Student will recognize women's status and rights from biblical times to the present day.

- Student will collect information on women's status and rights during the selected time period.
- Student will put events related to women's status and rights in sequence to form a timeline.
- Student will create awareness of the developments in women's status and rights throughout the time periods by combining the timelines.
- Student will look for connections between events.
- Student will raise his/her own awareness of processes and outside events that influenced progress.

Thinking Processes Developed
Future thinking

Thinking Strategies Developed
- Collecting information
- Classification and analysis
- Organizing in sequence
- Identifying connections
- Identifying processes

Learning Environment
- Computer lab/mobile phones
- Classroom

Opening/Exposure
- Presenting different time periods
- Presenting a template of a timeline

Teaching Strategies
- Future-based thinking
- Inquiry-based thinking

Learning Activities and Grouping
In plenary, Students and teacher will divide the time from the Bible up to now into 6–7 periods.

In groups, students will:

1 Select one period of time (teacher will make sure all periods are represented).

2 Collect information on significant events when doors were opened to women/changes occurred in their status and rights.
3 Select ten dates and organize them in sequence.
4 Write a short description under each date.

In plenary:

5 Combine the six or seven timelines and create a class timeline of events relating to women's status and rights.
6 Present the significant events detected in their timeline.

Learning Materials
– Timeline template
– Periods of time in history

Product/s
Timeline

Assessment
Timeline: At least 10 dates, a short explanation for each date, presented in the right sequence, oral explanation includes observation of connections between events, relating to the process of development of women's rights

Modification for Special Needs Students
Working in mixed ability groups

Enrichment for Able and Gifted Students
Explain how external events that may have triggered changes of women's rights

Lessons 9–10: Global Perspective

Debate
Content
Debate on women's rights

Aims
– Student will develop verbal skills.
– Student will recognize the basics/rules of debating.
– Student will experience presenting a point of view.

- Student will enhance his/her self-confidence in public speaking.
- Student will use self-evaluation to evaluate his/her performance.
- Student will experience giving productive feedback to peers.
- Student will be aware of his/her strengths and weaknesses regarding debating/public speaking and will consider areas of improvement.

Thinking Processes Developed
Creative thinking

Thinking Strategies Developed
- Identifying perspectives
- Identifying arguments
- Presenting arguments
- Encountering different angles
- Suggesting solutions

Learning Environment
Classroom

Opening/Exposure
- Principles, roles, and steps of debating.
  http://www.educationworld.com/a_lesson/03/lp304-01.shtml
- Practicing debating on school uniforms.

Learning Activities and Grouping
Topics for debate:

- Women should not be granted any additional rights.
- Women should stay at home, and not go out to work.
- Women should not be granted the right to vote.

Procedure:
- The class is arranged in 6 groups of 5 students.
- Each group represents one side – for or against a debate statement.

  Note: If the class is large (as in this case, 30 students) the teacher could serve as moderator, especially if it is the first attempt at debating an issue.

- Teacher as moderator is responsible for calling the debate to order, posing the debatable point/question, and introducing the debaters and their roles.

Group members' roles/responsibilities:

- Lead Debater/Constructor – presents the main points/arguments for his/her team's stand on the topic of the debate.
- Questioner/Cross-Examiner – poses questions about the opposing team's arguments to its Question Responder.
- Question Responder – takes over the role of the Lead Debater/Constructor as he/she responds to questions posed by the opposing team's Questioner/Cross-Examiner.
- Rebutter – responds on behalf of his/her team to as many of the questions raised in the cross-examination as possible.
- Summarizer – closes the debate by summarizing the main points of his/her team's arguments, especially attempts by the opposition to shoot holes in their arguments.
  http://www.educationworld.com/a_lesson/03/lp304-01.shtml

Note: The procedure and rules follow the format of the Lincoln-Douglas debates and are adapted to students' first-time experience/encounter with debating.

In groups, students will:

1 Collect information on the specific issue to be debated.
2 Affirm their previously decided position (for or against) and know who their opposing team is.
3 Present opening statement on the issue (based on accumulated knowledge and timeline).
4 Present arguments supporting their stand.
5 Raise questions.
6 Predict questions or arguments raised by opposing team which need to be addressed.
7 Prepare a closing statement – summarizing main points and questioning opposing team arguments.

Time limit for each round of two groups debating an issue will be 15 minutes.

- Self-assessment: Students will fill in a self-assessment sheet relating to their performance, pointing out strengths and weaknesses to be improved on in future debates.

– Peer evaluation: After each debate listeners will state which team was more convincing and explain why.

Learning Materials
– Debating worksheet – instructions, roles, procedure
– Self-assessment sheet

Product/s
Debate

Assessment
Debate procedure: students followed the instructions, students presented the issue well covering most important information, presented at least three arguments supporting their stand, answered questions posed by the opposing team, posed questions to the opposing team, concluded debate with summarizing main points, tried to undermine the credibility of the opposing team

Modification for Special Needs Students
– Mixed ability grouping
– Teacher paying special attention to shyness, hearing problems, lack of self-confidence

Enrichment for Able and Gifted Students
Serving as moderator controlling the debating process in the classroom (instead of the teacher)

Lessons 11–12: Time Perspective

Content
Women's rights problem solving

Aims
– Student will be aware of problems regarding women's rights in a timeline.
– Student will be exposed to the problem solving process.
– Student will be able to use the problem solving process to solve a problem regarding women's rights.
– Student will select one problem and define it.
– Student will suggest different solutions.

- Student will select the best solution based on pre-determined criteria.
- Student will suggest an action plan to apply the solution.

Thinking Processes Developed
Creative thinking – problem finding and problem solving

Thinking Strategies Developed
- Defining problem
- Suggesting solutions
- Finding criteria
- Selecting the best solution

Learning Environment
Classroom

Opening/Exposure
- Introducing students to the six steps of creative problem solving
- Examining the class timeline and looking for problems relating to women's rights

Teaching Strategies
Project-based learning

Learning Activities and Grouping
In groups, students will:

1. Select one problem.
2. Define the problem, starting with: How…?
   For example: How can we improve the status of women in our society? Or, How can we improve women's working conditions?
3. Brainstorm different solutions.
4. Determine criteria for selecting the best solution
5. Select the best solution based on pre-determined criteria.
6. Suggest an action plan to apply the solution.

In plenary:

7. Present the process, selected solution, and action plan.

Learning Materials
- Classroom timeline
- Steps of creative problem solving

Product/s
Presentation of process and action plan

Assessment
- Presentation of process and action plan: problem is defined correctly, at least 5 solutions, at least 4 criteria for selecting best solution, selected solution presented well, action plan is broken down into steps or levels of application
- Oral presentation: clear, accurate, focused.

Note: The teacher could ask students to hand in the draft of the problem-solving process, together with the action plan.

Modification for Special Needs Students
Working in mixed ability groups. Paying attention to the process, students could follow a worksheet explicitly stating the six steps of problem solving.

Enrichment for Able and Gifted Students
- Suggesting a more detailed action plan, or
- After listening to all problems presented by the different groups, gifted and able students will write a report trying to connect problems and solutions and suggest an overall plan for improving women's status and rights in society.

Lesson 13: Time Perspective

Content
Women's status and rights in the future

Aims
- Student will develop the ability to think about the future.
- Student will predict the future development of women's status and rights.

Thinking Processes Developed
Future thinking

Thinking Strategies Developed
Predicting development

Learning Environment
Classroom

Opening/Exposure
Presenting future scenario writing and criteria

Teaching Strategies
Future-based learning

Learning Activities and Grouping
In groups of 5, students will:

1. Project themselves into the future, selecting a time span (near -5 years; medium -10 years, far-30–50 years).
2. Write a future scenario based on accumulated information, following the pre-determined criteria.

In plenary:

3. Present the future scenario.
4. Discuss similarities and differences between scenarios.

Learning Materials
Future scenario writing

Product/s
Future scenario

Assessment
Future scenario criteria: It is located in the far or near future, one page long, mentions past, present and future, is written in first person, has two additional characters, has a plot, creative, correct and relevant events, it mentions a process

Modification for Special Needs Students
Mixed ability grouping

Enrichment for Able and Gifted Students
Adding characters to the scenario, elaborating on past and present and future.

5   Invited Guest

It is worthwhile adding two lessons before writing the future scenario, and inviting a female guest to speak to students about her activities to promote women's rights. This public figure could be an MP or activist in a local or international organization promoting women's rights. Students could prepare in advance a list of questions they would like to ask her. At the end of her presentation, based on the accumulated knowledge as a result of studying this unit, they could suggest additional areas which need attention.

6   Example Product

A dilemma faced by Tamar the biblical character
Tamar, Absalom's sister, was raped by Amnon. She fought and tried to prevent him from raping her. She told her brother, Absalom about the incident. She asked his opinion on whether to tell other people or keep quiet about it. Her brother suggested that she did not disclose this information and keep it to herself. Now it was her decision whether to follow his suggestion or not.

Unanimous decision based on the six thinking hats process
Using the six thinking hats, and considering all angles, options and consequences, the group decided that Tamar should not keep the rape incident to herself, although it is very risky, as women at that time were not allowed to have an opinion or go against any male.

Creative Product
My name is Tamar
And I do not live that far.
I hate my bitter share,
My brother does not care.
He says I have to hold it in
But I decided not to give in.
I will shout out to the world
Not matter what it holds.

Everybody will know how I feel
And even though it is after the fact
I will make Men think twice before they act

Note

The unit was developed by Sigal Smolnik with supervision of Hava Vidergor.

References

Ashman, A. (2008). *The genealogy of Eve: Daughters, mothers and gentile women in the bible*. Tel Aviv: Miskal. [in Hebrew]
Barak, A. (2013). Aharon Barak on the karioke stage. *Open University Journal, 1*, 23–26. [in Hebrew]
Bruner, R. (2007). Women's status in the bible. *Research in Education Society Technology and Science, 4*, 69–70. [in Hebrew]
Catz, H. (2006). Methodological perspectives in the study of women's status in the bible. *Beit Mikra, 51*(184), 72–84. [in Hebrew]
De Buboir, S. (2001). *The opposite sex: Facts and myths* (Vol. 1). Tel Aviv: Babylon. [in Hebrew]
Gallili, T. (2016). Students' permission to speak. *Free Lesson, 19*, 18–21. [in Hebrew]
Granot, M. (1982). The image of the woman in the bible. *Beit Mikra, 27*(89–90), 127–132. [in Hebrew]
Hammond, D. W., & Nessel, D. D. (2011). *The comprehension experience: Engaging readers through effective inquiry and discussion*. Portsmouth, NH: Heinemann.
Itzhak-Amiram, A. (2011). Woman's status and image in the bible. *Kesher Ayin, 208*, 32–36. [in Hebrew]
Mazor, M. (2011). How they speak. *Panim: A Journal for Culture Society and Education, 56*, 60–72. [in Hebrew]
Ministry of Education. (2015). Public speaking: A systematic program from first to twelfth grade in the spirit of meaningful learning. *1A, 9*, 3–14. [in Hebrew]
National Association of Colleges and Employers. (2012). *Job outlook 2013*. Bethlehem, PA: Author.
Palmer, E. (2014). Teaching speaking...presenting now. *Educational Leadership, 72*(3), 24–29.
Steinsaltz, A. (983). *Women in the bible*. Tel Aviv: Ministry of Defense. [in Hebrew]

PART 5

Multidimensional Curriculum for Special Needs

CHAPTER 15

Gifted Learners: Developing Leadership and Global Citizenship

This chapter introduces leadership to gifted students. It focuses on developing personal, global, and time perspectives. In the personal perspective, students investigate their own traits and goals, encounter traits of great leaders, learn how to present themselves preparing an 'elevator pitch', a short introduction of their favorite leader. The Model United Nations (MUN) is applied to introduce students to the global perspective and experience the responsibilities and actions involving representing countries in a mock UN assembly. It also develops future thinking through imaginary problem-solving simulation and future scenario writing prediction.

1   Leadership and the Gifted Student

Leadership and leadership development are viewed as collaborative, social and relational, and as a result, leadership in the future will be understood as the collaborative capacity of all members of an organization or community to accomplish critical tasks such as setting direction, creating alignment, and gaining commitment (Day, 2001). Scharmer (2009) identified listening as an essential individual skill, and conversing as a group skill involving debate, dialogue, and collective creativity. He claimed that these skills assist individuals to perform effectively in an environment of uncertainty and ambiguity and to reconcile the diversity of interests, needs and demands of multiple stakeholders in a global economy.

A study reported by Trilling and Fadel (2009) surveying 400 hiring executives of major corporations, asking whether high school graduates were ready to work, found that they thought students were not really prepared and lacked: oral and written communication skills; critical thinking and problem-solving skills; professionalism and work ethic; teamwork and collaboration; working in diverse teams; applying technology; leadership and project management skills (p. 7). Trilling and Fadel (2009) identified skills students will need in the future and placed them in three categories: learning and innovation, digital literacy, and career and life skills. Among *Learning and innovation skills* students will need: critical thinking and problem solving; communication and collaboration, and creativity and innovation. Among *Digital literacy skills* students will need: information literacy; media literacy, and information and communication technologies (ICT) literacy. Among *Career and life skills* students will need: flexibility and adaptability; initiative and self-direction; social and cross-cultural interaction; productivity and accountability; leadership and responsibility (Trilling & Fadel, 2009, p. xxvi).

Lee and Olszewski-Kubilius (2006) found that academically gifted students had greater leadership potential than other students; however, they did not have a significant difference in their level of emotional intelligence compared to heterogeneous groups of adolescents. Gifted male students showed a high level of adaptability in problem-solving and flexibility, while gifted females showed higher interpersonal abilities. An overall weakness was found in stress management, tolerance, and the ability to control impulses among both the male and female gifted students.

Vidergor and Sisk (2013) explained that

> as gifted students are provided with leadership activities to become more aware of and sensitive to the experiences of others from diverse cultures, they will become international and global citizens. As schools and centers integrate the cognitive, social, emotional, motivational and physical aspects of gifted students, they will be able to develop and demonstrate many of the characteristics identified by Singh (2003). (p. 52)

These characteristics include: (1) *Inquirers* – they possess natural curiosity and the skills to conduct purposeful constructive research and actively enjoy learning. (2) *Thinkers* – they exercise initiative in applying thinking skills critically and creatively to solve complex problems. Preparing students to be able to positively contribute in the 21st century will call for educators, businesses and governments to address the development of leadership to enable them to help solve the collective problems of a global world (Trilling & Fadel, 2009, p. 151).

According to Vidergor and Sisk (2013), gifted students are natural problem-seekers and problem-solvers, and as they are given opportunities to engage in real issues and problems that they care about, they will develop deeper understanding, become actively engaged and strengthen their desire and commitment to learn even more. Simulations provide opportunities to practice in a consequence-free environment with immediate feedback to address strengthening knowledge and understanding of one's inner world to enable the outer world to be addressed (Svobod & Whalem, 2005). Senge (2003) claimed that in an increasingly interdependent world, system thinking must become an educational priority. He stressed that business leaders, teachers and other professionals count on both wisdom of the past and their own experiences to create more inclusive ways of living and working globally in the present and in the future. Passig (2004) stressed that learning about the past is not enough; we should exploit and be able to develop an understanding of future possibilities and options. In order to survive in a fast–changing world, students need to make active use of their imagination to create images progressing beyond traditional paradigms, in order to discover, explore, invent and investigate new images in the present.

Sisk (2016) asked: How can we help gifted young people discover stronger senses of empowerment, ethics, and connection with others that will help them overcome the excessive materialism and individualism of today's Western culture? She argued that the gifted and talented suffer more from these problems, and advocated for the development of spiritual intelligence that brings into play intuitive processes, visualization, and other practices that are typically left unaddressed by formal education. Ambrose and Sternberg (2016b) said that

> students need to develop creative thinking skills to generate novel and compelling ideas for dealing with complex global problems; analytical skills to ascertain whether their new ideas are good ones; practical skills to implement their ideas and to persuade others of their usefulness; and wisdom-based skills to ensure that individuals use their knowledge and abilities to help promote a common good, by balancing their own, with others' and larger interests, over the long- as well as the short-term, through the infusion of positive ethical values. (p. 16)

Renzulli (2012, cited in Ambrose & Sternberg, 2016a), expressed the need to enable the gifted to discover worthy aspirations while preparing for leadership roles in the complex 21st-century. He stressed the importance of helping the gifted and talented develop and employ functions that will enable them to become effective planners, decision makers, and ethical leaders in novel, complex situations, which is of great importance in the growing 21st-century complex globalized world. Vidergor and Sisk (2013) translated many of the characteristics and skills gifted and talented students need to possess to become influential in various circles of life into a holistic leadership program starting from 3rd grade through to 12th grade.

2   Model United Nations

Model United Nations, also known as Model UN or MUN, is an extra-curricular activity in which students typically roleplay delegates to the United Nations and simulate UN committees. This activity takes place at MUN conferences, usually organized by a high school or college MUN club. At the end of most conferences, outstanding delegates in each committee are recognized and given an award certificate; the Best Delegate in each committee, however, receives a gavel. Thousands of middle school, high school, and college students across the country and around the world participate in Model United Nations, which involves substantial research, public speaking, debating, and writing skills, as well as critical thinking, teamwork, and leadership abilities (Ryan, 2007). Additional information can be found on http://bestdelegate.com/what-is-model-united-nations/

The educational value of this simulation is to expose the students to a different type of learning experience. By participating in this type of simulation, students will: hone their problem solving techniques; improve research and communication skills; and learn tolerance towards diverse groups who hold different opinions.

The Israel Middle East Model United Nations (TIMEMUN) is a student-led simulation of the United Nations in its 18th year at the American International School in Israel. In 2016, TIMEMUN hosted more than 600 students from Jewish and Arab schools, as well as participants from international schools in Israel. Students experience the intensity and rewards of dealing with global politics, researching and debating issues, drafting policy papers, and interacting with peers from different cultures and countries. In addition to honing their academic and leadership skills, students learn about cultural differences, and about how to view issues empathetically from multiple viewpoints. Additional information can be found on http://timemun.net

3 Example Unit and Lessons: Developing Leadership and Global Citizenship

3.1 *Unit Description*

The unit was designed for gifted students in different frameworks. The unit employs all three perspectives – personal, global and time, and is aimed at developing students' personal traits, global awareness, and future thinking.

The *first two lessons* raised students' awareness of their personal traits and short- and long-term goals, as well as of definitions of leadership. They learned how to use thinking maps to graphically/visually present information. In *Lessons 3–4* they practiced introducing themselves using the 30–60 second 'elevator pitch'. In *lessons 5–6* they researched a great leader of their choice and introduced him/her in three minutes. *Lessons 7–8* were devoted to becoming acquainted with different types of leadership. *Lessons 9–13* introduced Model UN and invited students to represent different countries in the Middle East regarding the issue of immigration, in a mock Council/General Assembly session. *Lessons 14–15* focused on a simulation of two imaginary countries named The Land of the Sphinx and the Land of the Rainbow, where students developed educational, environmental and projects in the year 2050. *The final lesson* was devoted to writing a future scenario relying on accumulated knowledge and combining the past and present, situated in 2050. *An extra unit* of six double lessons applying an action plan to solve a problem in the community, is suggested.

4 Lesson Plans

Student Level
9th grade gifted students

The Chosen Perspectives
Personal, global, and time perspectives

Unit and Lesson Length
16 lessons of 45 minutes each

Lessons 1–2: Introduction: Personal Perspective

Content
– Definition of leadership
– Personal traits and goals

Aims
– Student will identify his/her own weaknesses and strengths.
– Student will identify his/her personal goals.
– Student will compare traits of great leaders.
– Student will define leadership.

Thinking Processes Developed
Scientific thinking – inquiry

Thinking Strategies Developed
- Collecting information
- Organizing information
- Graphic representation

Learning Environment
Classroom

Opening/Exposure
- Worksheet: Who am I?
- Thinking maps

Teaching Strategies
Inquiry-based learning

Learning Activities and Grouping
Individually, students will:

1 Fill in a worksheet addressing personal traits, interests and hobbies, influential people in the student's life, short and long-term goals.

In pairs, students will:

2 Share the information.
3 Use the Double Bubble Map to find similarities and differences.

Individually, students will:

4 Choose a leader and write as many of his/her traits as possible using the Bubble Map.

In pairs, students will:

5 Use the Double Bubble Map to find similarities and differences between the two selected leaders.
6 Discuss how a person becomes a leader.
7 Use the Flow Map to illustrate how a person becomes a leader.
8 Define leadership using the Circle Map.
9 Write their own definition of leadership.

In plenary, students will:

10 Present the Double Bubble Map comparing two leaders.
11 Discuss suggested definitions of leadership.
12 Agree on one definition.

Learning Materials
- Worksheet – Who am I?
- Thinking maps

Product/s
Thinking maps

Assessment
Thinking maps: Each map has at least 5 items, Double Bubble and Flow Maps each have at least 7 items, are relevant and clear

Lessons 3–4: Personal Perspective

Content
Presenting myself to others

Aims
- Student will develop oral skills.
- Student will develop self-confidence.
- Student will practice self-presentation applying the elevator pitch.

Thinking Processes Developed
Scientific thinking

Thinking Strategies Developed
- Organizing information
- Classification
- Synthesis

Learning Environment
Classroom

Opening/Exposure
- Exposure to the elevator speech

- One-minute Elevator Pitch
  https://www.kent.edu/career/your-one-minute-elevator-pitch
- Examples of elevator pitches
  http://mcb.unco.edu/students/networking-night/examples-MCB-Pitch-Contest.aspx

Teaching Strategies
Inquiry-based learning

Learning Activities and Grouping
Individually, students will:

1. Review examples of elevator pitches.
2. Prepare a written form of his/her elevator pitch.
3. Practice the elevator pitch (30–60 seconds).

In pairs, students will:

4. Practice the speech, with one student presents himself/herself, and the other listening. Then students switch roles.
5. Analyze the speeches.

In plenary, students will:

6. Present their elevator pitches.
7. Give students feedback on performance and tips for further improvement.
8. Discuss the opportunities of using an elevator pitch in real life.

Learning Materials
Elevator pitch

Product/s
30–60 second elevator pitch

Assessment
Elevator pitch: covered age, place of residence, school, hobbies, traits, unique knowledge/ability, fluent, clear, established eye-contact, interesting

Modification for Doubly Exceptional Students
Video recording the speech

Lessons 5–6: *Personal Perspective*

Content
My great leader

Aims
- Student will enhance his/her oral skills.
- Student will explore the life of a great leader.
- Student will present the great leader to class.
- Student will be aware of his/her strengths and weaknesses regarding oral presentation.

Thinking Processes Developed
Scientific thinking – inquiry

Thinking Strategies Developed
- Collecting information
- Organizing information
- Oral representation

Learning Environment
- Computer lab/cell phones
- Classroom

Opening/Exposure
- Presenting the assignment – three-minute presentation of a selected great leader
- Mutually agreed upon criteria for evaluation of the oral presentation

Teaching Strategies
Inquiry-based learning

Learning Activities and Grouping
Individually, students will:

1. Select a great leader.
2. Collect information on the selected leader.
3. Organize the information.
4. Prepare a written presentation of the great leader.
5. Practice the presentation.

In plenary, students will:

6 Present the great leader to the class.
7 Evaluate the presentation (self-evaluation and peer evaluation according to pre-determined criteria).
8 Discuss the benefits of this experience for personal development.

Learning Materials
– Books
– Websites
– Self-evaluation worksheet

Product/s
Three-minute presentation of a great leader

Assessment
Presentation of a great leader: Explained relation/connection and reason for selection of the leader, fluent, covered the main biography of the leader, interesting, eye-contact, change of intonation, used anecdotes, expressed self-confidence in posture and volume of voice, stayed within the three-minute time limit

Modification for Doubly Exceptional Students
Video recording the presentation at home and showing it to the class. Oral self-evaluation

Lessons 7–8: Global Perspective

Content
Types of leadership

Aims
– Student will experience different types of leadership.
– Student will become acquainted with different types of leadership.
– Student will understand the difference between types of leadership and their consequences.

Thinking Processes Developed
Scientific thinking – inquiry

Thinking Strategies Developed
- Defining and identifying components
- Classification and analysis
- Comparison

Learning Environment
Classroom/computer lab

Opening/Exposure
- A game (types of leadership): The class is divided into three groups. Each group has a leader. The instructions for each leader change. One leader should be democratic, another represents dictatorship, and the third one anarchic. Students should follow the leader's orders and create a tower. In the debriefing, students reflect on the process and try to decide which type of leadership is more effective and why. They are also invited to talk about everyday life incidents demonstrating different types of leadership
- Exposure to the Divergent Thinking Map

Teaching Strategies
Inquiry-based learning

Learning Activities and Grouping
In groups, students will:

1. Pick one type of leadership.
2. Search for a definition online.
3. Give examples of leaders who used this type of leadership.

In plenary, students will:

4. Present the type of leadership.

In pairs, students will:

5. Compare the types of leadership using the Divergent Thinking Map.
6. Present the maps to the class.

Learning Materials
- Instructions for playing the game
- Internet websites

Product/s
Divergent Thinking Map

Assessment
Divergent Thinking Map: has at least three branches, each main branch has at least two sub-branches, oral explanation of types of leadership is clear, correct and focused

Modification for Doubly Exceptional Students
Map template

Lessons 9–13: Global Perspective: Model United Nations (MUN)

Content
Immigration – TIMEMUN aimulation

Aims
– Student will be exposed to a MUN simulation.
– Student will recognize the stance of a selected country regarding the issue of immigration.
– Student will experience writing a speech presenting the stance of the selected country.
– Student will experience delivering a speech presenting the stance of the selected country
– Student will develop oral skills.
– Student will develop cross-cultural and global awareness.

Thinking Processes Developed
– Scientific thinking – inquiry
– Creative thinking – problem solving

Thinking Strategies Developed
– Collecting information
– Organizing information
– Oral representation
– Defining problem
– Suggesting solutions
– Identifying perspectives
– Selecting the best solution

Learning Environment
- Classroom
- Computer lab

Opening/Exposure
- Teacher asks students to work in small groups and create a collage of global issues using newspaper headlines and or articles
- Teacher introduces MUN and TIMEMUN
- In plenary, students discuss which issue will be used for the MUN simulation

Teaching Strategies
Problem-based learning

Learning Activities and Grouping
In groups, students will:

1 Select a country
2 Conduct independent research on their country and its stance on the chosen issue.
3 Prepare written and oral statements using the following guidelines:

Writing the speech:

    a Know the details
    b Focus on topic
    c Create a one-minute speech (150 words)
    d Highlight important words that need to be stressed.
    e Make it interesting

Delivering the speech:

    a Practice and be prepared
    b Pay attention to body language
    c Pay attention to tone and pace
    d Show confidence
    e Overlook mistakes and go on

    http://bestdelegate.com/how-to-make-an-opening-speech/

Mock Council/General Assembly session:

4 Each group/country presents an oral statement using convincing arguments.
5 Each group/country presents a written statement.
6 Vote on the suggested motions

Discussion

7 Analyze the mock session using pre-determined criteria to assess performance.
8 Reflection.

Learning Materials
– Newspaper headlines and articles
– The TIMEMUN format

Product/s
Mock Council/General Assembly session

Assessment
– Written presentation: Knows the details, focuses on topic, within time and word limit (one-minute speech, 150 words), important words are stressed, interesting
– Speech delivery: Fluent, eye-contact, right pace and tone, showed confidence, overlooked mistakes, interesting, grabbing attention, presented relevant arguments/solutions to the issue

Modification for Doubly Exceptional Students
Open a page on Facebook and present your arguments. Invite representatives of other countries to comment and post pictures or film excerpts.
  Note: The MUN version provided can vary in structure and length depending on tudents' grade level and interest.
  Note

– Teacher and students are invited to join the MUN global classrooms or TIMEMUN conferences.
– A former ambassador can be invited as a guest telling about his experience in the UN.

Lessons 14–15: Time Perspective: Simulation

Content
Simulation of the future development of an imaginary country

Aims
- Student will develop his/her ability to think about the future.
- Student will acquire the skill of problem solving.
- Student will simulate living in an imaginary country.
- Student will suggest solutions to problems in the imaginary country.
- Student will develop different perspectives and angles of approaching a situation.

Thinking Processes Developed
Creative thinking

Thinking Strategies Developed
- Defining problem
- Suggesting solutions
- Identifying perspectives
- Selecting the best solution
- Encountering different angles
- Empathizing – being in the shoes of others

Learning Environment
Classroom

Opening/Exposure
Name one way that we might influence the future of our country. (How does our country shape our future? How can we influence the future of our country?)

Teaching Strategies
Problem-based learning – simulation

Learning Activities and Grouping
The Land of the Sphinx and the Land of the Rainbow (see Appendix)

The setting for the simulation game is the year 2050, and a minimum of 4 travelers are selected to visit the 2 countries: The Land of the Sphinx and the Land of the Rainbow.

Each country is asked to develop 3 projects to shape its future in the following felds:

1 Education;
2 Research;

3 Environment.

In small groups of 4–5, students will:

1 Identify projects in each area.
2 Develop the projects in writing.
3 Welcome the travelers.
4 Present the projects to the travelers and try to persuade them to stay in their country.

In plenary, students will:

5 Discuss the simulation

Learning Materials
Simulation: The Land of the Sphinx and the Land of the Rainbow (Sisk, 1985) (see Appendix).

Product/s
Three projects developed in groups

Assessment
Projects: clear, relate to a specific problem, written in points, suggest several solutions, identify the best solution, creative, interesting

Lesson 16: Time Perspective

Content
The future of our country

Aims
- Student will be exposed to future thinking.
- Student will practice future thinking on the topic of his/her country.
- Student will predict developments in different areas.

Thinking Processes Developed
Future thinking

Thinking Strategies Developed
Predicting development

Learning Environment
Classroom

Opening/Exposure
- What will our country look like 30 years from now?
- Introducing students to future scenario writing. Explaining they can draw on all they have learned about the past, present, future, personal, and global perspectives.

Teaching Strategies
Future-based learning

Learning Activities and Grouping
In groups of 3–4, students will:

1 Write a future scenario of the development of the country in the selected time span relating to different fields/areas/disciplines.

In plenary, students will:

2 Present the written future scenarios in class.
3 Discuss similarities and differences between the future scenarios.

Learning Materials
- Future scenario
- Accumulated knowledge

Product/s
Future scenario

Assessment
Future scenario: starting with the future, written in first person, there is at least one additional character, writing at least 2 pages, there is a plot, relating to the present and past and future, creative, correct language

Modification for Doubly Exceptional Students
Oral presentation of the scenario. Computer simulation of future scenario
   Note: The teacher could add to the suggested unit six double lessons for identifying a current problem and writing an action plan for im Pplementation, as well as implementing the plan in the community. This will promote student

leadership skills, social responsibility and teamwork. It should be accompanied by evaluation of the implementation and reflection on the process.

Adding the extra lessons creates a complete leadership course, which can be taught in pullout programs for a semester of 14 weeks.

References

Ambrose, D., & Sternberg, R. J. (Eds.). (2016a). *Giftedness and talent in the 21st century: Adapting to the turbulence of globalization* (Vol. 10). Rotterdam, The Netherlands: Sense Publishers.

Ambrose, D., & Sternberg, R. J. (Eds.). (2016b). *Creative intelligence in the 21st century: Grappling with enormous problems and huge opportunities* (Vol. 11). Rotterdam, The Netherlands: Sense Publishers.

Day, D. (2001). Leadership development: A review in context. *Leadership Quarterly, 11*(4), 581–613.

Karnes, F., & Bean, S. (2009). Developing the leadership potential of gifted students. In F. Karnes & S. Bean (Eds.), *Methods & materials for teaching the gifted*. Waco, TX: Prufrock Press.

Karnes, F., & Zimmerman, M. (2001). Employing visual learning to enhance the leadership of the gifted. *Gifted Child Today, 24*(1), 56–61.

Lee, S., & Olszewski-Kubilius, P. (2006). The emotional intelligence, moral judgment, and leadership of academically gifted adolescents. *Journal for the Education of the Gifted, 30*, 29–67.

Passig, D. (2004). Future time span as a cognitive skill in future studies. *Futures Research Quarterly, 19*(4), 27–47.

Scharmer, O. (2009). *Ten propositions on transforming the current leadership development paradigm*. Amherst, MA: Massachusetts Institute of Technology.

Senge, P. M. (2003). Creating desired futures in a global economy. *Reflections, 5*(1), 1–12.

Singh, N. (2003). How global is the curriculum? *Educational Leadership, 60*(2), 38–41.

Sisk, D. (1985). *The land of the Sphinx and land of the rainbow*. Tampa, FL: University of South Florida.

Sisk, D. (2016). Filling that empty space in the lives of people in a globalized world beset with turbulence and crises. In D. Ambrose & R. J. Sternberg (Eds.), *Giftedness and talent in the 21st century* (pp. 181–200). Rotterdam, The Netherlands: Sense Publishers.

Svoboda, S., & Whalen, J. (2005). Using experiential simulation to teach sustainability. *Greener Management International, 48*, 57–65.

Trilling, B. T., & Fadel, C. (2009). *21st century skills: Learning for life in our times.* San Francisco, CA: Jossey-Bass.

Vidergor, H. E., & Sisk, D. A. (2013). *Enhancing the gift of leadership: Innovative programs for all grade levels.* Ulm: International Center for Innovation in Education Press.

Appendix: Land of the Sphinx and Land of the Rainbow (Sisk, 1985)

Scenario: Land of the Sphinx

The *Land of the Sphinx* is inhabited by people who want to do what's right. You trust objectivity and logic. As people, you are concerned with the here and now. In making decisions, you want to do what is right. You pour over details, and every move is calculated. You like to do certain things at certain times, and tradition is essential. Time is very important and not to be wasted. As a group, you are always conservative and resolutions are important. Success comes from each person's ability and hard work. Schedules and routine lead to a course of action which is followed through to a finish. Order is very important

Scenario: Land of the Rainbow

The *Land of the Rainbow* people are interested in a deeper, larger, all-encompassing reality. You are people who view energy as power. You are impulsive and often make decisions by hunches. You are experimental and people are not required to conform in the Land of the Rainbow. You enjoy taking a risk and often make decisions on whether or not it feels good. Feelings are very important and, on the whole, you can be described as sensitive, optimistic and liberal. In problem solving, you try to get a broad perception of a problem and weigh evidence intuitively. You are concerned with the future. When you follow a hunch, there is often a sense of compulsion. Variety is important in the Land of the Rainbow. You need to deviate, to digress.

Travelers

The four of you have been chosen as travelers. You are seeking information from the people of the Land of the Sphinx and the Land of the Rainbow. You want to gather as much information about them as possible. Why do they do what they do? You want to find out the main thing that they need as a people. You will be recalled after 15 minutes to report what you have learned about each land. Ask questions and find out the single most important characteristic of each country. Write a statement that you think most reflects what the people are like in each country and what they need to survive. When you return from your journey, the four of you will share your knowledge. As a traveler, you are bold, open and courageous. You are driven by curiosity and desire, and you are seeking truth.

Evaluation Processing

1. How accurate were the travelers in ascertaining the need?
2. Were the travelers comfortable in the Lands? If so, why? If not, why not?
3. Were you comfortable in your Land as assigned? If so, why? If not, why not?
4. Can you see similarities between the traveler's quest for knowledge and a student's search for answers? Is the environment conducive to aspiration, curiosity, and desire? When people are bold, open, and courageous, does this always meet with approval?
5. What can we do to help travelers?
6. Which Land is shaping a future? Why?

CHAPTER 16

Learners at Risk: Economics and Globalization

Learners at risk need special attention and care in order to cope with difficulties in many areas resulting in the lack of emotional availability for studies. This chapter first introduces the topic of globalization selected for teaching 11th grade students at risk. It elaborates on a program for high school students at risk in Israel. Followed by the TASC model for teaching inquiry skills and problem solving, the unit based on MdCM illustrates how introduction to economics and the topic of globalization could be taught for a five-point (advanced level) matriculation exam, focusing on thinking skills and different perspectives.

1 Global Economics

Nowadays the world is in a state where many countries are entwined economically, and there is one world market in which technology, data, finance, trades, and employees flow from place to place quickly, regardless of distance. Technological developments such as the internet have accelerated the process, and as a result, many countries have reduced restrictions on imports and opened up the markets for free trade. This has created international competition and consumption of similar products and services from different countries around the globe. The World Trade Organization, and World Bank, and International Monetary Fund are organizations leading the global economy. Main activities are carried out by multinational companies such as McDonalds, Microsoft, Google, and many more. The developed countries are the beneficiaries of the global economy as these companies and organizations have bases in their territories. Developing countries have also benefited, as markets have opened for agricultural produce, and have created many opportunities for employment. Globalization processes accelerated after the end of the 'cold war' between Russia and the USA, which created suitable conditions for economic and cultural cooperation. Globalization creates economic inter-dependence, so that an economic crisis in one part of the world affects all countries involved around the world (Zimon & Hirsch, 2012).

The subject "Introduction to Economics" focuses on both micro and macro topics. At the micro level it stresses analysis of economic phenomena by following the activities of basic economic cells, which constitute the economic system in general. At the macro level, the focus is on examination of government actions to influence the level of activity in the market, i.e. monetary policy, fiscal policy, and supervision of price and salary policies.

The study of economics combines different disciplines to enable a real view of existing reality. It deals with human beings, society and its aspirations and values, and patterns of economic, social, and cultural functioning. It also creates meaning in learning throuh authentic experiences, developing multiple intelligences, and inquiry and representation of knowledge in varied ways (Ministry of Education, 2015). Its aim is to develop economic literacy, i.e. recognition of basic concepts in economy, understanding of economic processes, and building the foundations for economic thinking. Concepts and processes help students understand economic, personal, and national issues presented in the media, and how they affect decision-making at individual, corporate, and national levels. Studying economics exposes students to concepts and phenomena both theoretically and practically. Hence, learning strategies need to be varied and suited to the characteristics of the learned topics, as well as combine innovative technical means in suitable pedagogical ways, including alternative assessment. Topics are presented partly in a spiral construct, and partly as a puzzle, to lead students to economic thinking, and the understanding of the world of concepts it entails (Zimon & Hirsch, 2012).

2 Students At-Risk in High School

According to the Israeli Ministry of Education (2012), the decision to design programs from 9th grade was made in order to prevent students from dropping out of high school, reduce gaps, and increase the percentage of students with full matriculation among students at risk. Special programs were developed to identify difficulties and needs at the end of middle school, and help students overcome them, to enable a smooth transition into high school. The special programs and classes in high school offer students focused and significant learning scaffolding, which enables relatively easy integration into matriculation classes, with no additional help required. In these classes, students are offered extra lessons in math, English, and mother tongue. Individual detailed programs of study are designed for each student in each discipline, with evaluations, assessments, and other interventions based on performance. The rationale behind this program is that the student is the center of the learning process, and the program needs to fit his/her personality, needs, interests, and strengths. This is drawn from the belief the "every student can" (Ministry of Education, 2012).

Expectations from the implementation of the program in 9th grade were: improving student achievements in basic skills; increasing motivation; a smooth transition into high school and matriculation tracks; strengthening personal efficacy; developing learning strategies, nurturing social interpersonal relationships; and developing effective tools for caring for students at risk. In order to apply the program properly principles, homeroom teachers and discipline teachers need to: create an optimal social climate enabling significant functioning in class and school; build a suitable framework in 9th grade for students with adaptability and learning difficulties, whose achievements do not match the standards of their age as a result of personal and environmental deprivation; offer opportunities to experience success in learning and social function, which could increase the sense of self-efficacy; develop unique abilities; prevent dropout; develop values such as love of the land, and loyalty to country and its people; create a climate that nurtures fairness, tolerance, mutual respect, and acceptance of others; create a learning environment based on mutual help and social commitment; and construct adaptive learning environments in contents, instructional aids, and physical space (Ministry of Education, 2012).

3   Thinking Actively in a Social Context (TASC)

TASC was developed by Belle Wallace (Wallace, 2009; Wallace & Maker, 2004; Wallace, 2001, 2002) originally for elementary school students. It aimed at developing student inquiry skills along with social and reflective abilities. In this unit it is used with at-risk high school students and helps scaffold their learning and gives them a structured tool for inquiry and problem solving. The stages of TASC are explained by Wallace (2015) as follows:

Gather and Organize: What do I already know? This stage encourages learners to draw the fragments of their previous learning into the working memory. The important element in this stage is to visually construct connections between ideas using mind maps or thinking maps. It is also important to look for cross-curricular links through stories, drama, dance, music, numeracy, literacy, art, craft, and design, etc.

Identify: What am I going to do? Identifying the area of exploration personalizes learning and gives children a sense of ownership. Important questions include: What would you like to know about this topic? What questions could you ask? What do you want to achieve? What do you need to do this? Helping children to identify their own fields of interest and exploration creates motivation for learning, and generates the emotional involvement needed for attention and concentration. It also allows for differentiation, where some children can tackle simpler tasks, while others work in greater depth and breadth.

Generate: How many ways can I do it? The children suggest possible directions for the development of their activities and make their own decisions asking a number of key questions such as: How many ideas can I think of? Where can I find out? Who can I ask? What do other people think? How shall I present/communicate my work?

Decide: Which are the best ideas? In this stage the decision is focused on the end goal asking the following questions: What is the plan of action? Which ideas are important? How am I going to record my findings? What materials do I need? How much time do I have?

Implement: Let's do it! This is about putting the decision into action. Implementation involves planning, recording, and communicating to others.

Evaluate: How well did I do? Through evaluating themselves and their peers' work students use critical thinking, strengthen certain abilities, and acknowledge what they need to improve.

Communicate: Let's share what we have learned! This stage is about summarizing what students know and sharing ideas with others using different methods and skills. Learning new ideas and sharing with others adds to the collective knowledge.

Learn from Experience: What have we learned? At the end of a topic or project a metacognitive process of thinking about thinking, feeling and learning takes place centering around questions such as: What do I know now that I didn't know before? What new skills have I learned? How else can I use these skills? How can I improve my way of working? How can I improve how I work with others? (Wallace, 2015).

4 Example Unit and Lesson Plans: Economics and Globalization

4.1 *Unit Description*

The unit was designed for 11th grade high school students at risk. The lessons focused on globalization in general, and on economics in particular. Students were exposed to: areas contributing to the development of globalization such as technology and communication, transportation; political and economic changes; international trade, and the employment market which have all been influenced by globalization; discussion for or against globalization, problem solving in the job market, international companies; and prediction of globalization in the future.

The *first part* introduced students to the topic of globalization. They were asked to collect personal items and watched a video clip introducing the concept of globalization. They also raised hypotheses and used thinking maps to present data graphically. They illustrated the different areas and waves of globalization using a flow thinking map.

The *second part* of the unit focused on the global perspective. Students investigated the areas contributing to the development of globalization. Students used the TASC model to understand how national companies became international conglomerates. They also investigated international trade and the job market influenced by globalization and used the problem solving process to define and solve a problem regarding employment. They used the personal perspective in a process of decision-making, employing the six thinking hats to decide for or against globalization.

In the *third part* of the unit, the students used the time perspective to further investigate globalization. Each group focused on the development of one wave of globalization creating a timeline, and contributing their knowledge to combine timelines and show the different areas and events affecting globalization across time. At the end of the unit student projected themselves into the future and wrote a group future scenario relating to the expected areas that will influence and be influenced by future globalization.

Based on MdCM, the unit stressed scientific, creative, and future thinking, incorporating construction of concept, inquiry, problem solving, decision-making, data presentation, oral presentation, team work and more. This unit specifically illustrated the use of TASC as a structured model for thinking which could be used with older students at-risk to equip them with a tool for life.

5   **Lesson Plans**

Student Level
11th grade weak students, studying economics for matriculation exam (basic level)

The Chosen Perspectives
Global, personal, and time perspectives

Unit and Lesson Length
14 lessons of 45 minutes

Lessons 1–2: Introduction to Globalization

Content
Exposure to globalization (definitions and fields)

Aims
- Student will be exposed to the concept of globalization.
- Student will recognize definitions of globalization.
- Student will recognize the different fields/areas globalization deals with

Thinking Processes Developed
Scientific thinking – inquiry

Thinking Strategies Developed
- Collecting information
- Organizing information
- Identifying connections
- Graphic representation

Learning Environment
- Home
- Smart classroom

Opening/Exposure
- Homework assignment (prior to study): Filling in a table of songs and other items from different countries
- Video clip explaining globalization simply
  https://www.youtube.com/watch?v=JJonFD19eT8

Teaching Strategies
Inquiry-based learning

Learning Activities and Grouping
In groups, students will:

1 Write the data of group members in the table.

2 Classify the collected data.
3 Brainstorm associations.
4 Raise hypotheses regarding the topic of studies.

In plenary, students will:

5 Present table and associations.
6 Discuss definitions of globalization.
7 Discuss areas of globalization.
8 Present globalization and its areas in a Flow Map (with teacher's help).
9 Upload to a shared document.

Learning Materials
– Homework assignment
– Video clip

Product/s
– Flow Map (shared document)

Assessment
Flow Map: definition is clear, relates to at least one area of globalization

Lessons 3–4: Global Perspective

Content
Globalization waves

Aims
– Student will recognize different waves of globalization.
– Student will acquire tools for graphic representation of data.
– Student will use the double bubble thinking map to illustrate differences and similarities.

Thinking Processes Developed
Scientific thinking – inquiry

Thinking Strategies Developed
– Collecting information
– Organizing information
– Comparison

– Graphic representation

Learning Environment
Smart class

Opening/Exposure
Thinking maps – Double Bubble Map

Teaching Strategies
Inquiry-based learning

Learning Activities and Grouping
In groups of four, students will:

1. Explore the wave of globalization (read the article and look for more information online).
2. Focus on effects causing the wave of globalization.
3. Determine changes within the wave.
4. Show the areas in which changes occurred.

In plenary, students will:

5. Present the globalization wave (cause, changes, areas).

In groups, students will:

6. Draw a Double Bubble Map and compare all presented waves of globalization.

Learning Materials
– Summary of globalization wave (each group works on a different wave)
– Template of Double Bubble Map

Product/s
– Data on globalization wave
– Double Bubble Map

Assessment
– Data on globalization wave: presenting at least one cause, two changes, and at least two areas of change

– Double Bubble Map: Presenting at least two things in common between the different globalization waves, and at least three differences

Lessons 5–6: Global Perspective: TASC

Content
Developments contributing to globalization

Aims
– Student will develop an awareness of different areas of life contributing to globalization.
– Student will research the development of a selected company.
– Student will learn to work in a team.
– Student will present information using the flow thinking map.

Thinking Processes Developed
Scientific thinking

Thinking Strategies Developed
– Collecting information
– Organizing information
– Graphic representation
– Classification and analysis
– Organizing in sequence

Learning Environment
Smart classroom

Opening/Exposure
– Did You Know? YouTube video clip relating to the different areas and developments contributing to globalization
  https://www.youtube.com/watch?v=YmwwrGV_aiE
– TASC Thinking Wheel
  Introducing students to the structures wheel eight steps of researching any topic:
  1 Gather and organize
  2 Identify
  3 Generate
  4 Decide
  5 Implement

6 Evaluate
7 Communicate
8 Learn from experience (see figure in Appendix)

Teaching Strategies
Inquiry-based learning

Learning Activities and Grouping
In groups of 4, students will:

1 Select one company.
2 Work on TASC wheel.
3 Use the Flow Map as a final product, to present the development of the company.

In plenary, students will:

4 Present the process using TASC thinking wheel.
5 Present the product – Flow Map of development of the company.
6 Name areas/fields which contributed to globalization.

Learning Materials
– Did You Know? YouTube video clip
– A template of TASC Thinking Wheel
– Cardboard, scissors, glue, and colored felt pens

Product/s
– TASC Wheel
– Flow Map

Assessment
– TASC Wheel: all eight steps are filled in, used keywords, correct spelling, relevant information
– Flow Map: shows at least four different stages, shows years, relates to different periods of company development from local to global, accurate, correct spelling

Lessons 7–8: Global Perspective

Content
Areas affected by globalization:

- Employment market
- International trade market

Aims
- Student will recognize the six steps of problem solving.
- Student will apply the problem-solving steps.
- Student will recognize the areas affected by globalization.

Thinking Processes Developed
Creative thinking – problem finding and problem solving

Thinking Strategies Developed
- Defining problem
- Suggesting solution
- Finding criteria
- Selecting best solution

Learning Environment
Smart classroom

Opening/Exposure
- PPT presentation with problem solving steps. (See template of problem solving process in the Appendix of Chapter 7.)
- Practicing on real everyday issue requiring problem solving.
- Students will suggest areas affected by globalization and teacher will present them in a circle thinking map.

Teaching Strategies
Problem-based learning

Learning Activities and Grouping
In groups of four, students will:

1. Select one area.
2. Define problem.
3. Brainstorm at least 4 solutions.
4. Find at least four criteria for selecting the best solution.
5. Select the best solution.
6. Suggest an action plan to apply the best solution.

Note: Teacher could suggest all groups deal with the job market and relate to/define a different problem relating solely to it.

Examples of problems: low payment, gender underpayment, availability of jobs, job security etc.

Learning Materials
Problem solving steps

Product/s
Problem solving process and action plan

Assessment
Problem solving process and action plan: presented the problem, solutions, criteria, selected solution and action plan, was clear, within 5-minute time limit, action plan was presented in stages, applicable

Lessons 9–10: Time Perspective

Content
Development of globalization

Aims
- Student will recognize the development of globalization over time.
- Student will be able to place main events in the right sequence.
- Student will be able to explain each main event.

Thinking Processes Developed
Future thinking – constructing a concept

Thinking Strategies Developed
- Defining and identifying components
- Classification and analysis
- Organizing in sequence

Learning Environment
Computer lab

Opening/Exposure
Introducing the timeline template

Teaching Strategies
Future-based learning

Learning Activities and Grouping
In groups of four, students will:

1. Research globalization from its beginning to the present day.
2. Use a timeline template to mark at least ten main events.
3. Put the events in the right sequence.
4. Add a short explanation of the events.

In plenary, the students will:

5. Present the timeline to the class.
6. Combine all timelines into a class timeline representing the three waves of globalization.
7. With teacher's help, find connections between events.
8. With teacher's help, identify processes.

Learning Materials
- Internet websites
- Timeline template

Product/s
Timeline

Assessment
Timeline: at least 10 dates of events in globalization are mentioned, there is a short description of each event, it covers the three waves of globalization.

Lessons 11–12: Personal Perspective

Content
For or against globalization?

Aims
- Student will form an opinion on globalization.
- Student will identify different perspectives of globalization.
- Student will be acquainted with the six thinking hats.

– Student will practice applying the six thinking hats to a process requiring decision making.

Thinking Processes Developed
Creative thinking – decision making

Thinking Strategies Developed
– Identifying perspectives
– Encountering different angles
– Empathizing – being in the shoes of others

Learning Environment
Classroom

Opening/Exposure
– Video clip on advantages and disadvantages of globalization https://www.youtube.com/watch?v=q-V2OSRzZQA
– The six thinking hats guidelines
– Practice of the application of six thinking hats using an everyday issue such as being for or against school uniforms, or pocket money, or working after school hours etc.

Teaching Strategies
Problem-based learning – decision making

Learning Activities and Grouping
In groups of six, students will:

1 Define a dilemma.
2 Use the six thinking hats to solve the dilemma.
   Option – each student picks a different hat, or all hats are addressed by all group members.
3 Arrive at a unanimous decision. If they do not, they need to continue and convince group members to change their point of view.
4 Decide on a creative way of presenting their decision.
5 Present the decision in class.

Learning Materials
– Video clip on globalization
– The six thinking hats

Product/s
Presentation of process and decision using the six thinking hats

Assessment
Creative product: presented a clear decision, within a 3-minute time limit, presenting process, all group members participated

Lessons 13–14: Time Perspective

Content
Future of globalization

Aims
Student will predict the future of globalization based on previous knowledge

Thinking Processes Developed
Future thinking

Thinking Strategies Developed
Predicting developments

Learning Environment
Classroom

Opening/Exposure
- Poster presenting the future scenario and criteria for writing and evaluation
- Creative presentation of scenario: Criteria for evaluation

Teaching Strategies
Future-based learning

Learning Activities and Grouping
In groups of four, students will:

1 Revise the accumulated knowledge.
2 Select a time span.
3 Project themselves into the future.
4 Write a future scenario.
5 Check the scenario based on pre-determined criteria.

6   Prepare a short creative presentation of the future scenario.

In plenary, students will:

7   Present the future scenario creatively.
8   Evaluate their creative presentation of future scenario.
9   Discuss differences and similarities in future scenarios.

Learning Materials
– Accumulated knowledge
– Future scenario

Product/s
Future scenario

Assessment
Future scenario: it is located in the far or near future, one page long, mentions past, present and future, is written in first person, has two additional characters, has a plot, creative, correct and relevant events, it mentions a process

6   Future Scenario

To my best friend Adi,

Today is 20.5.2047 and I am celebrating my 47th birthday. I wish you were here on the moon to celebrate with me. Thank you for calling me. Seeing your hologram made it almost as perfect as if you were here in person. Talking to you made me remember many things I would like to share with you.

Last week I was on vacation in MOON PLAZA on the east side of the moon. I don't understand why you insist on living in Israel. I remember that back in 2015 the Minister of Interior Affairs deported 300 foreign workers because they did not have a visa. Nowadays, we work when we want to, if we possess the right qualifications. I don't understand why a human being needs to fight for employment. Now, everybody works everywhere and there are no borders between countries.

The world has become one unit and one culture. All other cultures disappeared. We have one language which is a combination of English and computer language, and my children do not want to speak any other language (although I tried to teach them Hebrew). I know that Israel is the only country that preserved Hebrew, and it is still taught in schools as a second language.

I am working in a global company called: "Global Manpower" and thought of persuading you to move from Israel to the moon and work as a data librarian in a chain of exclusive high schools. I remember you worked as a librarian in a public library in 2017. Librarians here get all books on 2 cm. size discs and scan them into the brains of the students. Everybody has a chip in their brains that puts the books in order according to subjects. People can delete the books or other data they do not need.

Do you remember that when we were in school we had a project on food and dishes from different cultures? My mother remembered that way back then, each neighborhood had its own way of life and special food that could be identified with the place. Now, all food is produced by one conglomerate and distributed on the same day to all parts of the world and the moon.

I wish it were different. I liked the differences between people, and different foods, and jobs. I like the world with less globalization. There are good things about it, but I think we have also lost our uniqueness.

Hope you come to visit on my next birthday.

Best wishes,
Ruth

Note

The unit was designed by Yael Shalom under the supervision of Hava Vidergor.

References

Ministry of Education. (2012). *Push for full matriculation*. Jerusalem: Shachar Division, Pedagogical Administration. [in Hebrew]

Ministry of Education. (2015). *Curriculum in administration and economics: Introduction to administration* (updated ed.). Jerusalem: Administration of Science and Technology, Business Management Department Supervision. [in Hebrew]

Wallace, B. (2001). *Teaching thinking skills across the primary curriculum*. London: David Fulton Publishers (A NACE-Fulton Pub).

Wallace, B. (2002). *Teaching thinking skills across the early years*. London: David Fulton Publishers (A NACE-Fulton Pub).

Wallace, B., & Maker, J., Cave, D., & Chandler, S. (2004). *Thinking skills and problem-solving: An inclusive approach*. London: David Fulton Publishers (A NACE-Fulton Pub).

Wallace, B. (2015). Using the TASC thinking and problem-solving framework to create a curriculum of opportunity across the full spectrum of human abilities: TASC – thinking actively in a social context. In H. E. Vidergor & C. R. Harris (Eds.), *Applied practice for educators of gifted and able learners* (pp. 113–130). Rotterdam, The Netherlands: Sense Publishers.

Wallace, B., Maker, J., & Zimmerman, B. (2009). *TASC international: Thinking actively in a social context: Theory and practice.*

Zimon, Y., & Hirsch, N. (2012). *Introduction to micro- and macro-economics with glossary* (new ed.). Tel Aviv: Ronel Publishing. [in Hebrew]

Appendix: TASC Wheel

TASC Wheel (© Belle Wallace, 2000, *reprinted here with permission*)

The following texts describe TASC used across the curriculum:

1 Wallace, B. (2002). *Teaching thinking skills across the middle years*. London: Taylor and Francis, Routledge.

2 Wallace, B. (2003). *Using history to develop thinking skills at key stage 2*. London: Taylor and Francis, Routledge.
3 Wallace, B., Cave, D., & Berry, A. (2008). *Teaching problem-solving and thinking skills through science*. London: Taylor and Francis, Routledge.

The reader is also referred to Wallace (2001, 2002) and Wallace et al. (2004).

Index

21st century   xiv, 3–5, 8, 10–12, 18, 19, 22, 122, 140, 181, 198, 274, 275
3D printers   14, 22, 222, 223, 242, 243

Able students   5, 25, 29, 30, 40, 42, 44, 46, 47, 50, 52, 53, 59, 61, 63, 64, 77, 78, 80, 82, 84, 171, 173, 175, 176, 178, 205, 206, 208, 211, 212, 215, 216, 218, 228, 231, 233, 235, 236, 238, 240, 242, 244, 245, 250, 266
Aims   xiv, 9, 11, 12, 23, 25, 27, 28, 35, 39, 40, 42, 44, 46, 48, 50, 52, 55–58, 60, 61, 63, 64, 66, 74, 75, 77, 79, 80, 82, 84, 89, 92, 94, 96, 98, 100, 102, 110, 111, 113, 114, 116, 118, 120, 121, 128–130, 132, 133, 135, 137, 138, 144, 145, 147, 148, 150–152, 155, 157, 158, 169–173, 175, 177, 182, 184, 185, 187, 188, 190, 192, 194, 203, 205, 207, 209, 211, 213, 215, 217, 220, 225–227, 229, 231, 233, 235, 237, 239, 240, 242, 244, 253, 254, 256, 258–261, 264, 266, 276, 277, 279, 281, 282, 284, 287, 288, 294, 295, 298, 299, 301, 303–307
Analogies   72
Application of thinking tools   35
Apps   22, 60, 62, 198, 203
Assessment tools   19, 21, 25, 29
Authenticity   168

Bible studies   xvi, 107, 251
Blended learning environment   4, 8, 14, 18, 22, 24, 28, 198, 199, 222, 225
Bring Your Own Device (BYOD)   22, 41, 65, 170, 172, 175, 198, 203, 205, 211, 215, 229, 232, 239, 241

Cell-phone   xv, 129, 222–246, 281
Classroom learning environment   199, 207
Collaboration across and beyond disciplines   181
Collaborative inquiry assignment   169
Community settlements   89–104, 215
Computer games   9
Concept maps   21, 71
Conceptual knowledge   55, 201
Conditional/situational knowledge   13
Constructivist approach   5, 181

Consumerism   xv, 55–68
Content dimension   7, 8
Creative problem-solving   xv, 5, 50, 169, 175, 182, 241, 265, 266
Creative thinking skills   6, 275
Creativity   3, 7–9, 11, 14, 23, 25, 90, 108, 126, 181, 222, 223, 273, 274
Critical thinking   3, 10, 11, 13, 61, 90, 142, 213, 273, 276, 296
Critical thinking skills   10, 74
Curriculum   xiv, xv, 3–14, 18–30, 35, 36, 56, 89, 125, 144, 162, 167, 182, 251, 310
Curriculum design   14, 18–30

Debating   xv, xvi, 22, 209, 210, 248, 250, 251, 261–264, 276
Decision-making   xv, 7, 10, 11, 46, 47, 56, 57, 72, 80–82, 107, 108, 132, 142, 156, 162, 163, 183, 185, 186, 198, 207, 209, 226, 235, 236, 252, 258, 294, 297, 306
Digital portfolio   37, 43, 47, 51
Dilemmas   4, 21, 46, 57, 81, 91, 96, 97, 99, 114–116, 132, 133, 145, 156, 162–164, 182, 185, 186, 226, 235, 251, 252, 258, 259, 268, 306
Divergent and convergent thinking   11, 61, 112, 145, 150, 151, 161, 283, 284

Effectiveness of the MdCM   12
EFL learners   70, 224
e-learning   25
Energy   xv, 20, 26, 167–179, 291
Engagement   23, 180, 200, 222
Enhancing leadership   xvi
Enrichment   13, 25, 29, 30, 40, 42, 44, 46, 47, 50, 52, 53, 59, 61, 63, 64, 66, 67, 77, 78, 80, 82, 84, 85, 93, 95, 97, 100, 101, 103, 111, 112, 114, 116, 118, 120, 121, 130, 131, 133, 135, 137, 138, 140, 147, 148, 150–152, 155, 157–159, 171, 173, 175, 176, 178, 185, 186, 188, 190, 192, 193, 195, 205, 206, 208, 211, 212, 215, 216, 218, 221, 228, 231, 233, 235, 236, 238, 240, 242, 244, 245, 254, 256, 257, 259, 261, 264, 266, 268
Entrepreneurship   21, 22, 167, 222, 242

Exposure   25, 27, 28, 37, 39, 41–43, 45, 46, 48, 50, 59, 60, 62, 63, 65, 66, 76, 77, 79, 81, 83, 84, 91, 92, 94, 96, 98, 100, 102, 110, 112, 113, 115, 116, 118, 121, 126, 129, 130, 132, 134, 136, 137, 139, 145–147, 149–151, 153, 155–157, 159, 170, 172, 174, 175, 184, 185, 187, 189, 191, 193, 194, 203, 205, 207, 209, 211, 213, 215, 217, 227, 229, 232, 234, 235, 237–239, 241, 243, 245, 253, 255, 256, 258, 260, 262, 265, 267, 278, 279, 281, 283, 285, 287, 289, 298, 300, 301, 303, 304, 306, 307
Extreme sports   70, 74, 75, 77, 78, 82–85

Flipped classroom   xv, 24, 198–201, 224, 225, 232
Flipped Classroom Model   199, 225
Flow charts   9, 37, 42–44
Flow of creativity   23
Formative assessment   21
Future orientation   xi, 10, 11
Future Problem-Solving Program (FPSP)   5, 11
Future scenarios   xiv, 21, 24, 26, 29, 35, 38, 52–54, 58, 66–68, 75, 84–86, 92, 102–104, 107, 121, 122, 125, 128, 139, 140, 142, 144, 145, 159, 160, 162–164, 169, 176, 177, 183, 193, 195, 202, 217, 218, 222, 226, 244–246, 251, 252, 267, 268, 273, 277, 289, 297, 307, 308
Future Thinking   xi, xiv, xvi, 3–14, 18–30, 37, 48, 52, 57, 58, 63, 66, 75, 82, 84, 100, 102, 109, 116, 120, 121, 128, 135, 138, 144, 157, 158, 177, 180, 183, 189, 192, 198, 215, 217, 222, 226, 239, 244, 260, 266, 273, 276, 288, 297, 304, 307
Future Thinking Centers   5
Future thinking literacy   xiv, xvi, 3–14, 18–30, 222

Game based learning   9, 22, 91, 151, 153, 164, 198, 283, 287
Genetics   xv, 13, 35–54
Gifted   xvi, 273–289
Gifted students   5, 25, 29, 30, 40, 42, 44, 46, 47, 50, 52, 53, 59, 61, 63, 64, 66, 67, 77, 78, 80, 82, 84, 85, 93, 95, 97, 100, 101, 103, 107, 111, 112, 114, 116, 118, 120, 121, 130, 131, 133, 135, 137, 138, 140, 147, 148, 150–152, 155, 157–159, 171, 173, 175, 176, 178, 185, 186, 188, 190, 192, 193, 195, 205, 206, 208, 211, 212, 215, 216, 218, 228, 231, 233, 235, 236, 238, 240, 242, 244, 245, 254, 256, 257, 259, 261, 264, 266, 268, 273–277
Global citizenship   24, 273–290
Global perspective   9, 11, 26, 38, 116, 118, 173–175, 202, 205–211, 213–215, 226, 261–264, 273, 282, 284
Globalization   xvi, 293–309
Graphic organizers   71, 201, 206, 207, 209, 211, 213, 229

Heterogeneous class   29, 30, 36, 38, 58, 202
High Order Thinking Skills (HOTS)   6, 7, 10, 12, 36
Higher-order thinking   4
Holisticity   168
Human rights   xv, 198–218, 220

Innovation   3, 25, 125, 223, 273, 274
Innovative teaching-learning strategies   12, 25
Inquiry   4, 6, 7, 10, 12, 20, 21, 24, 25, 27, 28, 35–37, 39, 41–45, 48, 56–60, 62, 76, 77, 79, 83, 92–94, 96, 109–113, 128–130, 132, 134, 144, 146, 147, 149, 150, 152, 162, 168, 169, 183–185, 187, 189, 204, 205, 213, 224, 227, 229, 250, 253–256, 260, 269, 274, 277, 278, 280–284, 293–295, 297–300, 302
Inquiry processes   10, 128
Interdisciplinary subjects   36
Inter-personal communication   125
Intrinsic motivation   9, 13
Inventive thinking   222, 223, 226

Jerusalem   xv, 13, 119, 122, 180–196
Jigsaw method   169, 174

Language arts   70–86, 222–246
Leadership skills   23, 276, 290
Learners at risk   xvi, 293–310
Learning environment   4, 8, 14, 18, 22–25, 27, 28, 39, 41, 43, 45, 46, 48, 50, 52, 59, 60, 62, 63, 65, 66, 76, 77, 79, 81, 83, 84, 92, 94, 96, 98, 100, 102, 110, 111, 113, 115, 116, 118, 121, 126, 129, 130, 132, 134, 136, 137, 139, 146, 147, 149–151, 153, 155, 157, 158, 170, 172, 174, 175, 177, 184, 185, 187,

189, 191, 193, 194, 198–200, 203, 205, 207, 209, 211, 213, 215, 217, 219, 222, 225, 227, 229, 232, 234, 235, 237, 239, 241, 242, 245, 253, 255, 256, 258, 260, 262, 265, 267, 278, 279, 281, 283, 285, 287, 289, 295, 298, 300, 301, 303, 304, 306, 307
Learning in Future Thinking Societies (LIFTS) Center   5, 13, 14
Learning materials   25, 28, 39, 41–43, 45, 47, 49, 51, 53, 59, 60, 62, 64, 65, 67, 76, 78, 80, 81, 83, 85, 93, 95, 97, 99, 101, 102, 111, 112, 114, 115, 117, 120, 121, 129, 131, 133, 134, 136, 138, 139, 146, 148, 149, 151, 152, 154, 156, 158, 159, 171, 172, 174, 176, 177, 184, 186, 188, 190, 192, 193, 195, 204, 206, 208, 210, 212, 214, 216–218, 228, 230, 232, 234, 236, 238, 240, 241, 243, 245, 254, 255, 257, 259, 261, 264, 266, 267, 279, 280, 282, 283, 286, 288, 289, 299, 300, 302, 304–306, 308
Life skills   xv, 142–164, 273, 274
LIFTS Center, see Learning in Future Thinking Societies (LIFTS) Center
Low order thinking skills   6

Mathematical concepts   55
MdCM, see Multidimensional Curriculum Model
Me, Myself and I   144, 145, 159, 160
Meaningful learning   3–5, 18, 22, 24, 70
Melioration   6, 21, 36, 222, 223, 242
Mock trial   xv, 198, 202, 213–215
Mock UN assembly   273
Model United Nations (MUN)   xvi, 273, 275, 276, 284–286
Modification   25, 29, 40, 42, 44, 46, 47, 49, 52, 53, 59, 61, 62, 64, 66, 67, 77, 78, 80, 82, 83, 85, 93, 95, 97, 100, 101, 103, 111, 112, 114, 116, 117, 120, 121, 130, 131, 133, 135, 136, 138, 139, 147, 148, 150–152, 154, 157–159, 171, 173, 175, 176, 178, 185, 186, 188, 190, 192, 193, 195, 204, 206, 208, 210, 212, 215, 216, 218, 228, 231, 233, 234, 236, 238, 240, 242, 244, 245, 254, 256, 257, 259, 261, 264, 266, 267, 280, 282, 284, 286, 289, 290
MOOCs   22, 198
Moral and ethical issues   198–218
Multi-age grouping   23

Multi/transdisciplinary   4, 167
Multi-categorical   19, 22, 24, 28, 37
Multidimensional Curriculum Model   xiv, xv, xvi, 3–14, 18, 20, 22–25, 27, 28, 30, 35, 36, 55, 57, 70, 89, 91, 107, 108, 125, 142, 144, 167, 169, 180, 182, 198, 222, 248, 251, 293, 297
Multidisciplinary concepts   8
Multiple intelligences   23, 294
Music education   125, 126

New knowledge   6, 8, 18, 22, 35, 73, 74, 169, 172, 227, 244

Peer evaluation   19, 22, 24, 29, 37, 264, 282
Personal perspective   9, 11, 36–38, 42–47, 58–63, 75, 77–82, 91, 95–100, 109, 111–116, 128, 130–135, 145–157, 163, 183, 185–188, 202, 225, 226, 229, 231–238, 254–259, 273, 277–282, 297, 305, 306
Personalized learning   4
Phenomenon-based learning   14, 25, 167–170
Physics   35, 168, 169, 171, 222, 224–226, 231
Positive self-image   142
Pre-designed tools   9
Prediction models   9
Prior knowledge   74
Problem-based learning   xv, 14, 22, 24, 28, 37, 47, 65, 98, 115, 118, 132, 137, 153, 156, 167, 175, 186, 191, 198, 209, 211, 235, 241, 258, 285, 287, 303, 306
Problem finding   8, 10, 12, 20, 23, 50, 98, 109, 118, 137, 175, 191, 211, 240, 265, 303
Problem solving/Problem-solving processes   xv, 3, 5–8, 10–12, 20, 21, 29, 36, 50, 51, 57, 64–66, 72, 73, 98–100, 107–109, 118–121, 123, 124, 137, 138, 143–145, 153, 169, 175, 176, 180, 182, 183, 190–192, 198, 201, 202, 207, 211, 212, 218–220, 222, 224, 240–242, 251, 252, 264–266, 273, 274, 276, 284, 287, 291, 293, 295, 297, 303, 304
Problem-solving simulation   218–220, 273
Process dimension   8
Product   xiv, 3, 6, 8–10, 18–22, 24–27, 29, 37, 38, 40, 42, 44, 45, 47, 49, 51, 53, 56–59, 61, 62, 64–68, 74, 76, 78, 80–83, 85, 86, 93, 95, 97, 99, 101, 103, 111, 112, 114, 115, 117, 120, 121, 129, 131, 133, 135, 136, 138, 139, 142, 145, 146, 148–152, 154, 156,

Product (cont.)   158–160, 163, 171, 172, 174, 176, 177, 183, 184, 186, 188, 190, 192–195, 203, 204, 206, 208, 210, 212, 214, 216, 218, 222, 223, 225, 228, 230, 233, 234, 236, 238, 240, 242–245, 250, 254, 255, 257–259, 261, 264, 266–269, 279, 280, 282, 284, 286, 288, 289, 293, 299, 300, 302, 304, 305, 307, 308
Product dimension   8, 9
Productive failure   201
Productive thinking   7, 8
Productive thinking skills   8
Project-based learning   4, 14, 22, 28, 30, 63, 65, 67, 81, 169, 172, 174, 194, 198, 200, 213, 218, 243, 250, 265
Public speaking   213, 248–252, 262, 276
Pullout program   30, 290

Real-world phenomena   167
Reflection   4, 14, 19, 22, 286, 290
Revised Bloom's taxonomy   6, 223

S.C.A.M.P.E.R.   21, 223, 226, 242–244
Scaffolding learning   168
Scenarios   xiv, 9, 11, 21, 24, 26, 29, 35, 38, 50–53, 58, 66–68, 75, 81, 84–86, 92, 102, 103, 107, 121, 122, 125, 128, 139, 140, 142, 144, 145, 159, 160, 162, 163, 169, 176–178, 183, 193, 195, 196, 202, 217, 218, 222, 226, 235, 244–246, 251, 252, 267, 268, 273, 277, 289, 291, 297, 307, 308
Scientific inquiry skills   7
Scientific thinking–inquiry   10–12, 41, 42, 44, 48, 58, 92, 94, 96, 109–111, 113, 128–130, 132, 147, 187, 253, 254, 256, 277, 281, 282, 284, 298, 299
Scientific-technological literacy   35
Social responsibility   3, 18, 22, 23, 25, 290
Social studies   xv, xvi, 89–104, 180, 248–269
Social-emotional capabilities   142
Student level   25, 26, 38, 58, 75, 92, 109, 128, 145, 169, 183, 202, 225, 226, 250, 252, 277, 297

Tablets   22, 160, 198, 232, 234
Teacher's role   22
Teaching English   70, 71
Teaching strategies   xiv, 6, 8, 22, 23, 25, 26, 28, 30, 39, 41, 43, 45, 47, 48, 50, 52, 59, 60, 62, 63, 65, 67, 76, 77, 79, 81, 83, 84, 93, 94, 96, 98, 100, 102, 110, 112, 113, 115, 116, 118, 121, 129, 130, 132, 134, 136, 137, 139, 146, 147, 149, 150, 152, 153, 156, 157, 159, 170, 172, 174, 175, 177, 184, 186, 187, 189, 191, 193, 194, 204, 205, 207, 209, 211, 213, 216, 217, 227, 229, 232, 234, 235, 237, 239, 241, 243, 245, 248, 253, 255, 256, 258, 260, 265, 267, 278, 280, 281, 283, 285, 287, 289, 298, 300, 302, 303, 305–307
Technology   xi, xv, 3, 4, 8, 14, 18, 20, 22–24, 27, 35–54, 101, 108, 122, 167, 168, 181, 198, 200, 201, 222, 223, 226, 229, 273, 274, 293, 296
TEDEx   22
Thinking Actively in a Social Context (TASC)   xvi, 21, 27–29, 293, 295–297, 301–304
Thinking hats   xv, 10, 21, 29, 38, 46, 47, 57, 75, 80–82, 89–91, 96–99, 104, 109, 114, 115, 128, 132, 133, 144, 145, 155, 156, 162, 163, 182, 185, 186, 202, 207, 208, 226, 235, 236, 251, 252, 258, 259, 268, 297, 305–307
Thinking maps   xv, 21, 24, 29, 37, 39, 40, 60, 61, 70–75, 77–80, 94, 95, 109–112, 142, 144, 145, 150–152, 161, 206, 207, 209, 211, 213, 253, 254, 276, 278, 279, 283, 284, 295, 297, 299–301, 303
Thinking processes   xiv, 10–14, 19, 20, 22, 25, 27, 28, 37, 39, 41, 42, 44, 46, 48, 50, 52, 57, 58, 60, 61, 63, 65, 66, 71, 75, 77, 79, 81, 82, 84, 90, 92, 94, 96, 98, 100, 102, 109–111, 113, 114, 116, 118, 121, 129, 130, 132, 133, 135, 137, 138, 145, 147, 148, 150–152, 155, 157, 158, 169, 170, 172, 173, 175, 177, 184, 185, 187, 189, 191, 192, 194, 198, 203, 205, 207, 209, 211, 213, 215, 217, 223, 227, 229, 231, 233, 235, 237, 239, 240, 242, 244, 253, 254, 256, 258, 260, 262, 265, 266, 277, 279, 281, 282, 284, 287, 288, 298, 299, 301, 303, 304, 306, 307
Thinking skills   xii, xiv, 3, 6–8, 10, 12, 14, 21, 35, 36, 70, 71, 74, 102, 128, 144, 181, 202, 217, 222, 223, 225, 274, 275, 293, 310, 311
Three-stage application of thinking hats   91
Time perspective   xiv, xv, 4, 6, 9, 10, 12, 25, 26, 38, 48, 50–53, 57, 58, 63–67, 75, 82–85, 91, 92, 100–103, 109, 116–121, 128, 135–140, 145, 157–159, 163, 169, 176–178,

INDEX 317

183, 188–193, 202, 215–218, 225, 226, 239–245, 252, 259–261, 264–268, 273, 277, 286–290, 297, 304, 307, 308
Timeline   21, 24, 29, 38, 48, 49, 57, 64, 75, 83, 100, 101, 109, 116, 117, 120, 128, 135, 136, 139, 172, 183, 188–192, 202, 215, 216, 226, 239, 240, 252, 260, 261, 263–266, 297, 304, 305
Transdisciplinary   xiv, xv, 3, 4, 18–20, 23, 25, 26, 180–196

Transdisciplinary perspective   xiv, xv, 3, 4, 167, 180–196, 242

Unit of study   25–30, 70, 218, 249

Whole language approach   74, 225
WICS model   108
Wild Cards   11, 53, 178
Women's status and rights   xvi, 248–269
Written scenarios   9

www.ingramcontent.com/pod-product-compliance
Lightning Source LLC
Chambersburg PA
CBHW070230230426
43664CB00014B/2261